Buffy the vampire slayer™

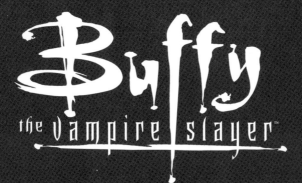

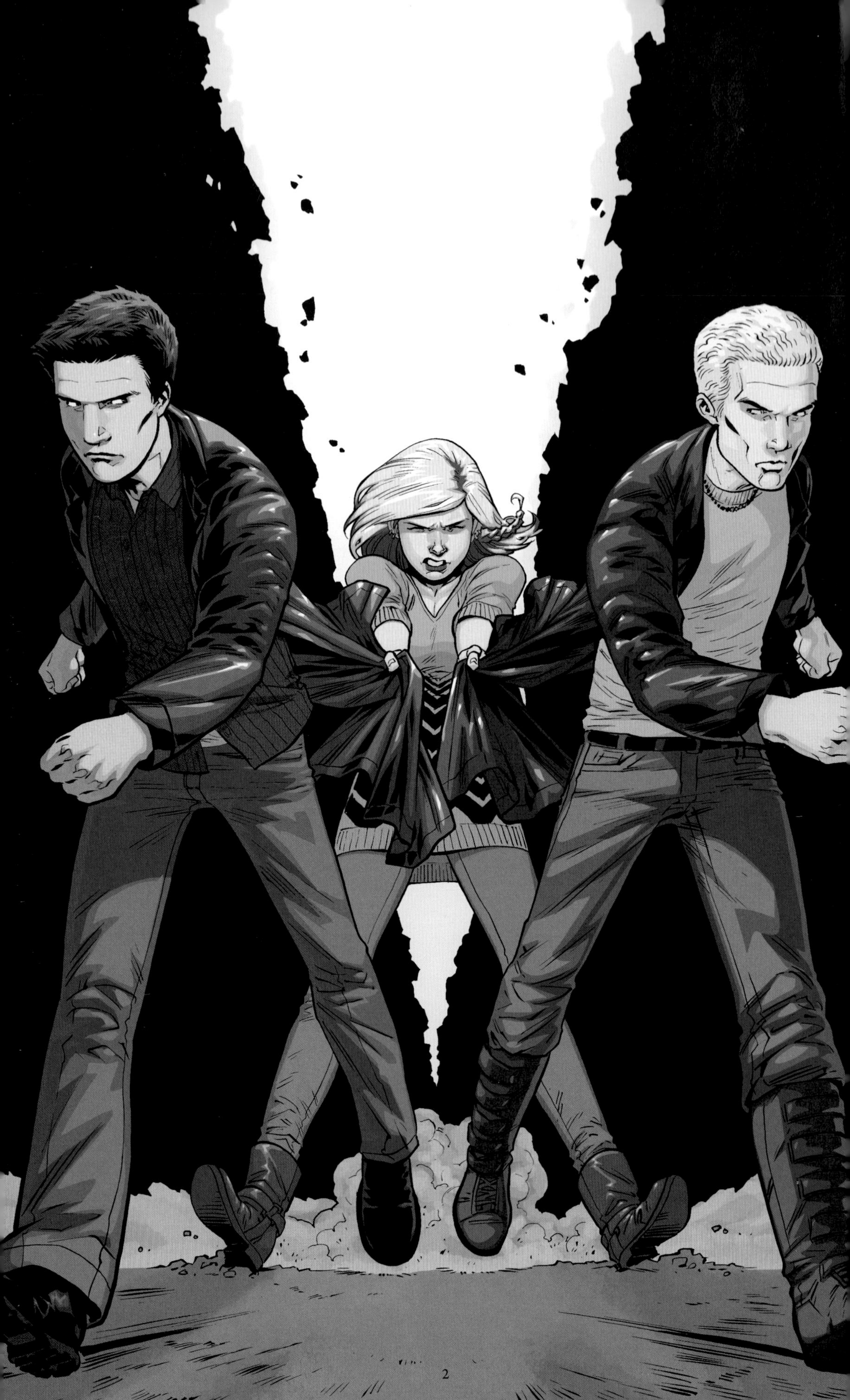

Buffy the Vampire Slayer™

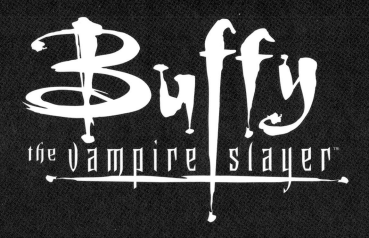

SEASON 10 · VOLUME 4

OLD DEMONS

SCRIPT · CHAPTERS 1–3, 5
CHRISTOS GAGE

SCRIPT · CHAPTER 4
CHRISTOS GAGE & NICHOLAS BRENDON

ART · CHAPTERS 1–4
REBEKAH ISAACS

ART · CHAPTER 5
MEGAN LEVENS

COLORS DAN JACKSON
LETTERS RICHARD STARKINGS & COMICRAFT'S JIMMY BETANCOURT
COVER AND CHAPTER BREAK ART STEVE MORRIS

EXECUTIVE PRODUCER JOSS WHEDON

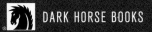

DARK HORSE BOOKS

PRESIDENT & PUBLISHER: MIKE RICHARDSON · EDITORS: SIERRA HAHN & JIM GIBBONS
ASSISTANT EDITORS: FREDDYE MILLER & SPENCER CUSHING · COLLECTION
DESIGNER: JUSTIN COUCH · DIGITAL ART TECHNICIAN: CHRISTIANNE GOUDREAU

Special thanks to NICOLE SPIEGEL *and* JOSH IZZO *at Twentieth Century Fox,*
DANIEL KAMINSKY, *and* SCOTT ALLIE.

The art on page 2 is the variant cover for *Buffy* Season 10 #18, by Rebekah Isaacs with Dan Jackson.

This story takes place after the events in *Buffy the Vampire Slayer* Season 9, created by Joss Whedon.

DARKHORSE.COM

First edition: February 2016
ISBN 978-1-61655-802-4

1 3 5 7 9 10 8 6 4 2
Printed in China

Published by Dark Horse Books, a division of Dark Horse Comics, Inc.
10956 SE Main Street, Milwaukie, OR 97222

BUFFY THE VAMPIRE SLAYER SEASON 10 VOLUME 4: OLD DEMONS

This volume reprints the comic book series *Buffy the Vampire Slayer* Season 10 #16–#20, from Dark Horse Comics.

Neil Hankerson, Executive Vice President · Tom Weddle, Chief Financial Officer · Randy Stradley, Vice President of Publishing · Michael Martens, Vice President of Book Trade Sales · Matt Parkinson, Vice President of Marketing · David Scroggy, Vice President of Product Development · Dale LaFountain, Vice President of Information Technology · Cara Niece, Vice President of Production and Scheduling · Ken Lizzi, General Counsel · Davey Estrada, Editorial Director · Dave Marshall, Editor in Chief · Scott Allie, Executive Senior Editor · Chris Warner, Senior Books Editor · Cary Grazzini, Director of Print and Development · Lia Ribacchi, Art Director · Mark Bernardi, Director of Digital Publishing

To find a comics shop in your area, call the Comic Shop Locator Service toll-free at
(888) 266-4226. International Licensing: 503-905-2377.

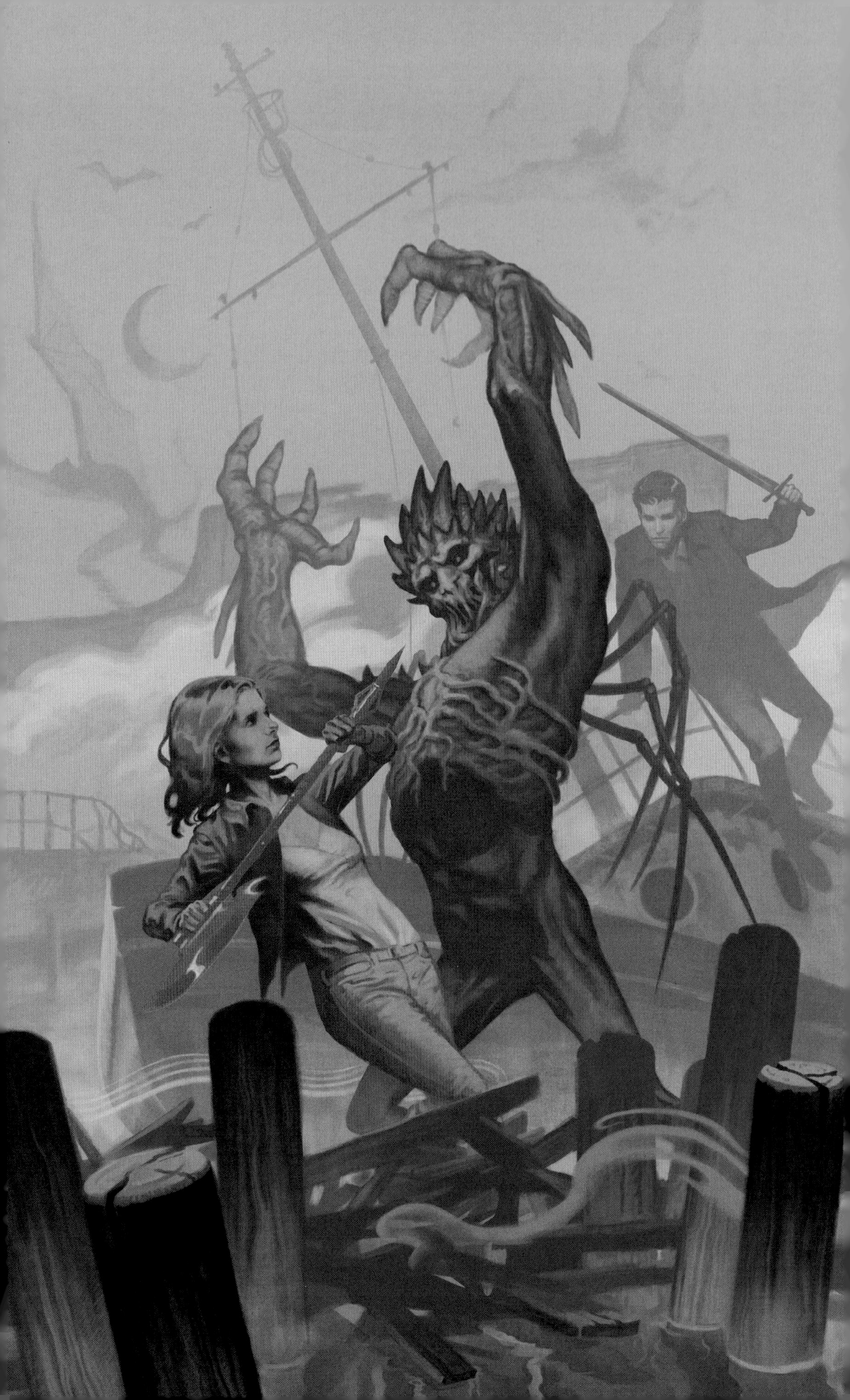

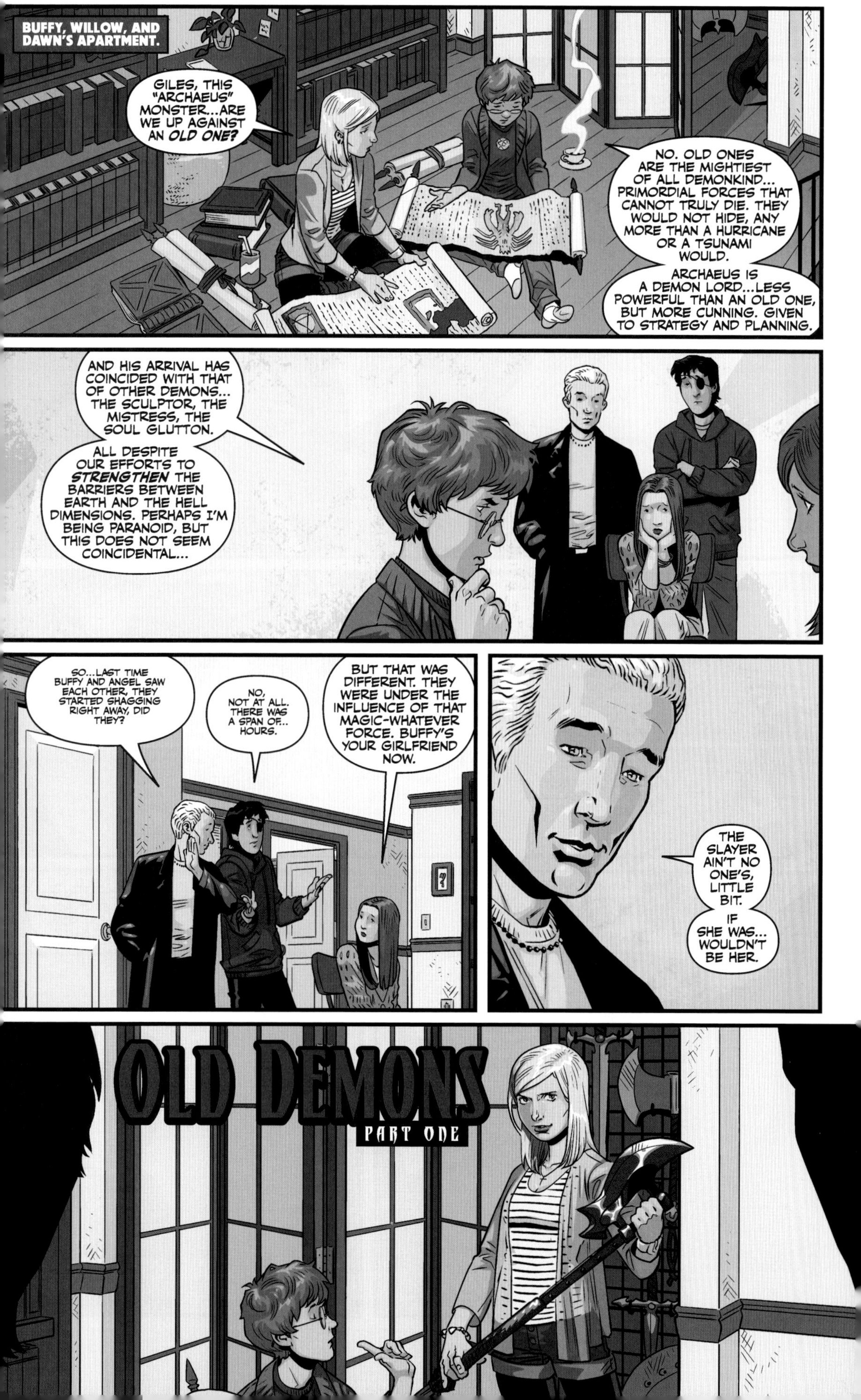
BUFFY, WILLOW, AND DAWN'S APARTMENT.
GILES, THIS "ARCHAEUS" MONSTER...ARE WE UP AGAINST AN *OLD ONE?*
NO. OLD ONES ARE THE MIGHTIEST OF ALL DEMONKIND... PRIMORDIAL FORCES THAT CANNOT TRULY DIE. THEY WOULD NOT HIDE, ANY MORE THAN A HURRICANE OR A TSUNAMI WOULD.
ARCHAEUS IS A DEMON LORD...LESS POWERFUL THAN AN OLD ONE, BUT MORE CUNNING. GIVEN TO STRATEGY AND PLANNING.
AND HIS ARRIVAL HAS COINCIDED WITH THAT OF OTHER DEMONS... THE SCULPTOR, THE MISTRESS, THE SOUL GLUTTON.
ALL DESPITE OUR EFFORTS TO *STRENGTHEN* THE BARRIERS BETWEEN EARTH AND THE HELL DIMENSIONS. PERHAPS I'M BEING PARANOID, BUT THIS DOES NOT SEEM COINCIDENTAL...
SO...LAST TIME BUFFY AND ANGEL SAW EACH OTHER, THEY STARTED SHAGGING RIGHT AWAY, DID THEY?
NO, NOT AT ALL. THERE WAS A SPAN OF.. HOURS.
BUT THAT WAS DIFFERENT. THEY WERE UNDER THE INFLUENCE OF THAT MAGIC-WHATEVER FORCE. BUFFY'S YOUR GIRLFRIEND NOW.
THE SLAYER AIN'T NO ONE'S, LITTLE BIT.
IF SHE WAS... WOULDN'T BE HER.
OLD DEMONS
PART ONE

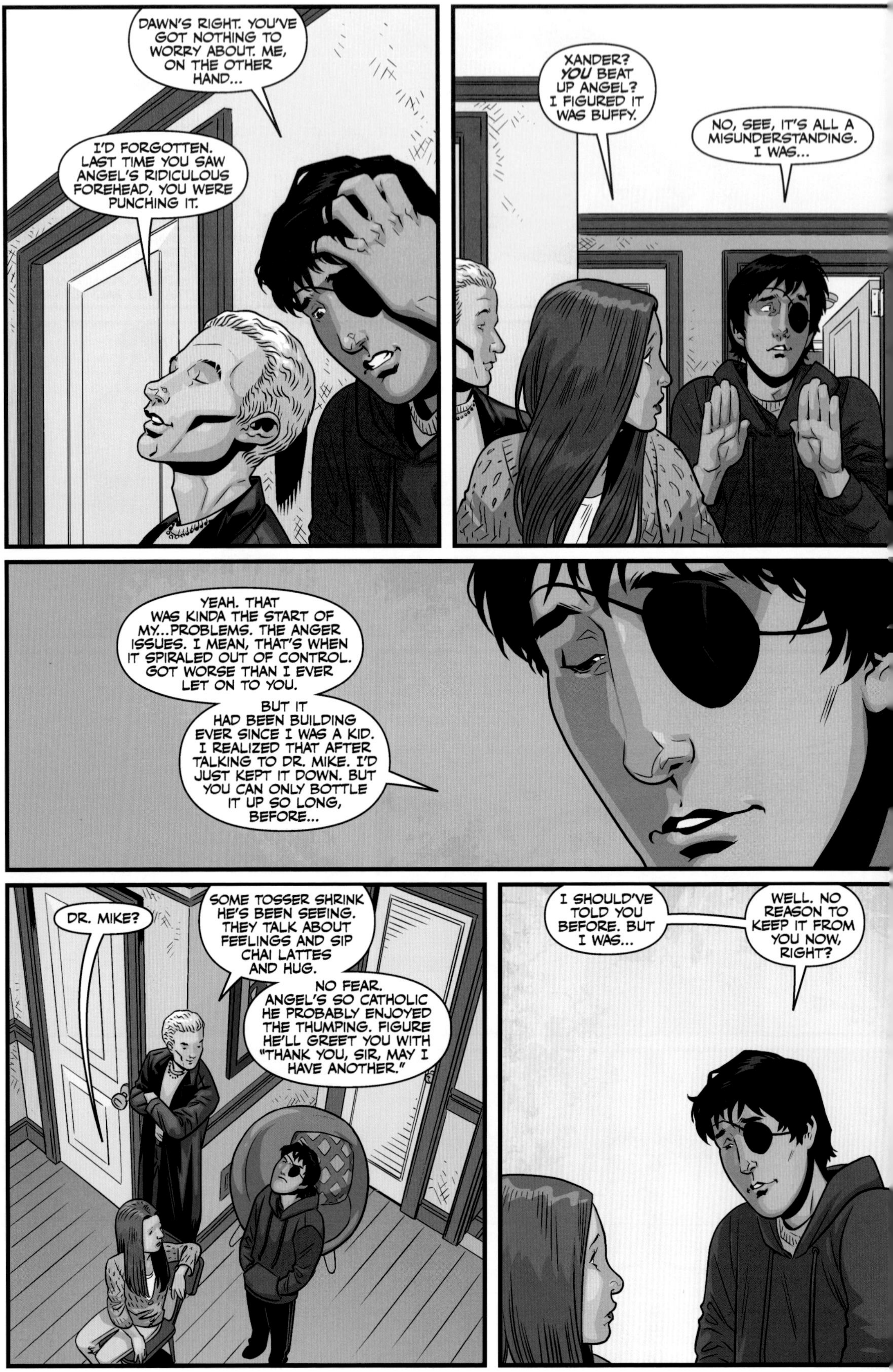
DAWN'S RIGHT. YOU'VE GOT NOTHING TO WORRY ABOUT. ME, ON THE OTHER HAND...
I'D FORGOTTEN. LAST TIME YOU SAW ANGEL'S RIDICULOUS FOREHEAD, YOU WERE PUNCHING IT.
XANDER? YOU BEAT UP ANGEL? I FIGURED IT WAS BUFFY.
NO, SEE, IT'S ALL A MISUNDERSTANDING. I WAS...
YEAH. THAT WAS KINDA THE START OF MY...PROBLEMS. THE ANGER ISSUES. I MEAN, THAT'S WHEN IT SPIRALED OUT OF CONTROL. GOT WORSE THAN I EVER LET ON TO YOU.
BUT IT HAD BEEN BUILDING EVER SINCE I WAS A KID. I REALIZED THAT AFTER TALKING TO DR. MIKE. I'D JUST KEPT IT DOWN. BUT YOU CAN ONLY BOTTLE IT UP SO LONG, BEFORE...
DR. MIKE?
SOME TOSSER SHRINK HE'S BEEN SEEING. THEY TALK ABOUT FEELINGS AND SIP CHAI LATTES AND HUG.
NO FEAR. ANGEL'S SO CATHOLIC HE PROBABLY ENJOYED THE THUMPING. FIGURE HE'LL GREET YOU WITH "THANK YOU, SIR, MAY I HAVE ANOTHER."
I SHOULD'VE TOLD YOU BEFORE. BUT I WAS...
WELL. NO REASON TO KEEP IT FROM YOU NOW, RIGHT?

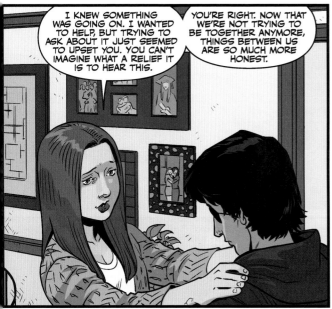

I KNEW SOMETHING WAS GOING ON. I WANTED TO HELP, BUT TRYING TO ASK ABOUT IT JUST SEEMED TO UPSET YOU. YOU CAN'T IMAGINE WHAT A RELIEF IT IS TO HEAR THIS.

YOU'RE RIGHT. NOW THAT WE'RE NOT TRYING TO BE TOGETHER ANYMORE, THINGS BETWEEN US ARE SO MUCH MORE HONEST.

YEAH. I WAS RIGHT.

YAY ME.

RIGHT. WE DON'T HAVE TIME TO WAIT FOR THE REAR GUARD. I'M GONNA GO OUT THERE AND TRACK THE BASTARD DOWN.

DON'T BE A FOOL. YOU WOULDN'T STAND A CHANCE.

THEN WHAT GOOD IS ANGEL? I'VE HAD IT WITH WAITIN' AROUND FOR SOME WANKER TO COME RIDIN' IN LIKE THE CAVALRY WHEN THERE AIN'T A DAMN THING HE CAN DO THAT *I CAN'T--*

SPIKE.

GOT A MINUTE?

9

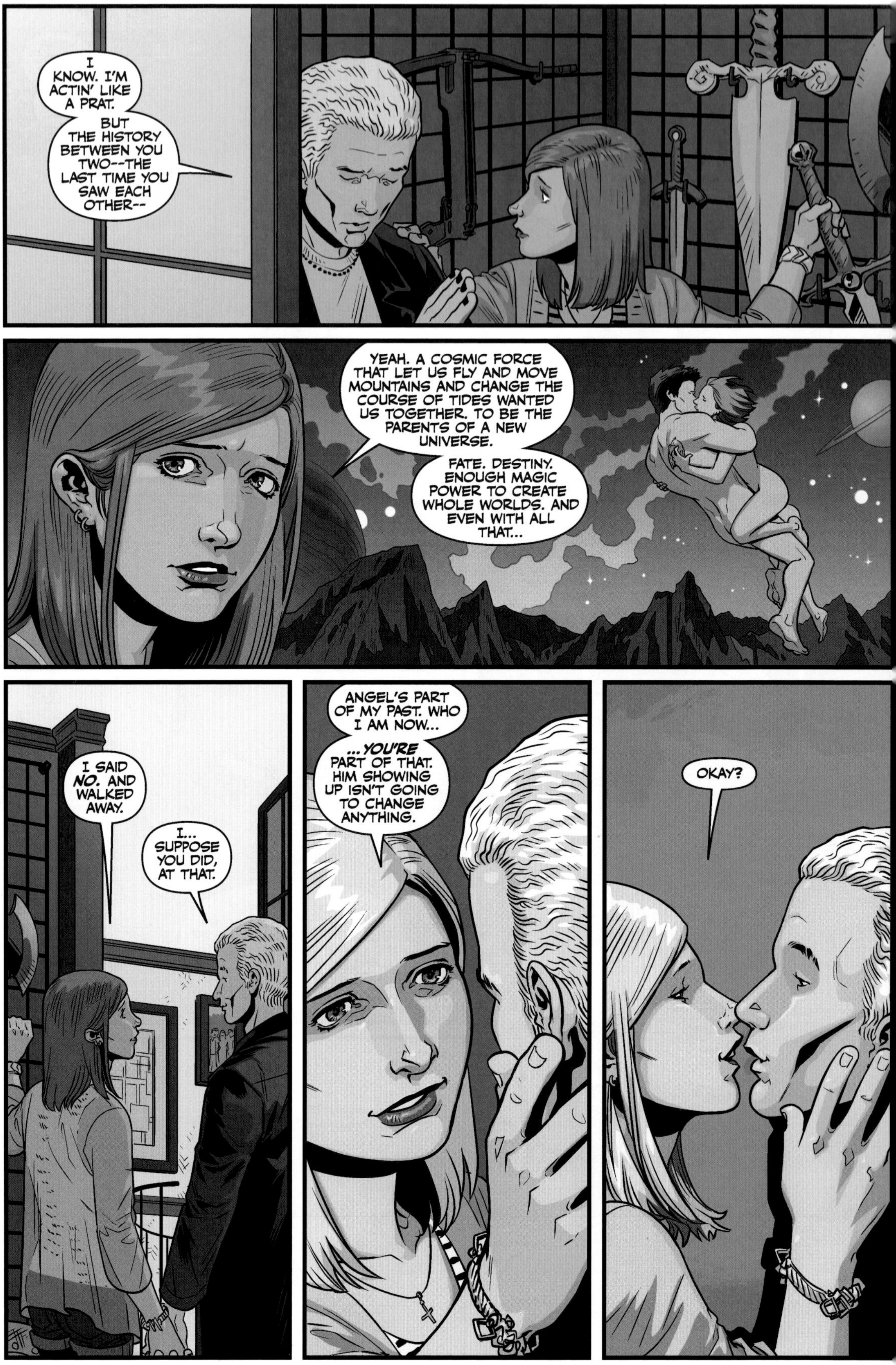
I KNOW. I'M ACTIN' LIKE A PRAT.
BUT THE HISTORY BETWEEN YOU TWO--THE LAST TIME YOU SAW EACH OTHER--
YEAH. A COSMIC FORCE THAT LET US FLY AND MOVE MOUNTAINS AND CHANGE THE COURSE OF TIDES WANTED US TOGETHER. TO BE THE PARENTS OF A NEW UNIVERSE.
FATE. DESTINY. ENOUGH MAGIC POWER TO CREATE WHOLE WORLDS. AND EVEN WITH ALL THAT...
I SAID *NO.* AND WALKED AWAY.
I... SUPPOSE YOU DID, AT THAT.
ANGEL'S PART OF MY PAST. WHO I AM NOW...
...YOU'RE PART OF THAT. HIM SHOWING UP ISN'T GOING TO CHANGE ANYTHING.
OKAY?

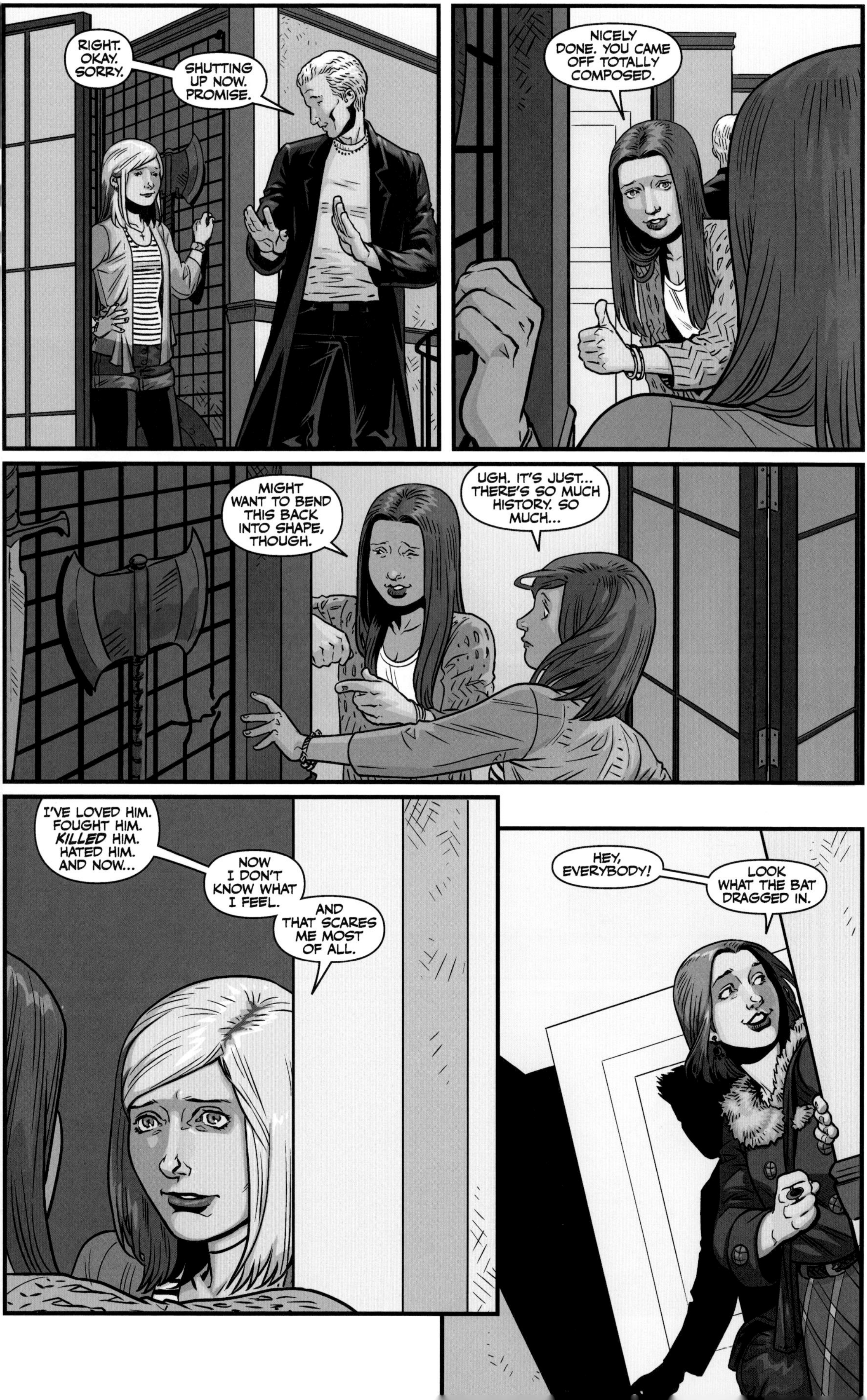
RIGHT. OKAY. SORRY.
SHUTTING UP NOW. PROMISE.
NICELY DONE. YOU CAME OFF TOTALLY COMPOSED.
MIGHT WANT TO BEND THIS BACK INTO SHAPE, THOUGH.
UGH. IT'S JUST... THERE'S SO MUCH HISTORY. SO MUCH...
I'VE LOVED HIM. FOUGHT HIM. *KILLED* HIM. HATED HIM. AND NOW...
NOW I DON'T KNOW WHAT I FEEL.
AND THAT SCARES ME MOST OF ALL.
HEY, EVERYBODY!
LOOK WHAT THE BAT DRAGGED IN.

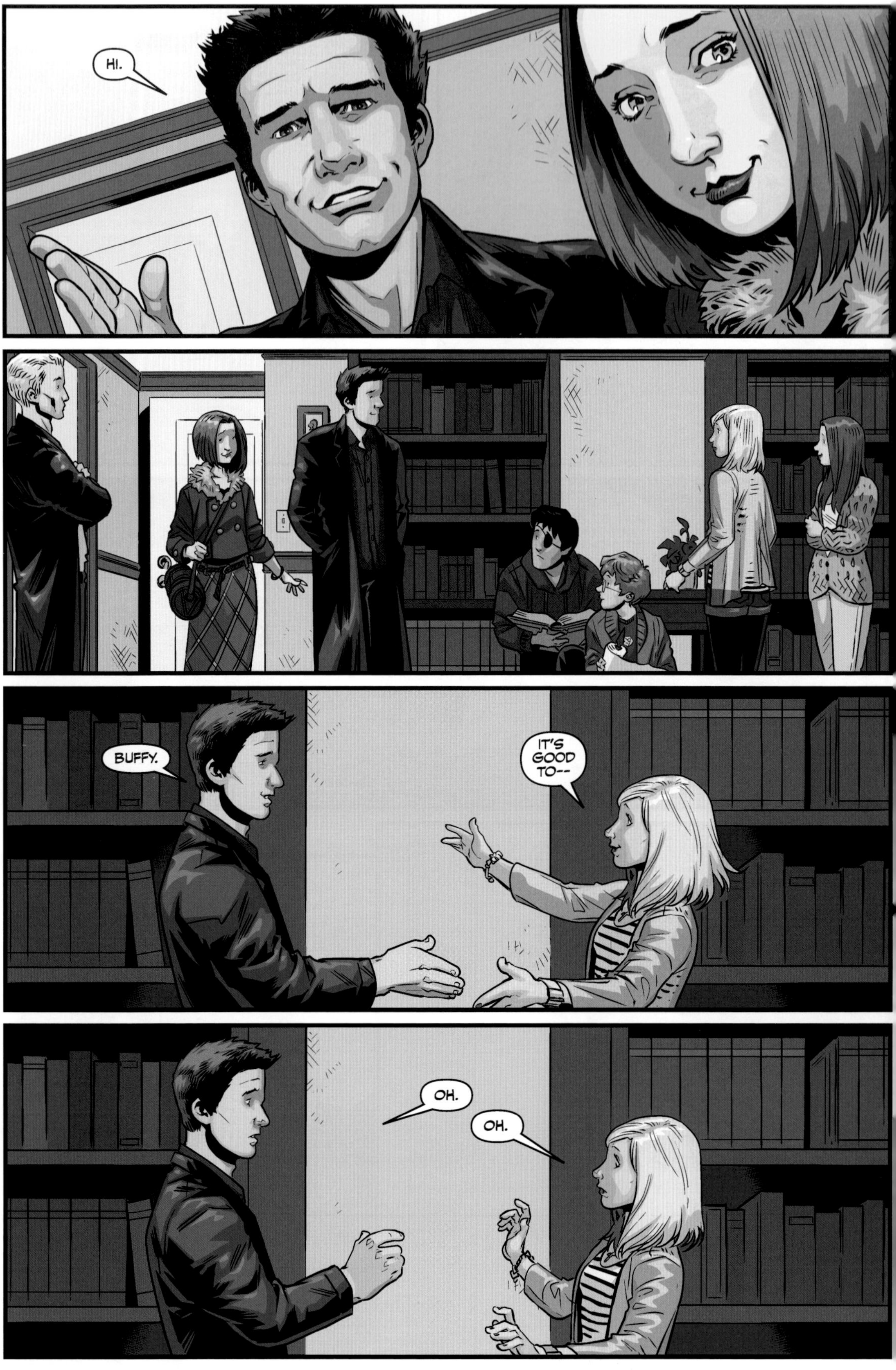
HI.
BUFFY.
IT'S GOOD TO--
OH.
OH.

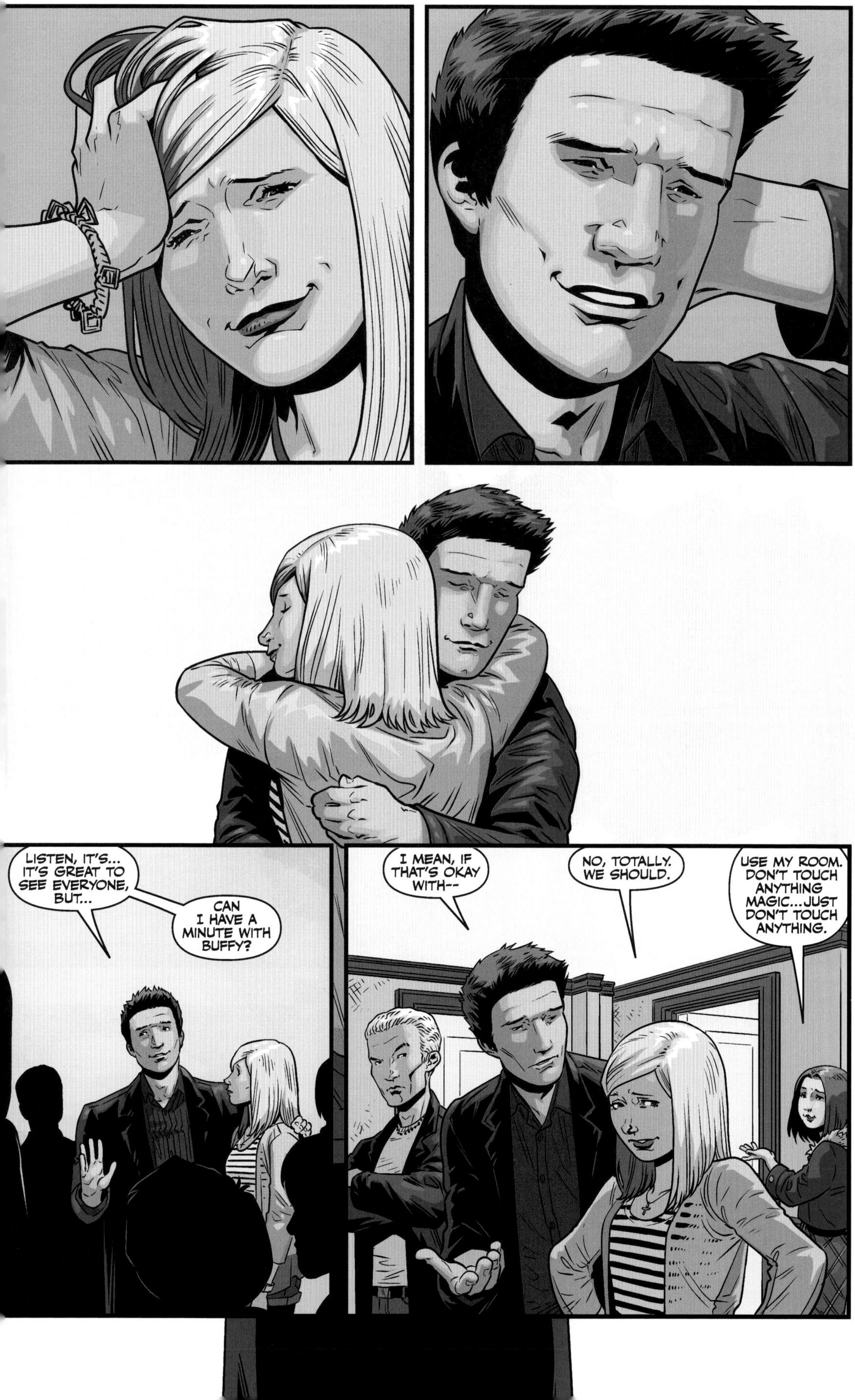

LISTEN, IT'S... IT'S GREAT TO SEE EVERYONE, BUT...
CAN I HAVE A MINUTE WITH BUFFY?
I MEAN, IF THAT'S OKAY WITH--
NO, TOTALLY. WE SHOULD.
USE MY ROOM. DON'T TOUCH ANYTHING MAGIC...JUST DON'T TOUCH ANYTHING.

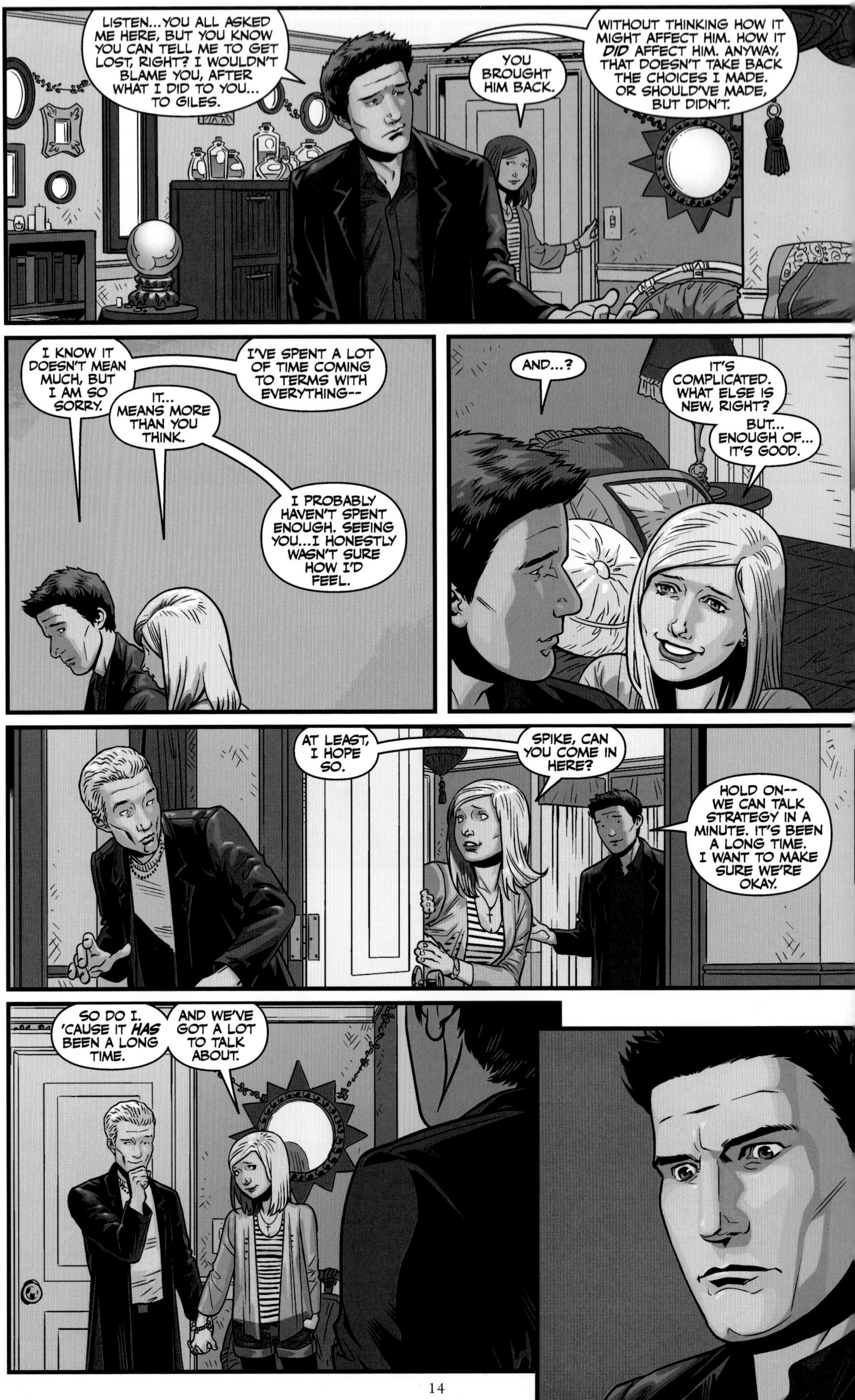
LISTEN...YOU ALL ASKED ME HERE, BUT YOU KNOW YOU CAN TELL ME TO GET LOST, RIGHT? I WOULDN'T BLAME YOU, AFTER WHAT I DID TO YOU... TO GILES.
YOU BROUGHT HIM BACK.
WITHOUT THINKING HOW IT MIGHT AFFECT HIM. HOW IT DID AFFECT HIM. ANYWAY, THAT DOESN'T TAKE BACK THE CHOICES I MADE. OR SHOULD'VE MADE, BUT DIDN'T.
I KNOW IT DOESN'T MEAN MUCH, BUT I AM SO SORRY.
IT... MEANS MORE THAN YOU THINK.
I'VE SPENT A LOT OF TIME COMING TO TERMS WITH EVERYTHING--
I PROBABLY HAVEN'T SPENT ENOUGH. SEEING YOU...I HONESTLY WASN'T SURE HOW I'D FEEL.
AND...?
IT'S COMPLICATED. WHAT ELSE IS NEW, RIGHT?
BUT... ENOUGH OF... IT'S GOOD.
AT LEAST, I HOPE SO.
SPIKE, CAN YOU COME IN HERE?
HOLD ON-- WE CAN TALK STRATEGY IN A MINUTE. IT'S BEEN A LONG TIME. I WANT TO MAKE SURE WE'RE OKAY.
SO DO I. 'CAUSE IT HAS BEEN A LONG TIME.
AND WE'VE GOT A LOT TO TALK ABOUT.

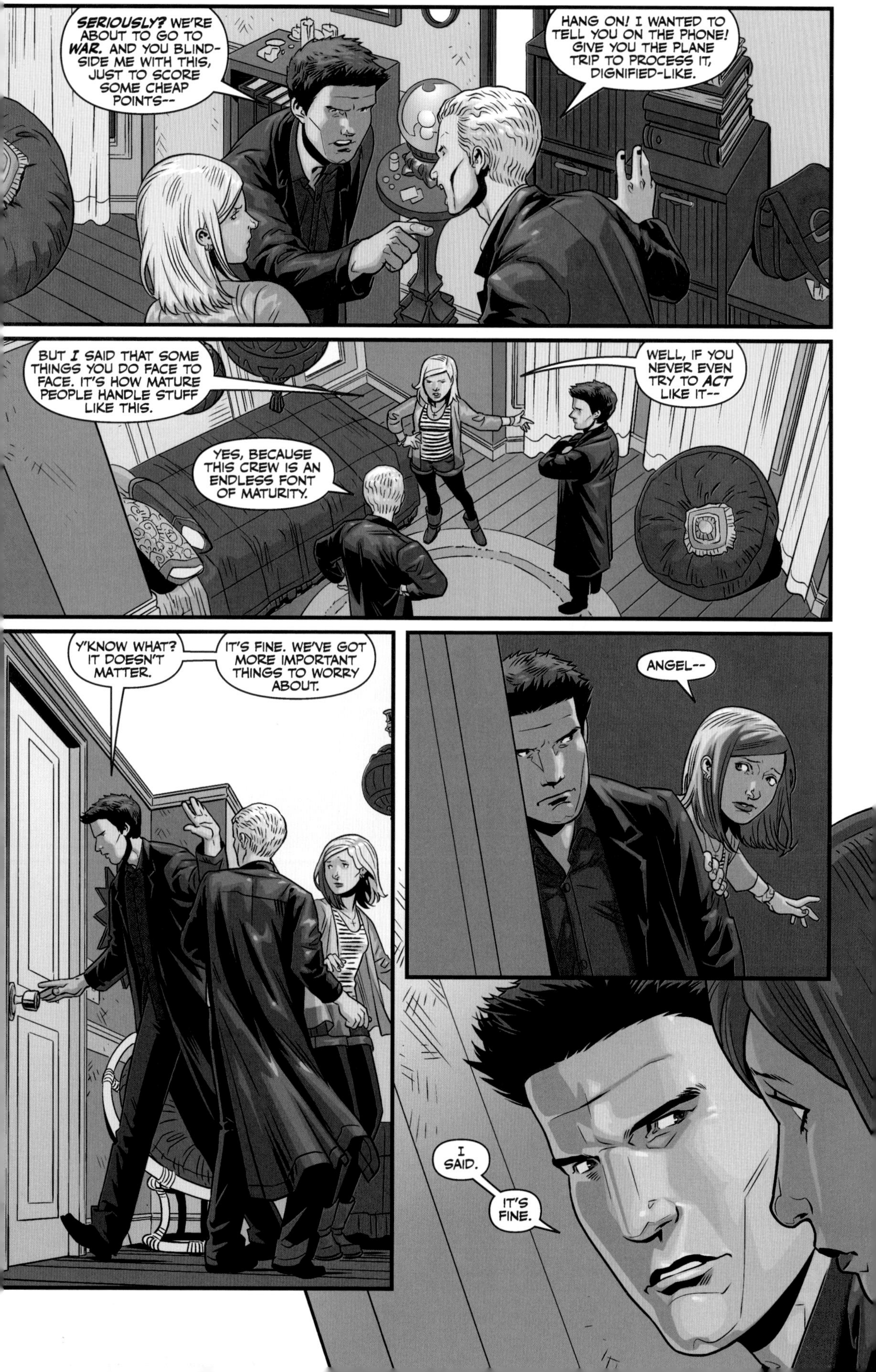
SERIOUSLY? WE'RE ABOUT TO GO TO WAR. AND YOU BLIND-SIDE ME WITH THIS, JUST TO SCORE SOME CHEAP POINTS--
HANG ON! I WANTED TO TELL YOU ON THE PHONE! GIVE YOU THE PLANE TRIP TO PROCESS IT, DIGNIFIED-LIKE.
BUT I SAID THAT SOME THINGS YOU DO FACE TO FACE. IT'S HOW MATURE PEOPLE HANDLE STUFF LIKE THIS.
WELL, IF YOU NEVER EVEN TRY TO ACT LIKE IT--
YES, BECAUSE THIS CREW IS AN ENDLESS FONT OF MATURITY.
Y'KNOW WHAT? IT DOESN'T MATTER.
IT'S FINE. WE'VE GOT MORE IMPORTANT THINGS TO WORRY ABOUT.
ANGEL--
I SAID.
IT'S FINE.

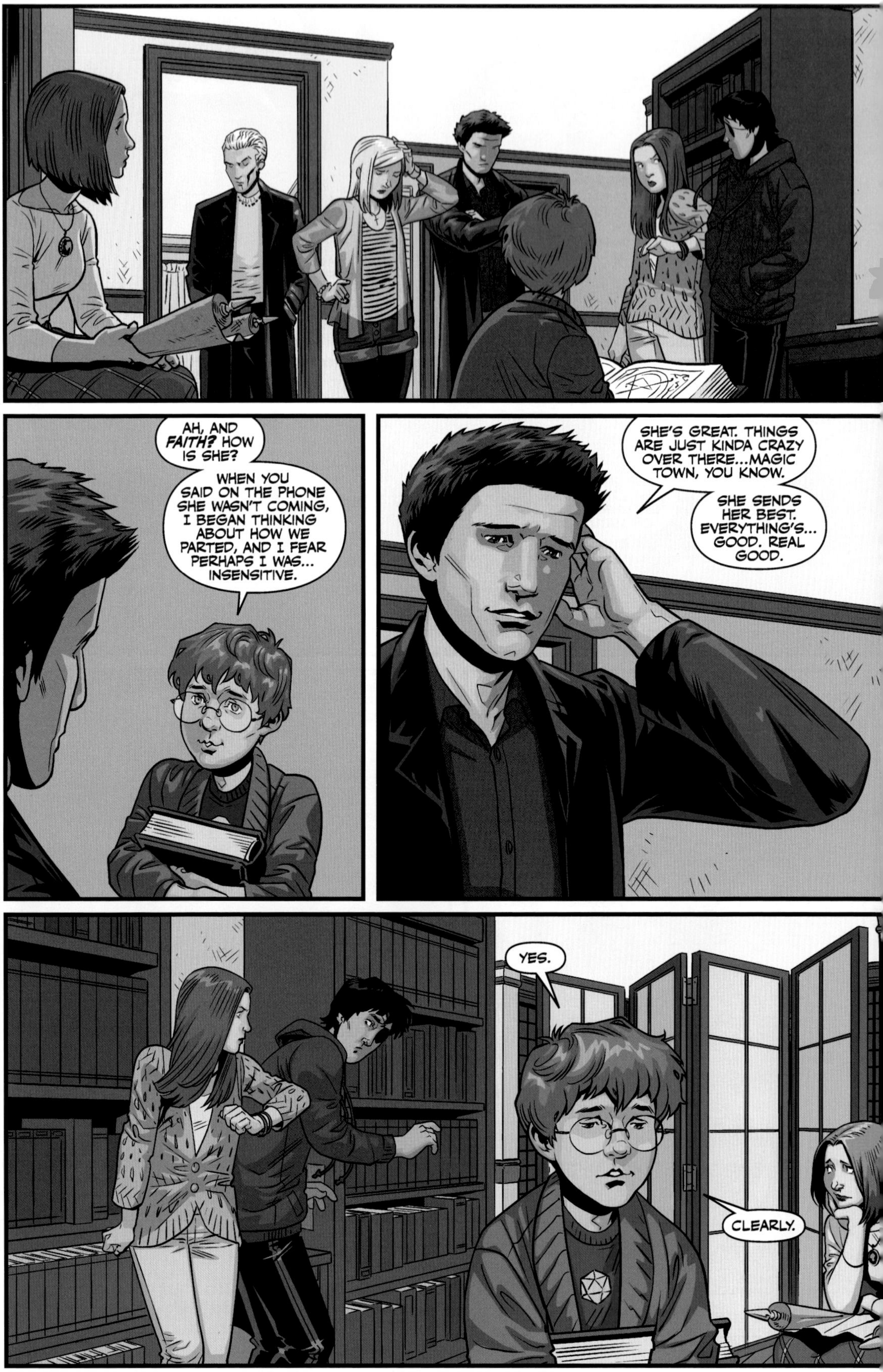

AH, AND FAITH? HOW IS SHE?
WHEN YOU SAID ON THE PHONE SHE WASN'T COMING, I BEGAN THINKING ABOUT HOW WE PARTED, AND I FEAR PERHAPS I WAS... INSENSITIVE.
SHE'S GREAT. THINGS ARE JUST KINDA CRAZY OVER THERE...MAGIC TOWN, YOU KNOW.
SHE SENDS HER BEST. EVERYTHING'S... GOOD. REAL GOOD.
YES.
CLEARLY.

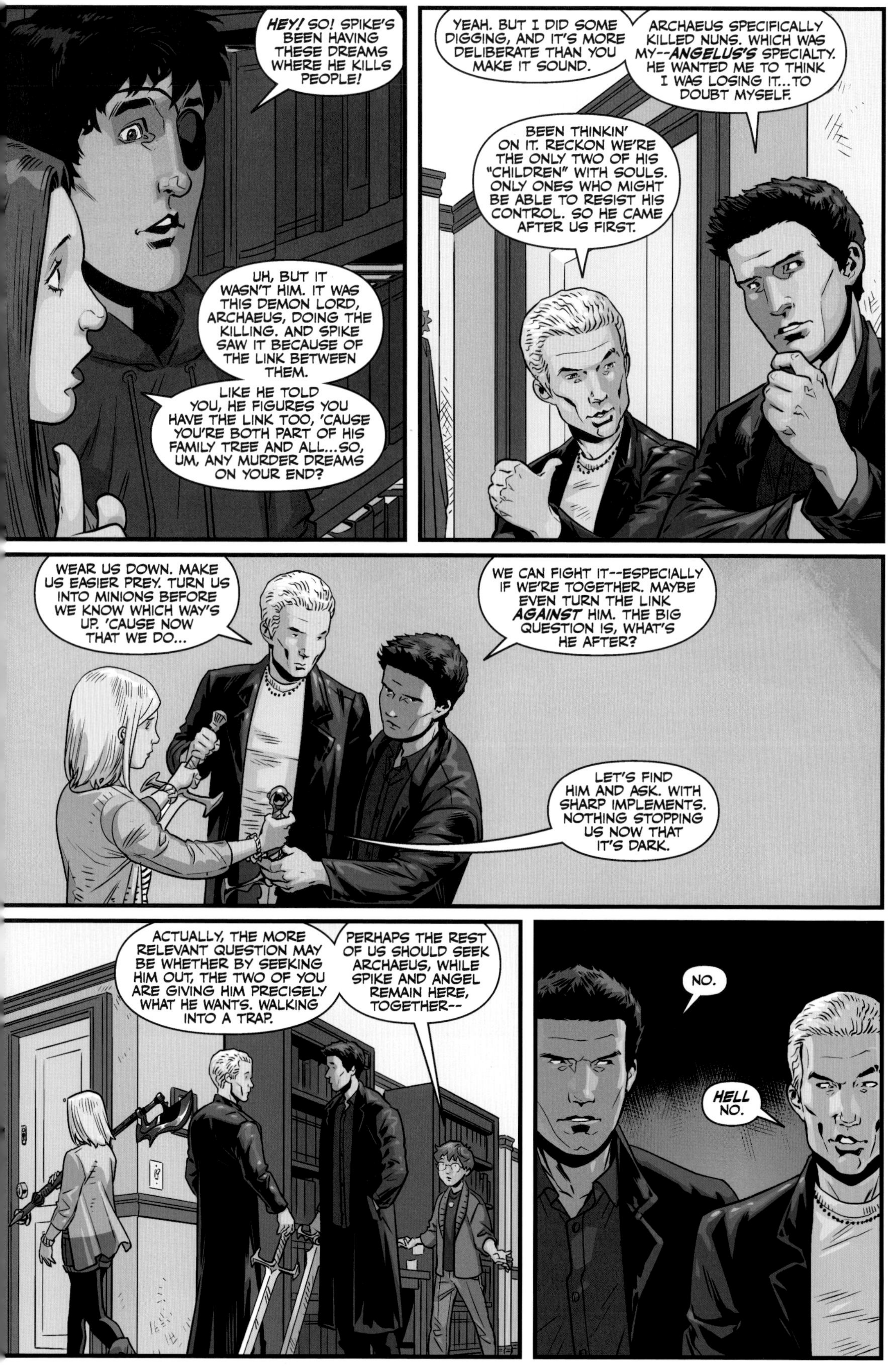
HEY! SO! SPIKE'S BEEN HAVING THESE DREAMS WHERE HE KILLS PEOPLE!
UH, BUT IT WASN'T HIM. IT WAS THIS DEMON LORD, ARCHAEUS, DOING THE KILLING. AND SPIKE SAW IT BECAUSE OF THE LINK BETWEEN THEM.
LIKE HE TOLD YOU, HE FIGURES YOU HAVE THE LINK TOO, 'CAUSE YOU'RE BOTH PART OF HIS FAMILY TREE AND ALL...SO, UM, ANY MURDER DREAMS ON YOUR END?
YEAH. BUT I DID SOME DIGGING, AND IT'S MORE DELIBERATE THAN YOU MAKE IT SOUND.
ARCHAEUS SPECIFICALLY KILLED NUNS. WHICH WAS MY--ANGELUS'S SPECIALTY. HE WANTED ME TO THINK I WAS LOSING IT...TO DOUBT MYSELF.
BEEN THINKIN' ON IT. RECKON WE'RE THE ONLY TWO OF HIS "CHILDREN" WITH SOULS. ONLY ONES WHO MIGHT BE ABLE TO RESIST HIS CONTROL. SO HE CAME AFTER US FIRST.
WEAR US DOWN. MAKE US EASIER PREY. TURN US INTO MINIONS BEFORE WE KNOW WHICH WAY'S UP. 'CAUSE NOW THAT WE DO...
WE CAN FIGHT IT--ESPECIALLY IF WE'RE TOGETHER. MAYBE EVEN TURN THE LINK AGAINST HIM. THE BIG QUESTION IS, WHAT'S HE AFTER?
LET'S FIND HIM AND ASK. WITH SHARP IMPLEMENTS. NOTHING STOPPING US NOW THAT IT'S DARK.
ACTUALLY, THE MORE RELEVANT QUESTION MAY BE WHETHER BY SEEKING HIM OUT, THE TWO OF YOU ARE GIVING HIM PRECISELY WHAT HE WANTS. WALKING INTO A TRAP.
PERHAPS THE REST OF US SHOULD SEEK ARCHAEUS, WHILE SPIKE AND ANGEL REMAIN HERE, TOGETHER--
NO.
HELL NO.

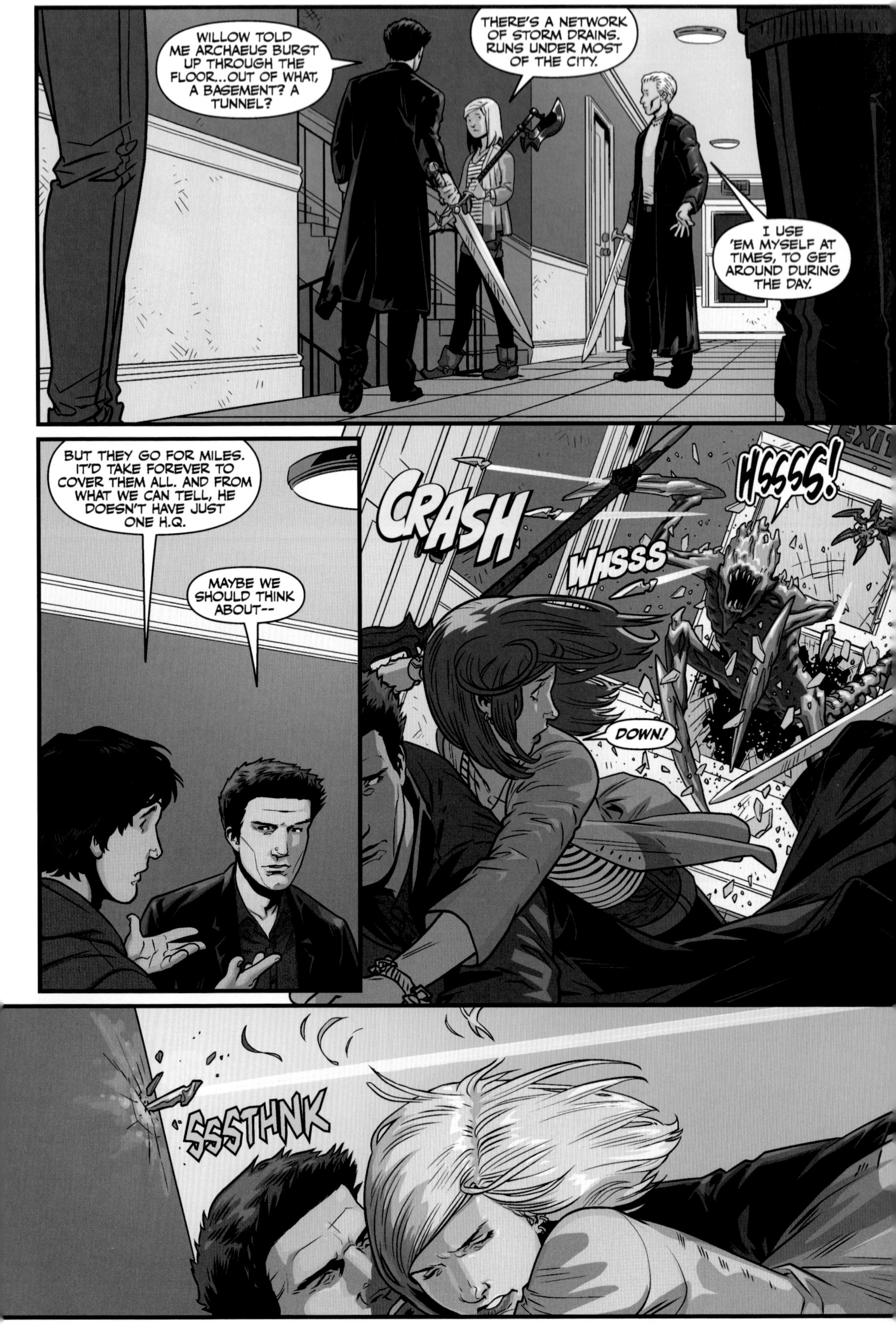
WILLOW TOLD ME ARCHAEUS BURST UP THROUGH THE FLOOR...OUT OF WHAT, A BASEMENT? A TUNNEL?
THERE'S A NETWORK OF STORM DRAINS. RUNS UNDER MOST OF THE CITY.
I USE 'EM MYSELF AT TIMES, TO GET AROUND DURING THE DAY.
BUT THEY GO FOR MILES. IT'D TAKE FOREVER TO COVER THEM ALL. AND FROM WHAT WE CAN TELL, HE DOESN'T HAVE JUST ONE H.Q.
MAYBE WE SHOULD THINK ABOUT--
EXIT
CRASH
HSSSS!
WHSSS
DOWN!
SSSTHNK

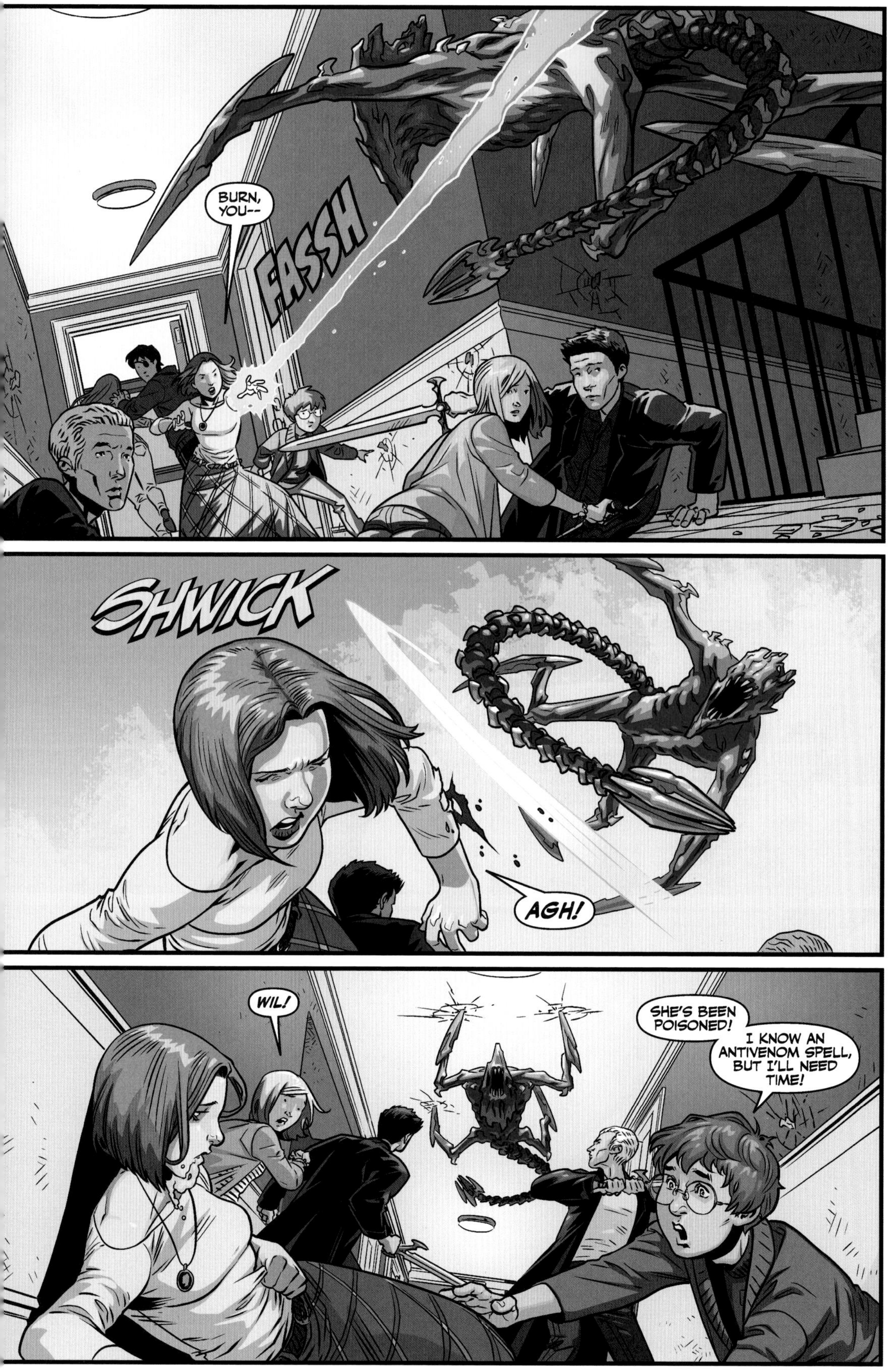
BURN, YOU--
FASSH
SHWICK
AGH!
WIL!
SHE'S BEEN POISONED!
I KNOW AN ANTIVENOM SPELL, BUT I'LL NEED TIME!

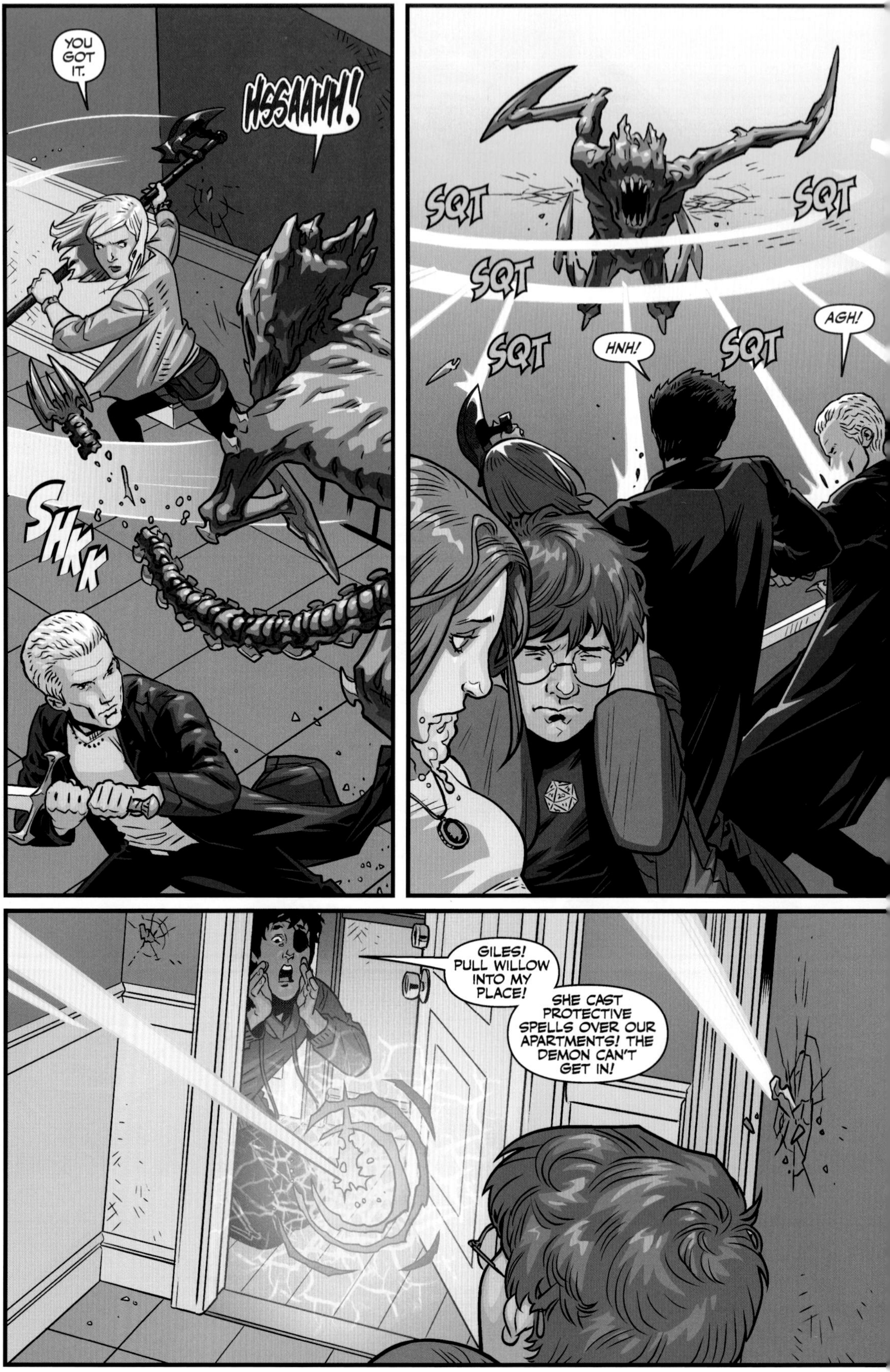
YOU GOT IT.
HSSAAHH!
SHKK
SQT
SQT
SQT
SQT
SQT
HNH!
AGH!
GILES! PULL WILLOW INTO MY PLACE!
SHE CAST PROTECTIVE SPELLS OVER OUR APARTMENTS! THE DEMON CAN'T GET IN!

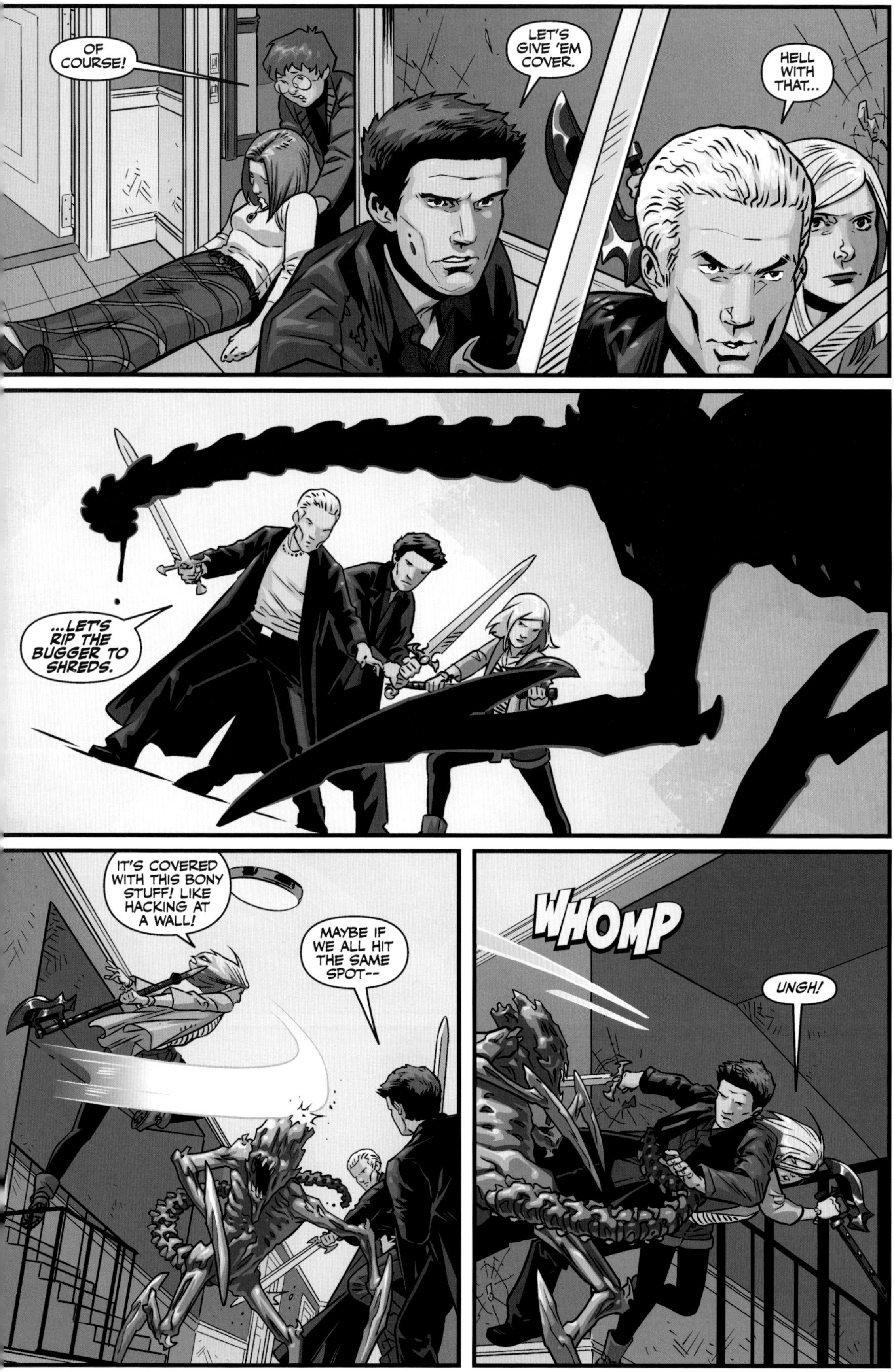
OF COURSE!
LET'S GIVE 'EM COVER.
HELL WITH THAT...
...LET'S RIP THE BUGGER TO SHREDS.
IT'S COVERED WITH THIS BONY STUFF! LIKE HACKING AT A WALL!
MAYBE IF WE ALL HIT THE SAME SPOT--
WHOMP
UNGH!

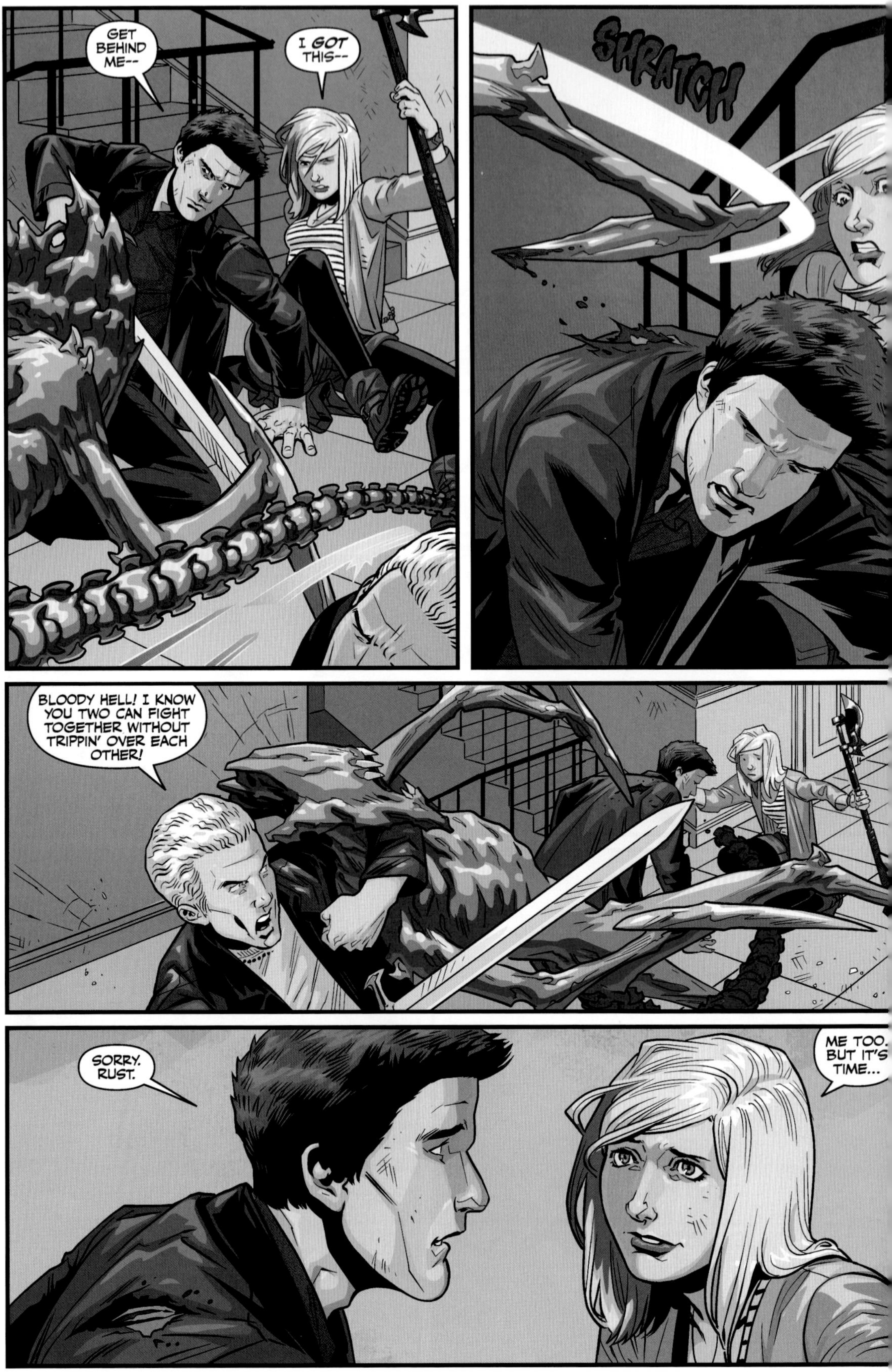
GET BEHIND ME--
I GOT THIS--
SHRATCH
BLOODY HELL! I KNOW YOU TWO CAN FIGHT TOGETHER WITHOUT TRIPPIN' OVER EACH OTHER!
SORRY. RUST.
ME TOO. BUT IT'S TIME...

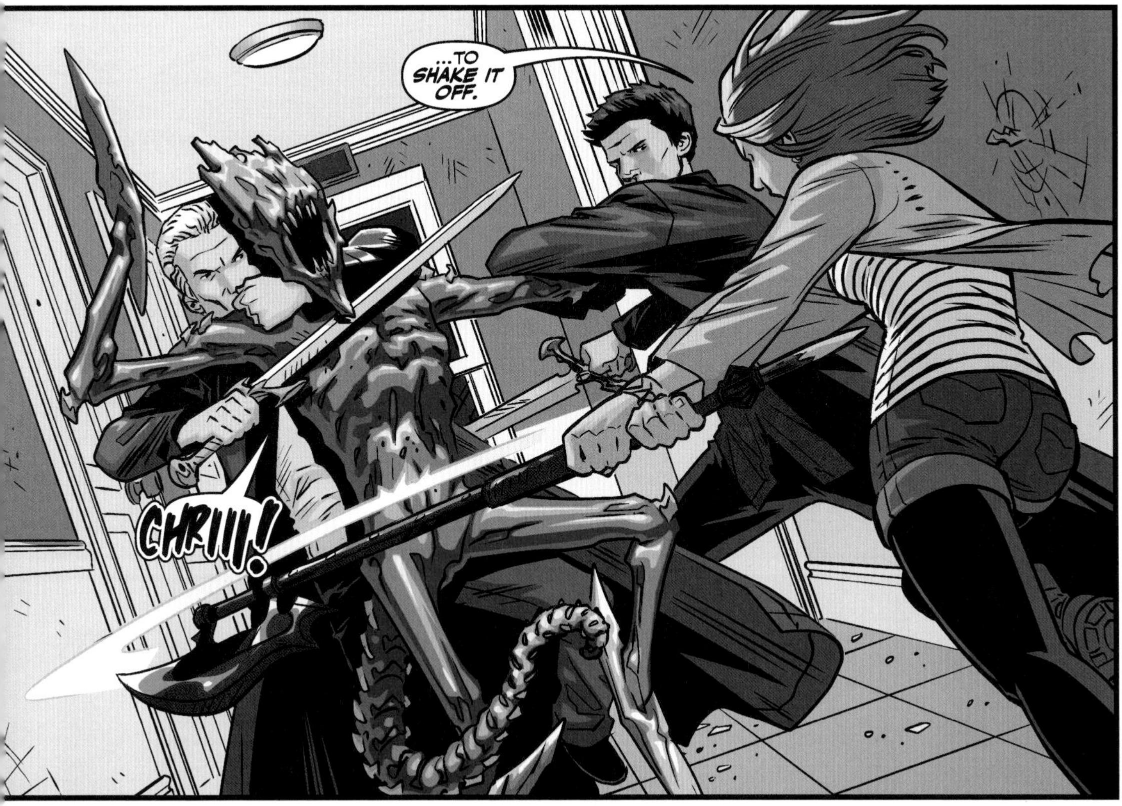
...TO SHAKE IT OFF.
CHRIIII!

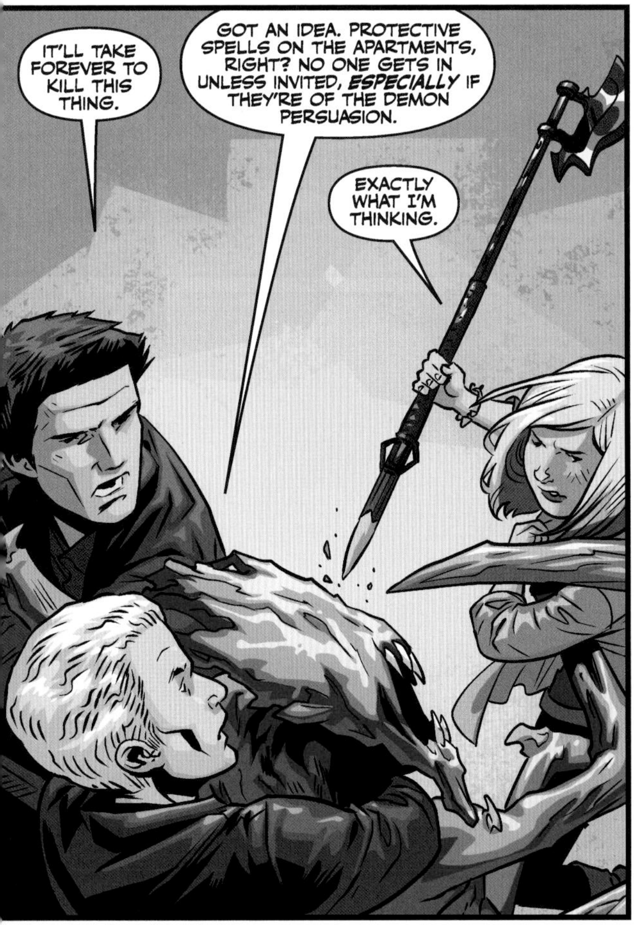
IT'LL TAKE FOREVER TO KILL THIS THING.
GOT AN IDEA. PROTECTIVE SPELLS ON THE APARTMENTS, RIGHT? NO ONE GETS IN UNLESS INVITED, ESPECIALLY IF THEY'RE OF THE DEMON PERSUASION.
EXACTLY WHAT I'M THINKING.

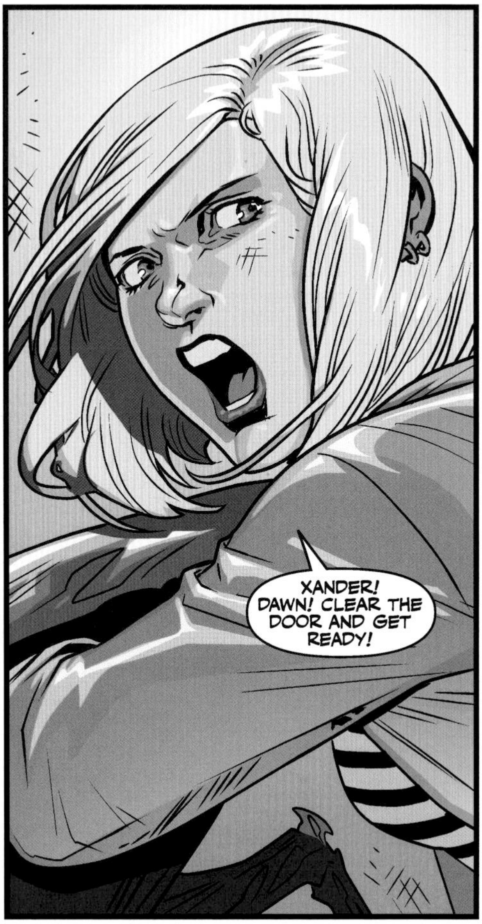
XANDER! DAWN! CLEAR THE DOOR AND GET READY!

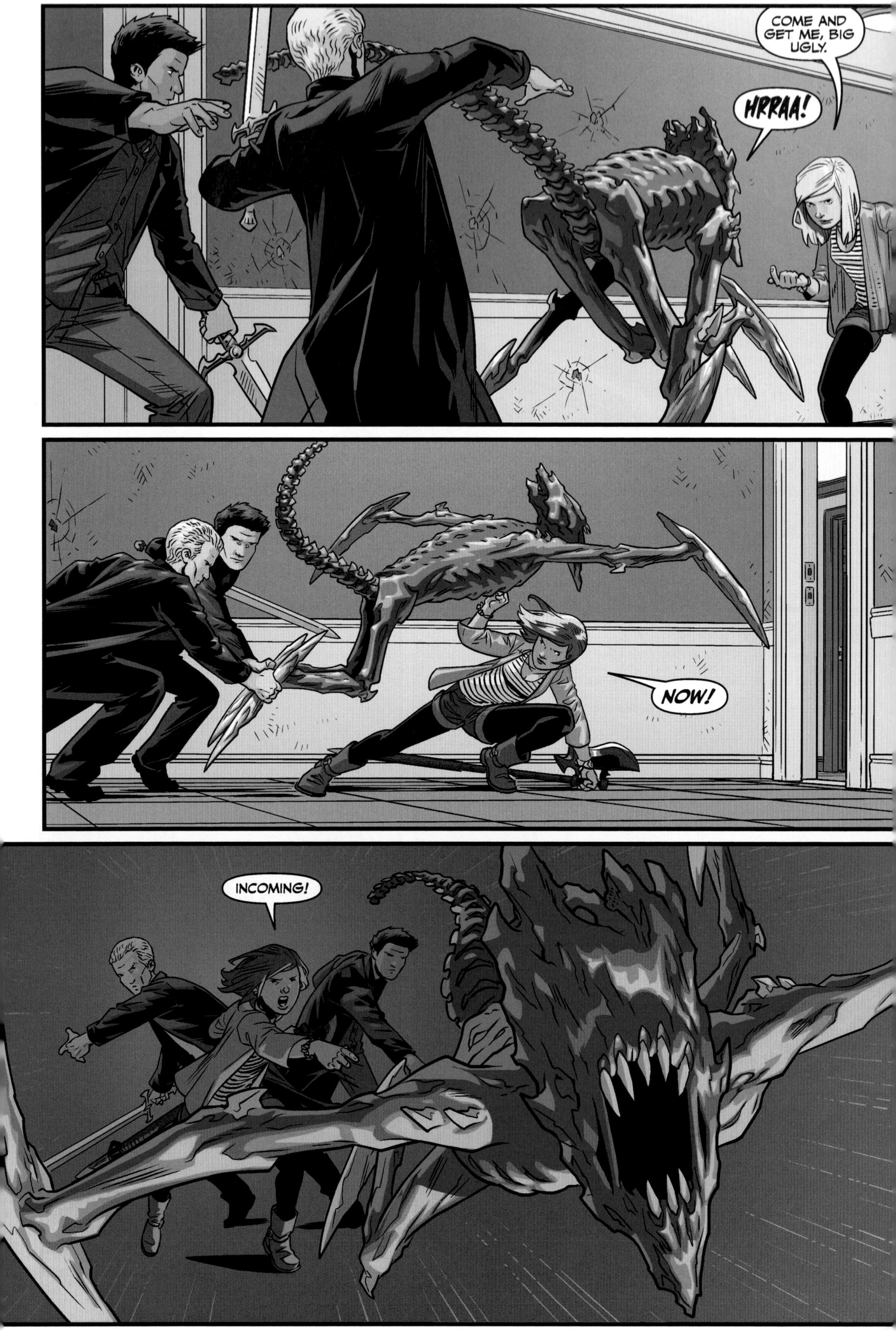
COME AND GET ME, BIG UGLY.
HRRAA!
NOW!
INCOMING!

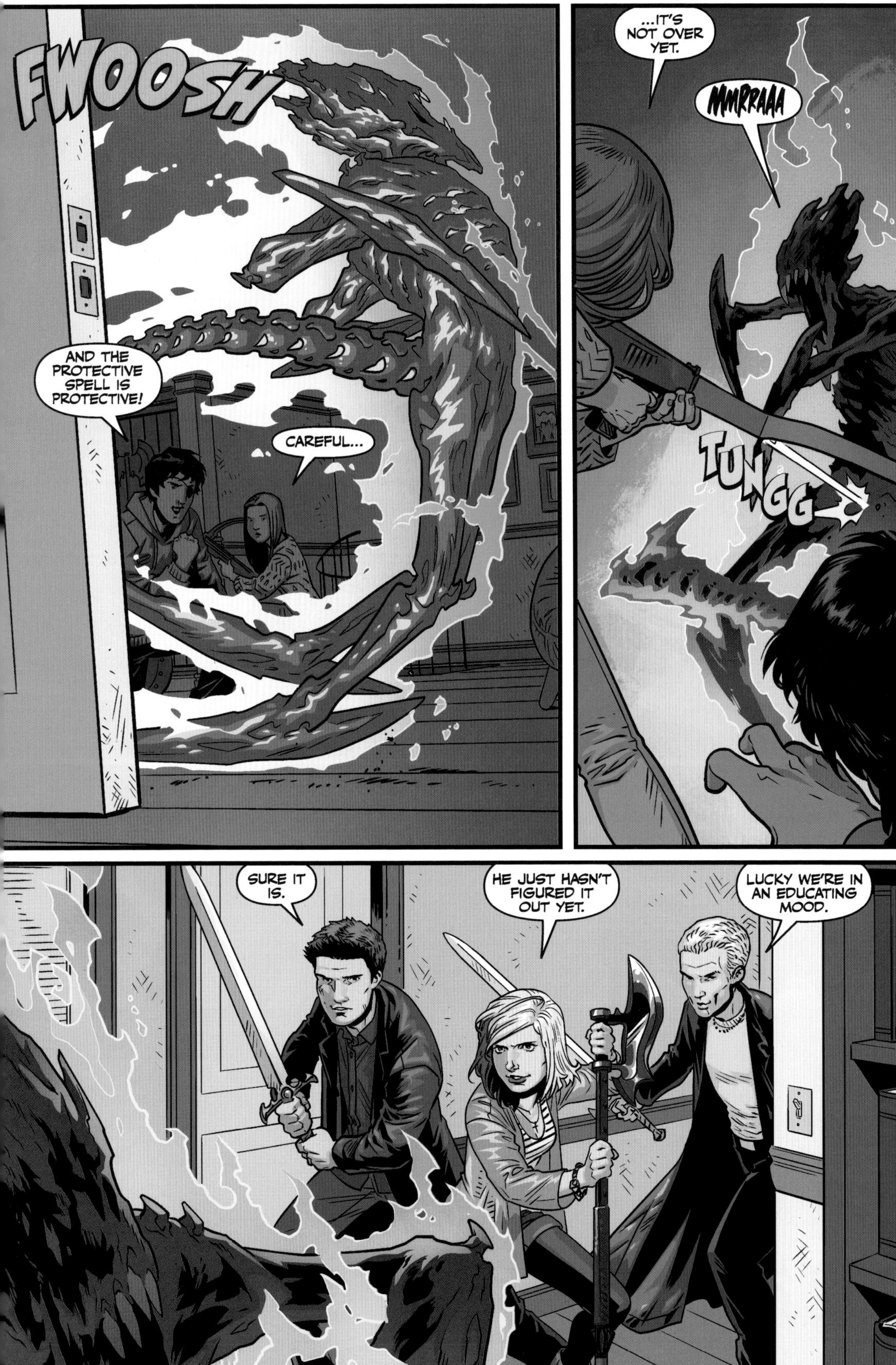
FWOOSH
AND THE PROTECTIVE SPELL IS PROTECTIVE!
CAREFUL...
...IT'S NOT OVER YET.
MMRRAAA
TUNGG
SURE IT IS.
HE JUST HASN'T FIGURED IT OUT YET.
LUCKY WE'RE IN AN EDUCATING MOOD.

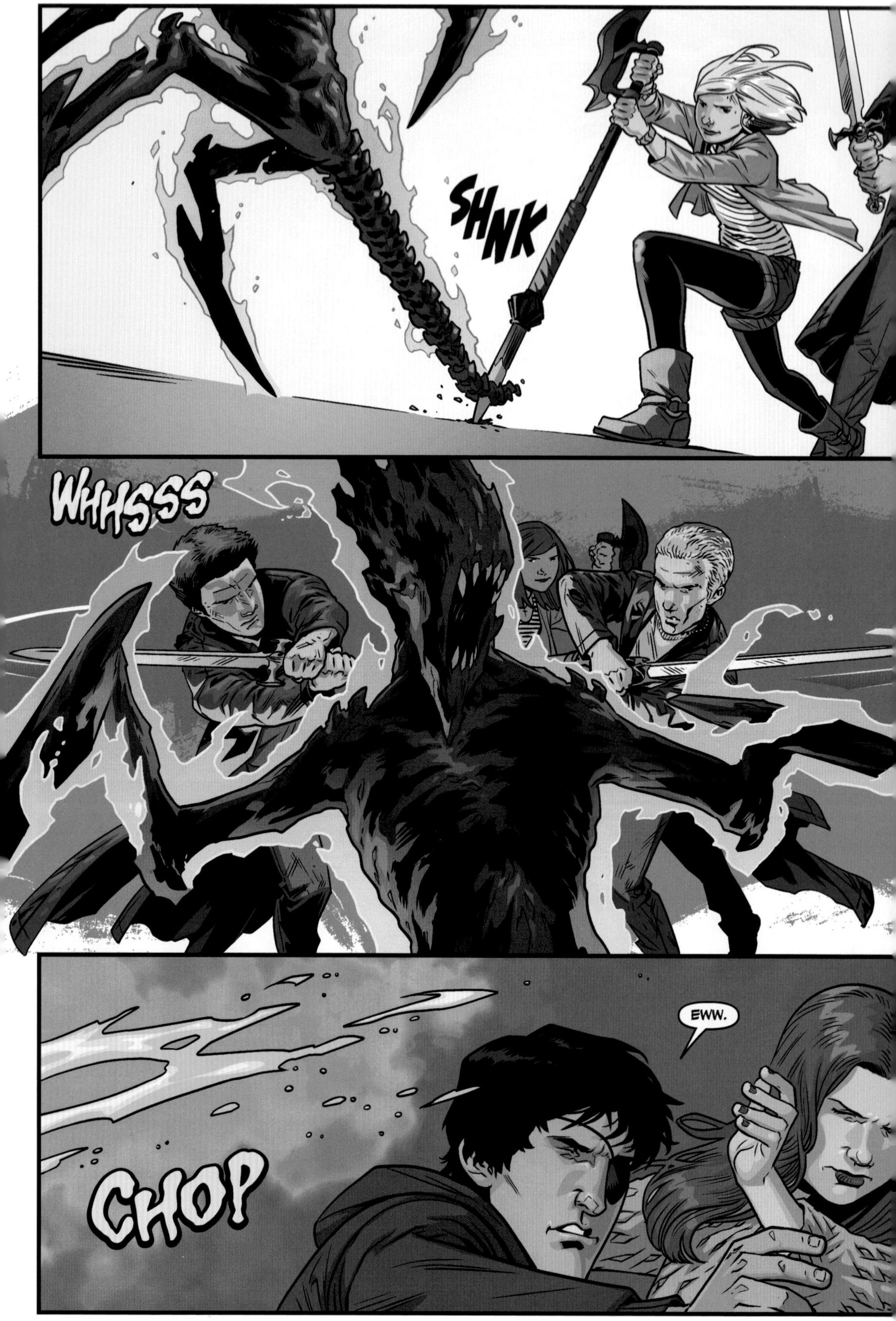
SHNK
WHHSSS
EWW.
CHOP

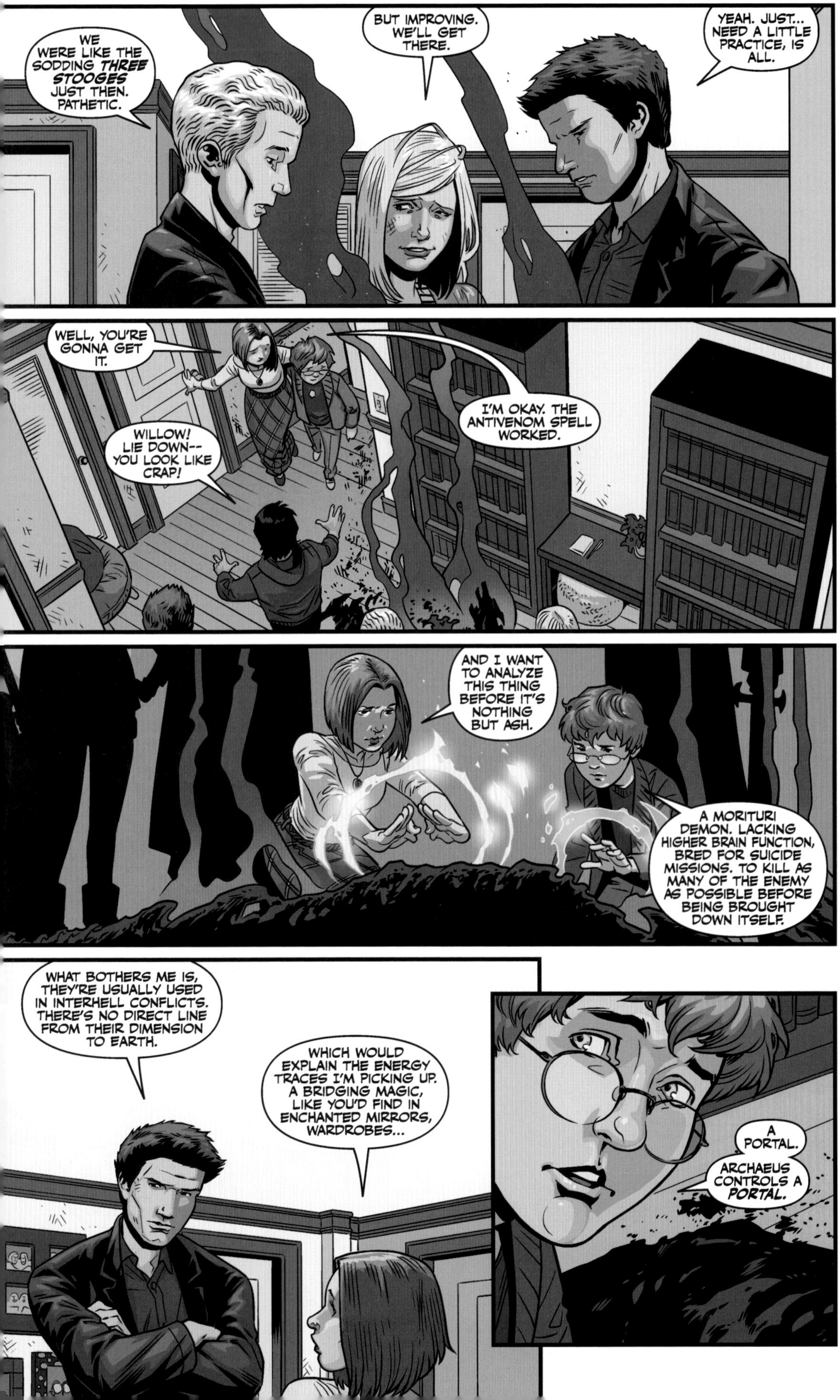
WE WERE LIKE THE SODDING *THREE STOOGES* JUST THEN. PATHETIC.
BUT IMPROVING. WE'LL GET THERE.
YEAH. JUST... NEED A LITTLE PRACTICE, IS ALL.
WELL, YOU'RE GONNA GET IT.
I'M OKAY. THE ANTIVENOM SPELL WORKED.
WILLOW! LIE DOWN-- YOU LOOK LIKE CRAP!
AND I WANT TO ANALYZE THIS THING BEFORE IT'S NOTHING BUT ASH.
A MORITURI DEMON. LACKING HIGHER BRAIN FUNCTION, BRED FOR SUICIDE MISSIONS. TO KILL AS MANY OF THE ENEMY AS POSSIBLE BEFORE BEING BROUGHT DOWN ITSELF.
WHAT BOTHERS ME IS, THEY'RE USUALLY USED IN INTERHELL CONFLICTS. THERE'S NO DIRECT LINE FROM THEIR DIMENSION TO EARTH.
WHICH WOULD EXPLAIN THE ENERGY TRACES I'M PICKING UP. A BRIDGING MAGIC, LIKE YOU'D FIND IN ENCHANTED MIRRORS, WARDROBES...
A PORTAL.
ARCHAEUS CONTROLS A *PORTAL.*

WHAT, THE BIG BAD'S GOT AN EXPRESS TRAIN TO EARTH? I THOUGHT WE SHUT ALL THAT DOWN.

NO, WE MADE IT MORE DIFFICULT. BUT DEMONS CAN STILL CROSS OVER THROUGH NATURAL ENTRY POINTS, LIKE HELLMOUTHS...OR BY USING CERTAIN POWERFUL MYSTIC ARTIFACTS.

IT'S MAKING SENSE NOW. THE UPTICK IN DEMON ACTIVITY...ARCHAEUS GATHERING POWER. IF HE'S GOT SOMETHING THAT CAN OPEN A LINE TO HELL DIMENSIONS...

HE LETS THE CREEPY-CRAWLIES THROUGH, AND THEY OWE HIM A FAVOR. THE BLIGHTER'S LIKE THE DON CORLEONE OF DEMONS.

THIS UNDERMINES ALL OUR EFFORTS TO PROTECT EARTH. WE MUST STOP ARCHAEUS, AT ANY COST.

YEAH, UH... DOES IT STRIKE ANYONE THAT MAYBE HE KINDA WANTED US TO ARRIVE AT THAT CONCLUSION?

OF COURSE. BUT THAT DOESN'T MAKE THE SITUATION ANY LESS URGENT.

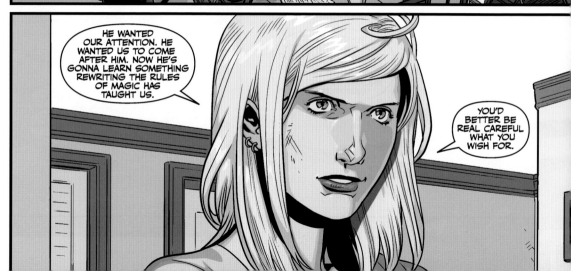

HE WANTED OUR ATTENTION. HE WANTED US TO COME AFTER HIM. NOW HE'S GONNA LEARN SOMETHING REWRITING THE RULES OF MAGIC HAS TAUGHT US.

YOU'D BETTER BE REAL CAREFUL WHAT YOU WISH FOR.

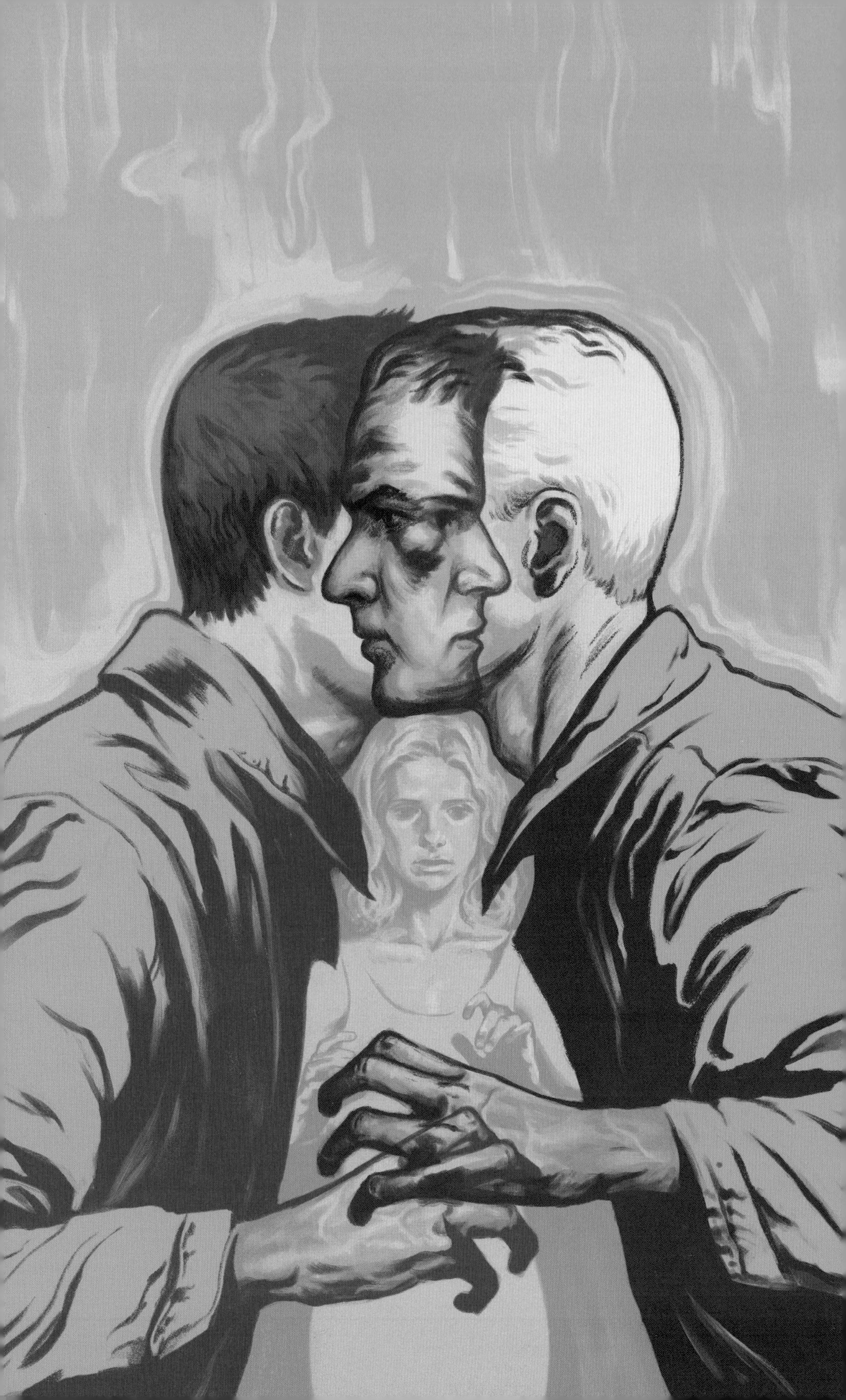

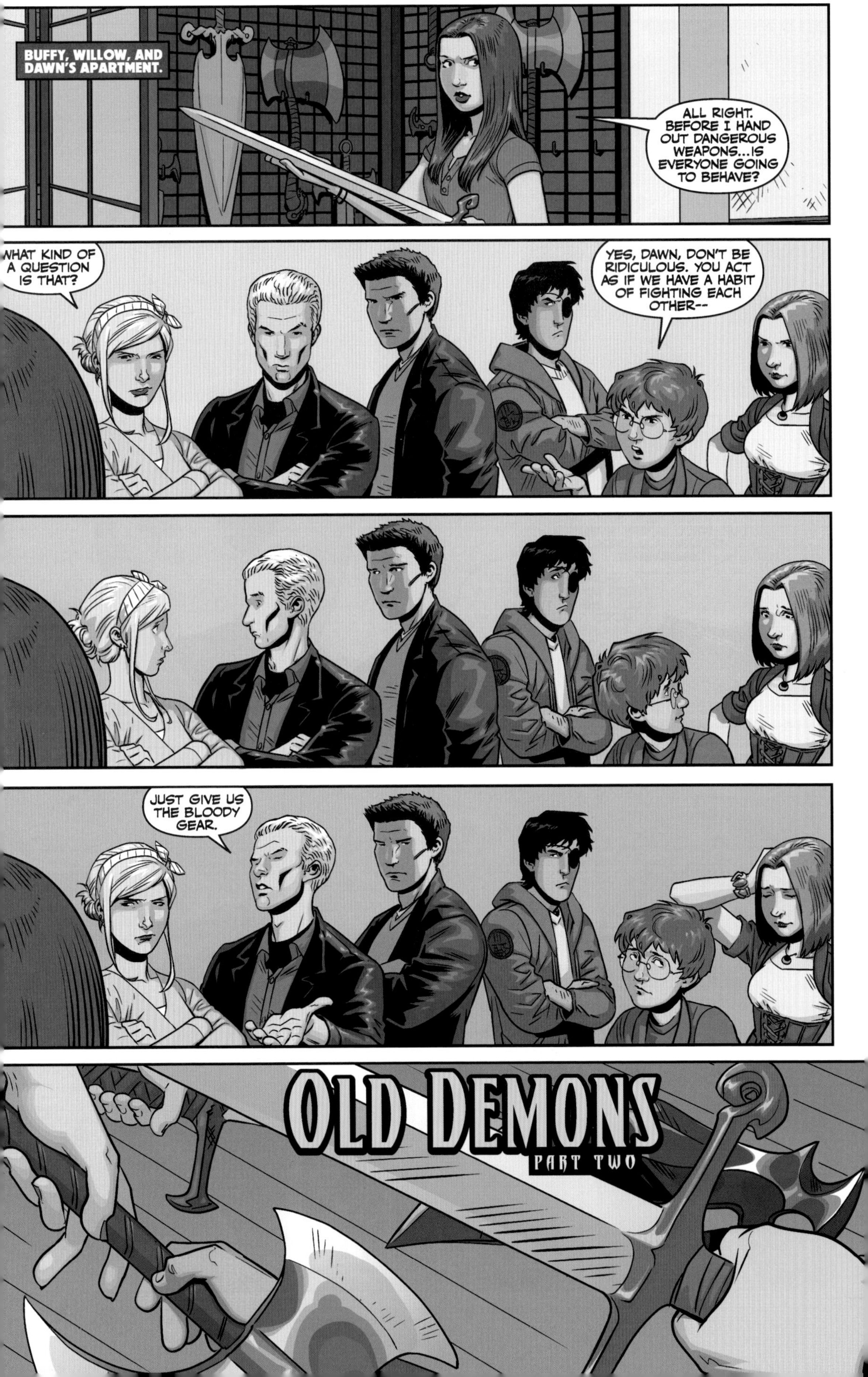
BUFFY, WILLOW, AND DAWN'S APARTMENT.
ALL RIGHT. BEFORE I HAND OUT DANGEROUS WEAPONS...IS EVERYONE GOING TO BEHAVE?
WHAT KIND OF A QUESTION IS THAT?
YES, DAWN, DON'T BE RIDICULOUS. YOU ACT AS IF WE HAVE A HABIT OF FIGHTING EACH OTHER--
JUST GIVE US THE BLOODY GEAR.
OLD DEMONS
PART TWO

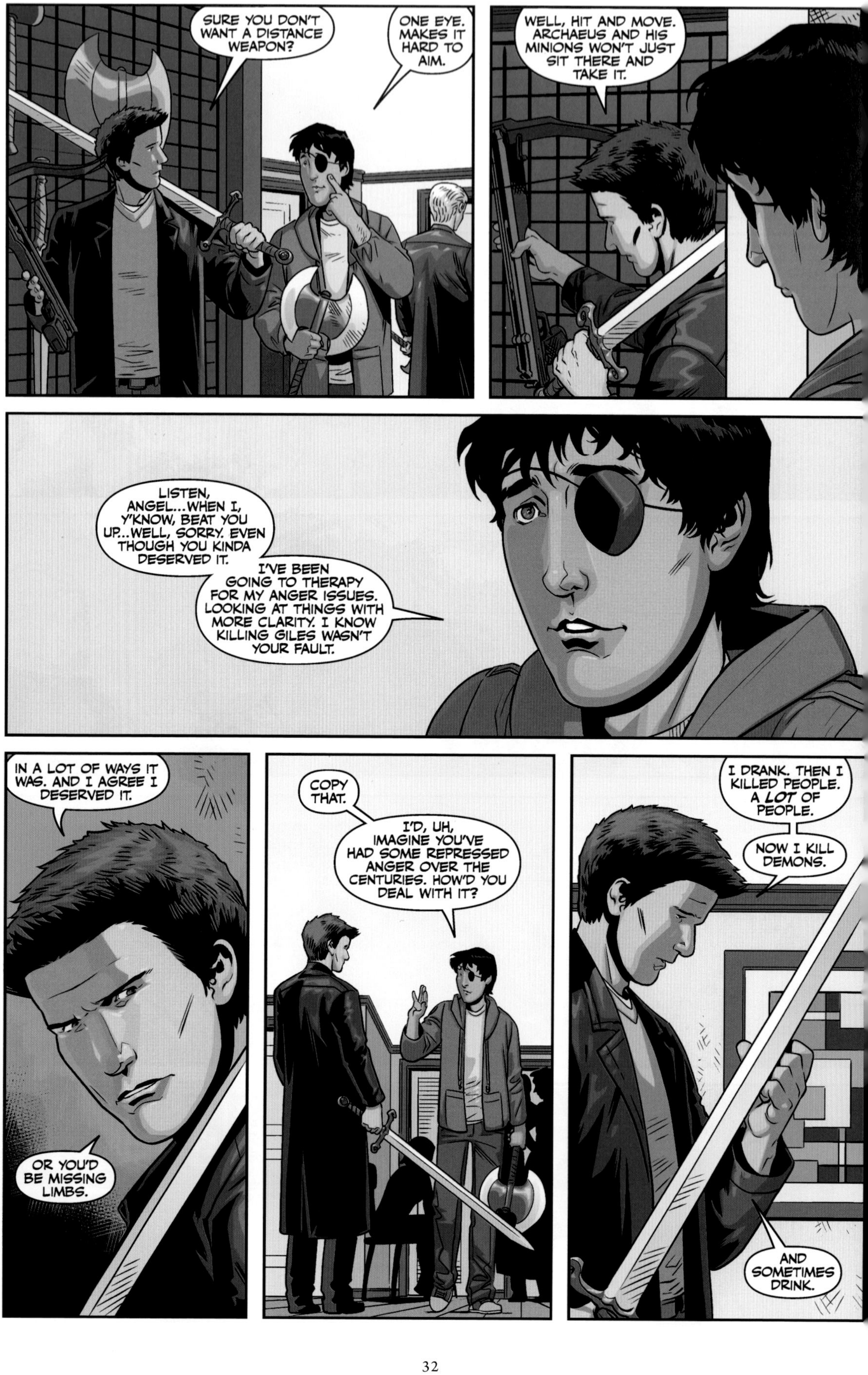
SURE YOU DON'T WANT A DISTANCE WEAPON?
ONE EYE. MAKES IT HARD TO AIM.
WELL, HIT AND MOVE. ARCHAEUS AND HIS MINIONS WON'T JUST SIT THERE AND TAKE IT.
LISTEN, ANGEL...WHEN I, Y'KNOW, BEAT YOU UP...WELL, SORRY. EVEN THOUGH YOU KINDA DESERVED IT.
I'VE BEEN GOING TO THERAPY FOR MY ANGER ISSUES. LOOKING AT THINGS WITH MORE CLARITY. I KNOW KILLING GILES WASN'T YOUR FAULT.
IN A LOT OF WAYS IT WAS. AND I AGREE I DESERVED IT.
OR YOU'D BE MISSING LIMBS.
COPY THAT.
I'D, UH, IMAGINE YOU'VE HAD SOME REPRESSED ANGER OVER THE CENTURIES. HOW'D YOU DEAL WITH IT?
I DRANK. THEN I KILLED PEOPLE. A *LOT* OF PEOPLE.
NOW I KILL DEMONS.
AND SOMETIMES DRINK.

INTERESTING APPROACH. Y'KNOW, I BET THEY HAVE GOOD THERAPISTS IN LONDON--

WOULDN'T THAT BE PAINFUL?

GOT A LOT OF CHURCHES, TOO. I'D GO TO ONE OF THEM FIRST.

EXACTLY.

HEY, DAWN. WILLOW MENTIONED YOUR MEMORIES GOT SHAKEN UP. DO YOU... STILL KNOW WHO I AM?

ACTUALLY, YES. ALL MY ARTIFICIAL MEMORIES ARE SHIPSHAPE. WHICH IS SO WEIRD.

WE'VE BARELY EVER *REALLY* MET, BUT I REMEMBER YOU BEING AROUND. HAVING THE BIGGEST CRUSH ON YOU WHEN YOU AND BUFFY WERE...

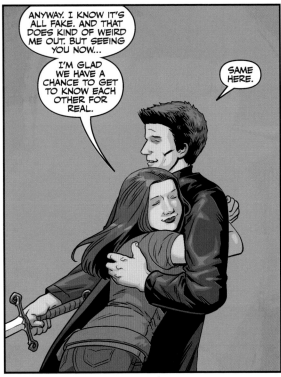

ANYWAY. I KNOW IT'S ALL FAKE. AND THAT DOES KIND OF WEIRD ME OUT. BUT SEEING YOU NOW...

I'M GLAD WE HAVE A CHANCE TO GET TO KNOW EACH OTHER FOR REAL.

SAME HERE.

DRINKING AND KILLING DEMONS.

ALWAYS WILLING TO TRY NEW MODALITIES.

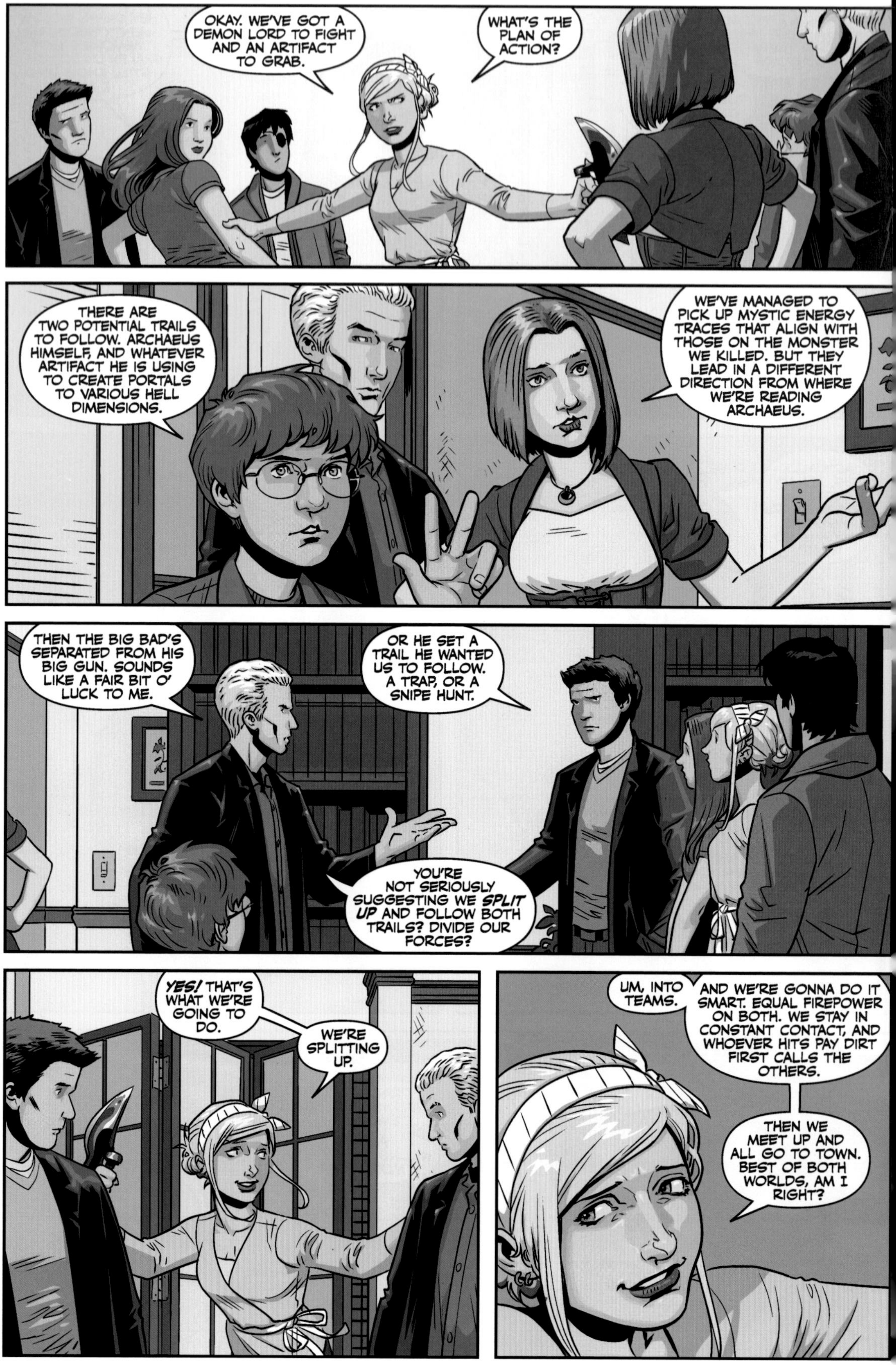
OKAY. WE'VE GOT A DEMON LORD TO FIGHT AND AN ARTIFACT TO GRAB.
WHAT'S THE PLAN OF ACTION?
THERE ARE TWO POTENTIAL TRAILS TO FOLLOW. ARCHAEUS HIMSELF, AND WHATEVER ARTIFACT HE IS USING TO CREATE PORTALS TO VARIOUS HELL DIMENSIONS.
WE'VE MANAGED TO PICK UP MYSTIC ENERGY TRACES THAT ALIGN WITH THOSE ON THE MONSTER WE KILLED. BUT THEY LEAD IN A DIFFERENT DIRECTION FROM WHERE WE'RE READING ARCHAEUS.
THEN THE BIG BAD'S SEPARATED FROM HIS BIG GUN. SOUNDS LIKE A FAIR BIT O' LUCK TO ME.
OR HE SET A TRAIL HE WANTED US TO FOLLOW. A TRAP, OR A SNIPE HUNT.
YOU'RE NOT SERIOUSLY SUGGESTING WE *SPLIT UP* AND FOLLOW BOTH TRAILS? DIVIDE OUR FORCES?
YES! THAT'S WHAT WE'RE GOING TO DO.
WE'RE SPLITTING UP.
UM, INTO TEAMS.
AND WE'RE GONNA DO IT SMART. EQUAL FIREPOWER ON BOTH. WE STAY IN CONSTANT CONTACT, AND WHOEVER HITS PAY DIRT FIRST CALLS THE OTHERS.
THEN WE MEET UP AND ALL GO TO TOWN. BEST OF BOTH WORLDS, AM I RIGHT?

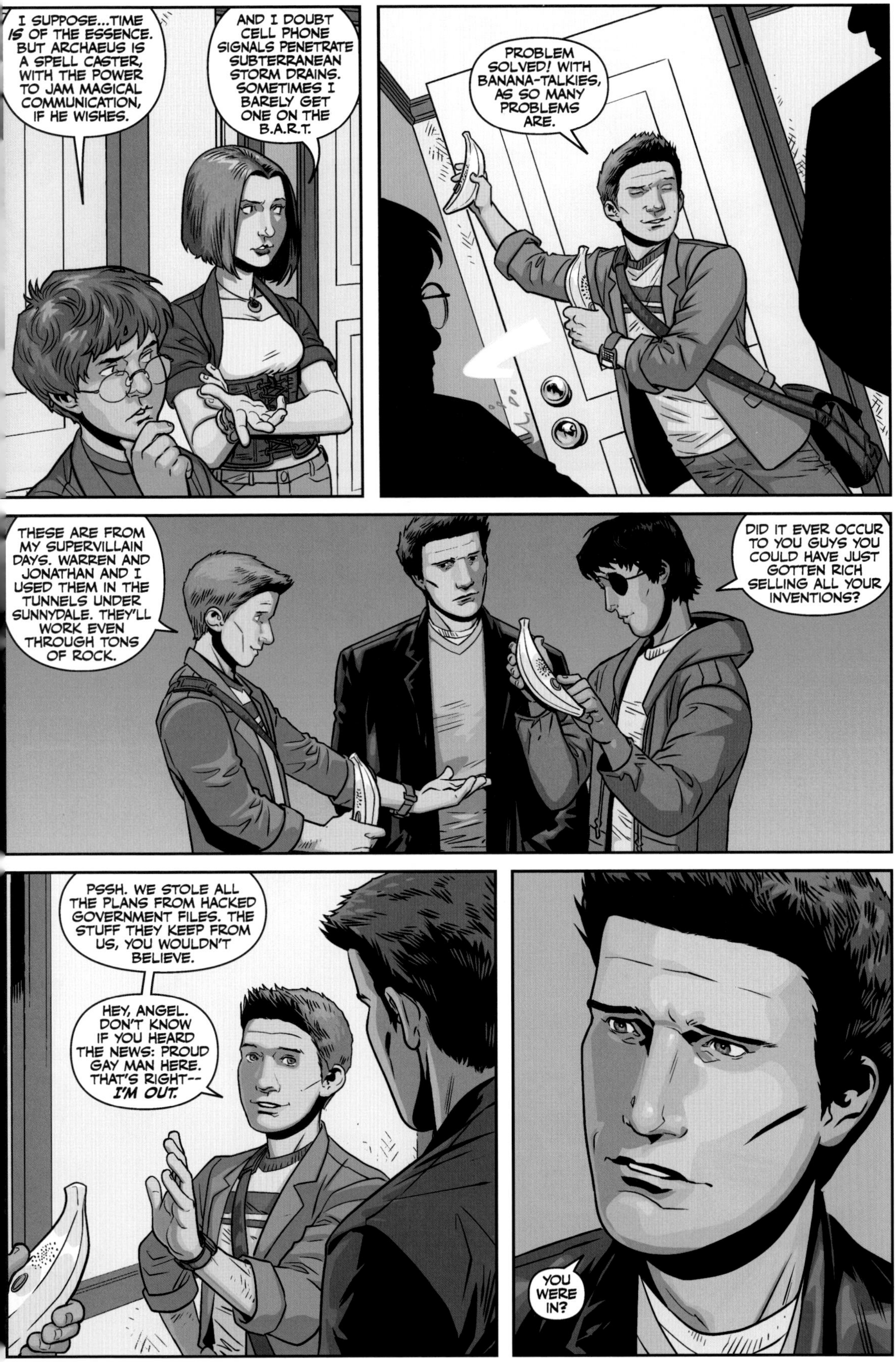
I SUPPOSE...TIME *IS* OF THE ESSENCE. BUT ARCHAEUS IS A SPELL CASTER, WITH THE POWER TO JAM MAGICAL COMMUNICATION, IF HE WISHES.
AND I DOUBT CELL PHONE SIGNALS PENETRATE SUBTERRANEAN STORM DRAINS. SOMETIMES I BARELY GET ONE ON THE B.A.R.T.
PROBLEM SOLVED! WITH BANANA-TALKIES, AS SO MANY PROBLEMS ARE.
THESE ARE FROM MY SUPERVILLAIN DAYS. WARREN AND JONATHAN AND I USED THEM IN THE TUNNELS UNDER SUNNYDALE. THEY'LL WORK EVEN THROUGH TONS OF ROCK.
DID IT EVER OCCUR TO YOU GUYS YOU COULD HAVE JUST GOTTEN RICH SELLING ALL YOUR INVENTIONS?
PSSH. WE STOLE ALL THE PLANS FROM HACKED GOVERNMENT FILES. THE STUFF THEY KEEP FROM US, YOU WOULDN'T BELIEVE.
HEY, ANGEL. DON'T KNOW IF YOU HEARD THE NEWS: PROUD GAY MAN HERE. THAT'S RIGHT-- *I'M OUT.*
YOU WERE IN?

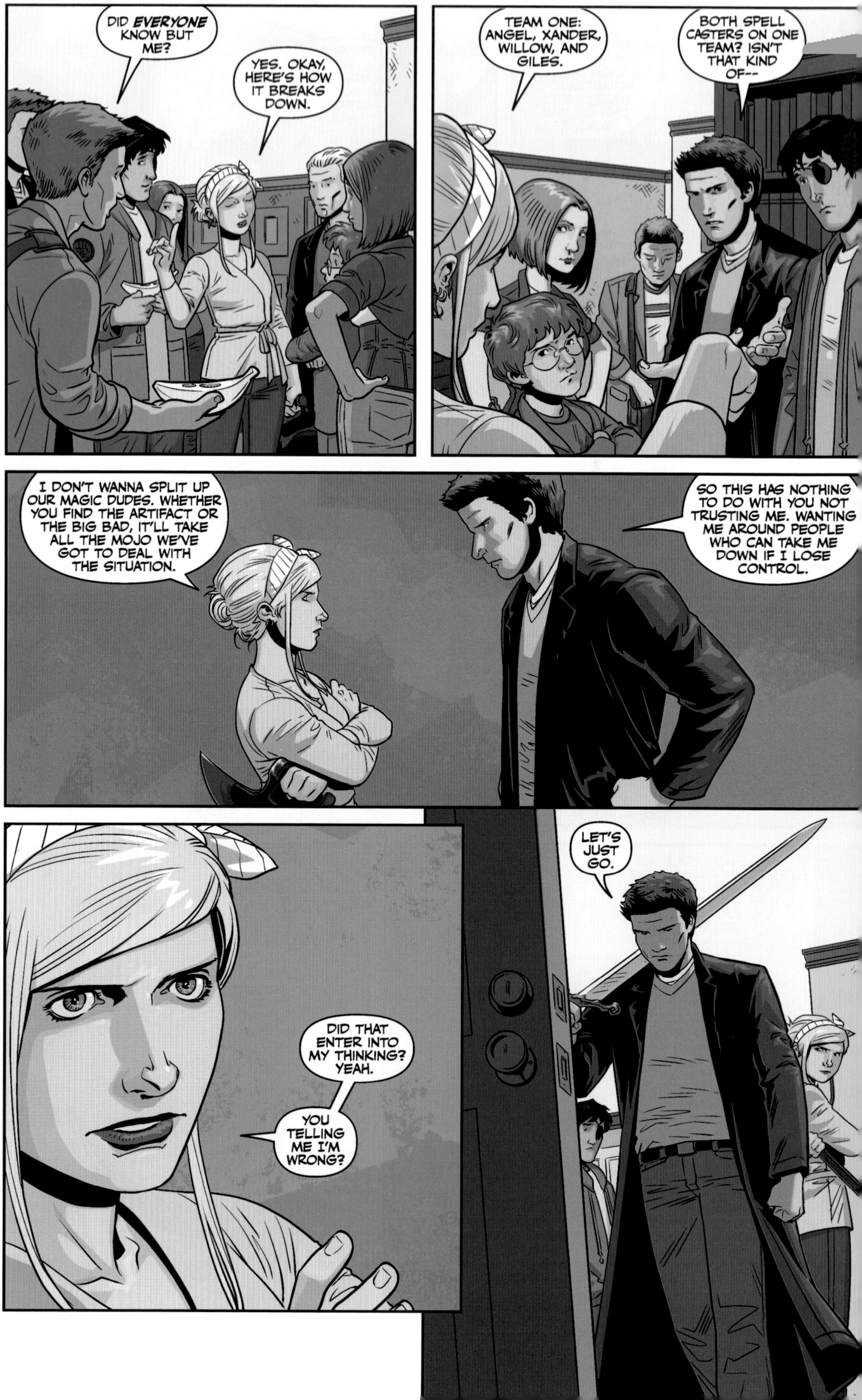
DID *EVERYONE* KNOW BUT ME?
YES. OKAY, HERE'S HOW IT BREAKS DOWN.
TEAM ONE: ANGEL, XANDER, WILLOW, AND GILES.
BOTH SPELL CASTERS ON ONE TEAM? ISN'T THAT KIND OF--
I DON'T WANNA SPLIT UP OUR MAGIC DUDES. WHETHER YOU FIND THE ARTIFACT OR THE BIG BAD, IT'LL TAKE ALL THE MOJO WE'VE GOT TO DEAL WITH THE SITUATION.
SO THIS HAS NOTHING TO DO WITH YOU NOT TRUSTING ME. WANTING ME AROUND PEOPLE WHO CAN TAKE ME DOWN IF I LOSE CONTROL.
DID THAT ENTER INTO MY THINKING? YEAH.
YOU TELLING ME I'M WRONG?
LET'S JUST GO.

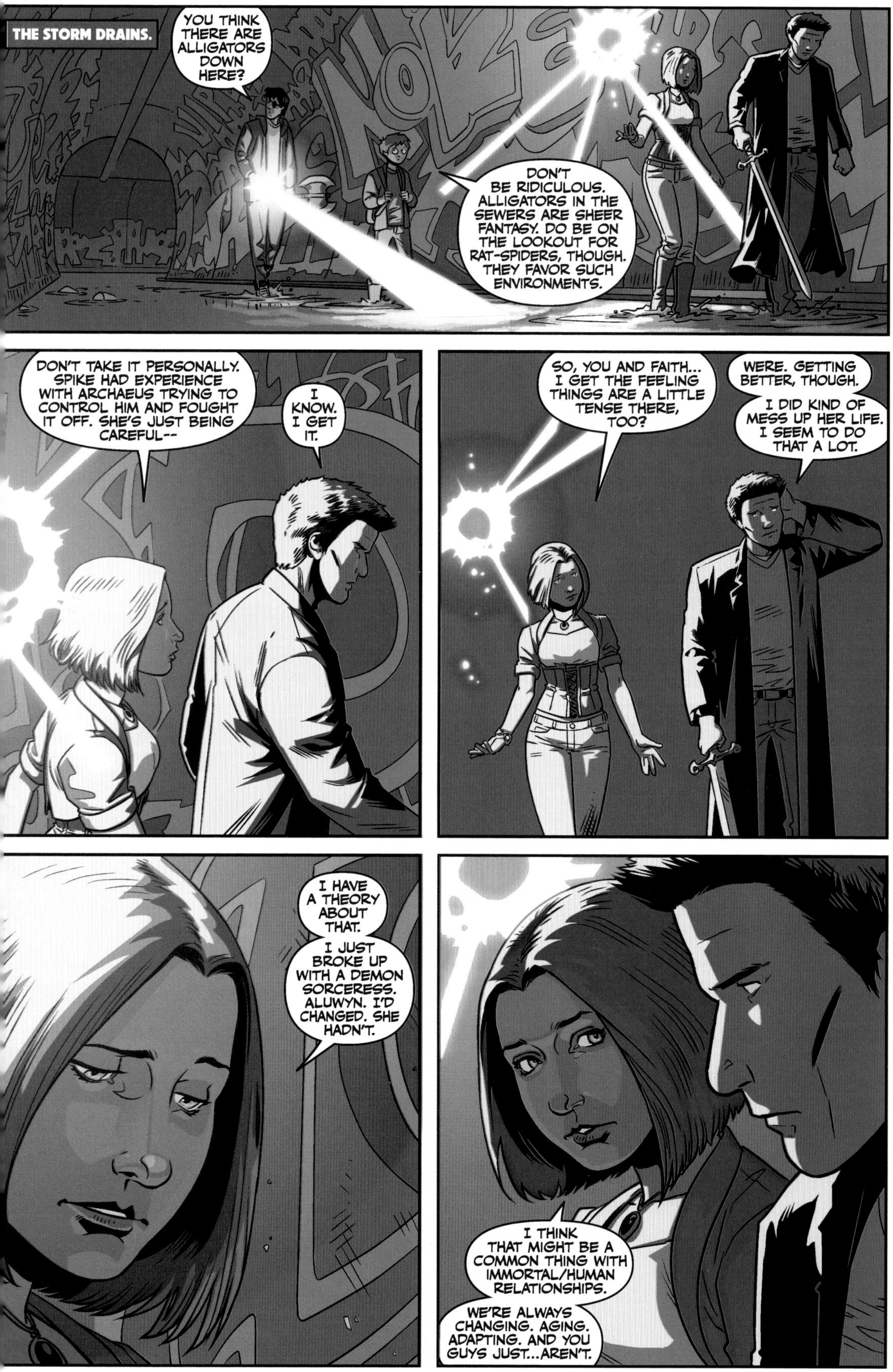
THE STORM DRAINS.
YOU THINK THERE ARE ALLIGATORS DOWN HERE?
DON'T BE RIDICULOUS. ALLIGATORS IN THE SEWERS ARE SHEER FANTASY. DO BE ON THE LOOKOUT FOR RAT-SPIDERS, THOUGH. THEY FAVOR SUCH ENVIRONMENTS.
DON'T TAKE IT PERSONALLY. SPIKE HAD EXPERIENCE WITH ARCHAEUS TRYING TO CONTROL HIM AND FOUGHT IT OFF. SHE'S JUST BEING CAREFUL--
I KNOW. I GET IT.
SO, YOU AND FAITH... I GET THE FEELING THINGS ARE A LITTLE TENSE THERE, TOO?
WERE. GETTING BETTER, THOUGH.
I DID KIND OF MESS UP HER LIFE. I SEEM TO DO THAT A LOT.
I HAVE A THEORY ABOUT THAT.
I JUST BROKE UP WITH A DEMON SORCERESS. ALUWYN. I'D CHANGED. SHE HADN'T.
I THINK THAT MIGHT BE A COMMON THING WITH IMMORTAL/HUMAN RELATIONSHIPS.
WE'RE ALWAYS CHANGING. AGING. ADAPTING. AND YOU GUYS JUST...AREN'T.

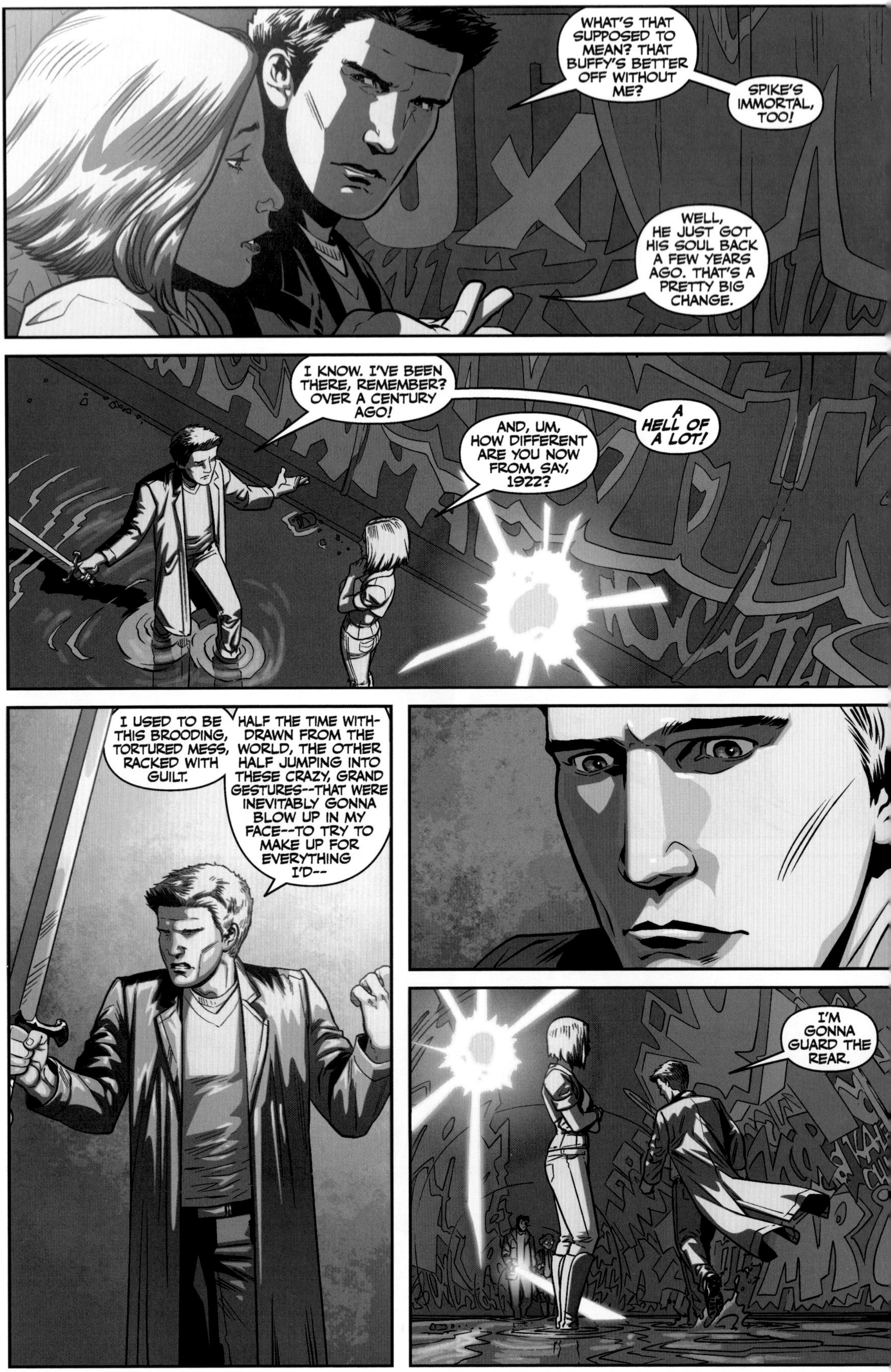
WHAT'S THAT SUPPOSED TO MEAN? THAT BUFFY'S BETTER OFF WITHOUT ME?
SPIKE'S IMMORTAL, TOO!
WELL, HE JUST GOT HIS SOUL BACK A FEW YEARS AGO. THAT'S A PRETTY BIG CHANGE.
I KNOW. I'VE BEEN THERE, REMEMBER? OVER A CENTURY AGO!
A HELL OF A LOT!
AND, UM, HOW DIFFERENT ARE YOU NOW FROM, SAY, 1922?
I USED TO BE THIS BROODING, TORTURED MESS, RACKED WITH GUILT.
HALF THE TIME WITH-DRAWN FROM THE WORLD, THE OTHER HALF JUMPING INTO THESE CRAZY, GRAND GESTURES--THAT WERE INEVITABLY GONNA BLOW UP IN MY FACE--TO TRY TO MAKE UP FOR EVERYTHING I'D--
I'M GONNA GUARD THE REAR.

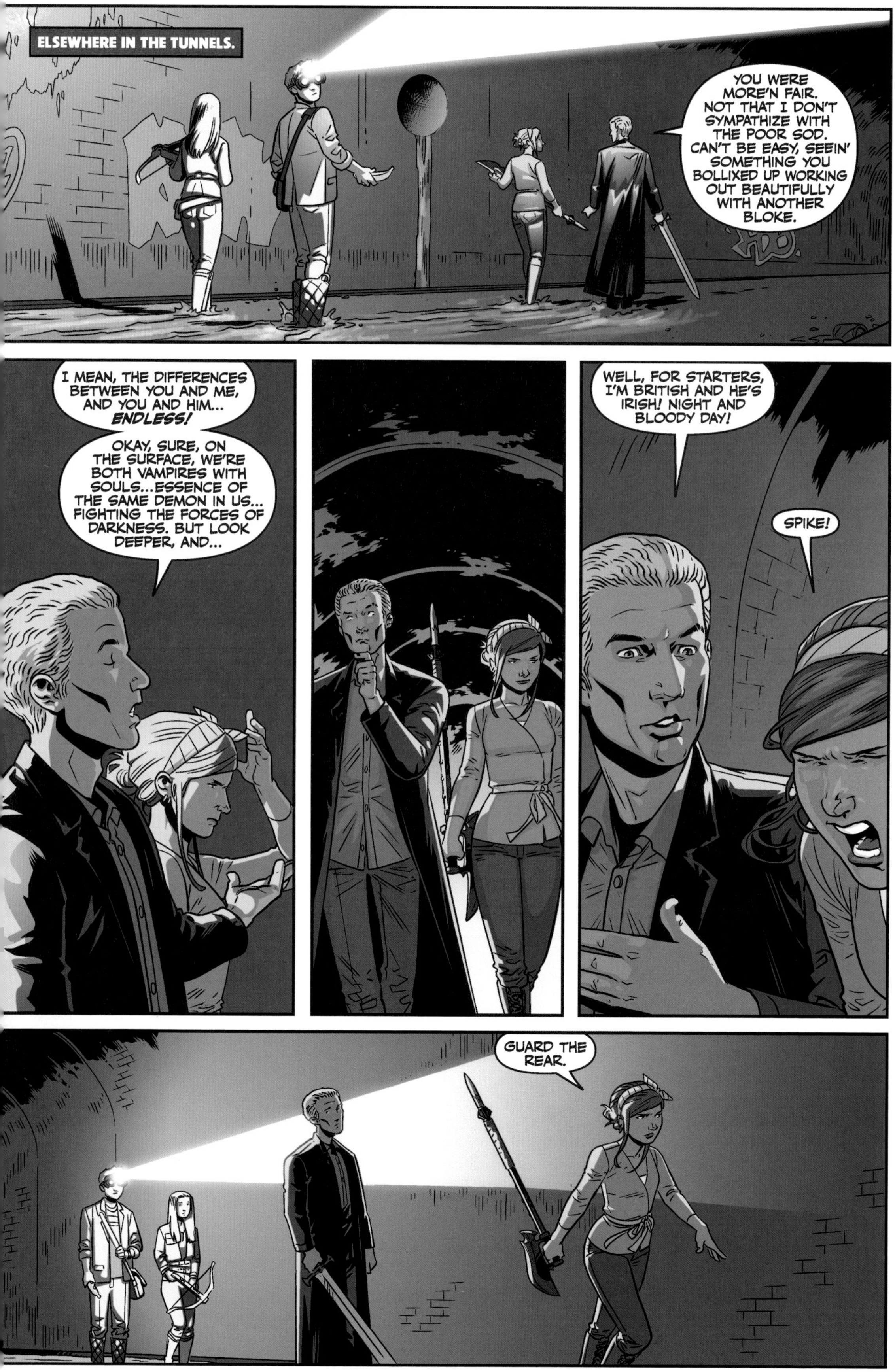
ELSEWHERE IN THE TUNNELS.
YOU WERE MORE'N FAIR. NOT THAT I DON'T SYMPATHIZE WITH THE POOR SOD. CAN'T BE EASY, SEEIN' SOMETHING YOU BOLLIXED UP WORKING OUT BEAUTIFULLY WITH ANOTHER BLOKE.
I MEAN, THE DIFFERENCES BETWEEN YOU AND ME, AND YOU AND HIM... ENDLESS!
OKAY, SURE, ON THE SURFACE, WE'RE BOTH VAMPIRES WITH SOULS...ESSENCE OF THE SAME DEMON IN US... FIGHTING THE FORCES OF DARKNESS. BUT LOOK DEEPER, AND...
WELL, FOR STARTERS, I'M BRITISH AND HE'S IRISH! NIGHT AND BLOODY DAY!
SPIKE!
GUARD THE REAR.

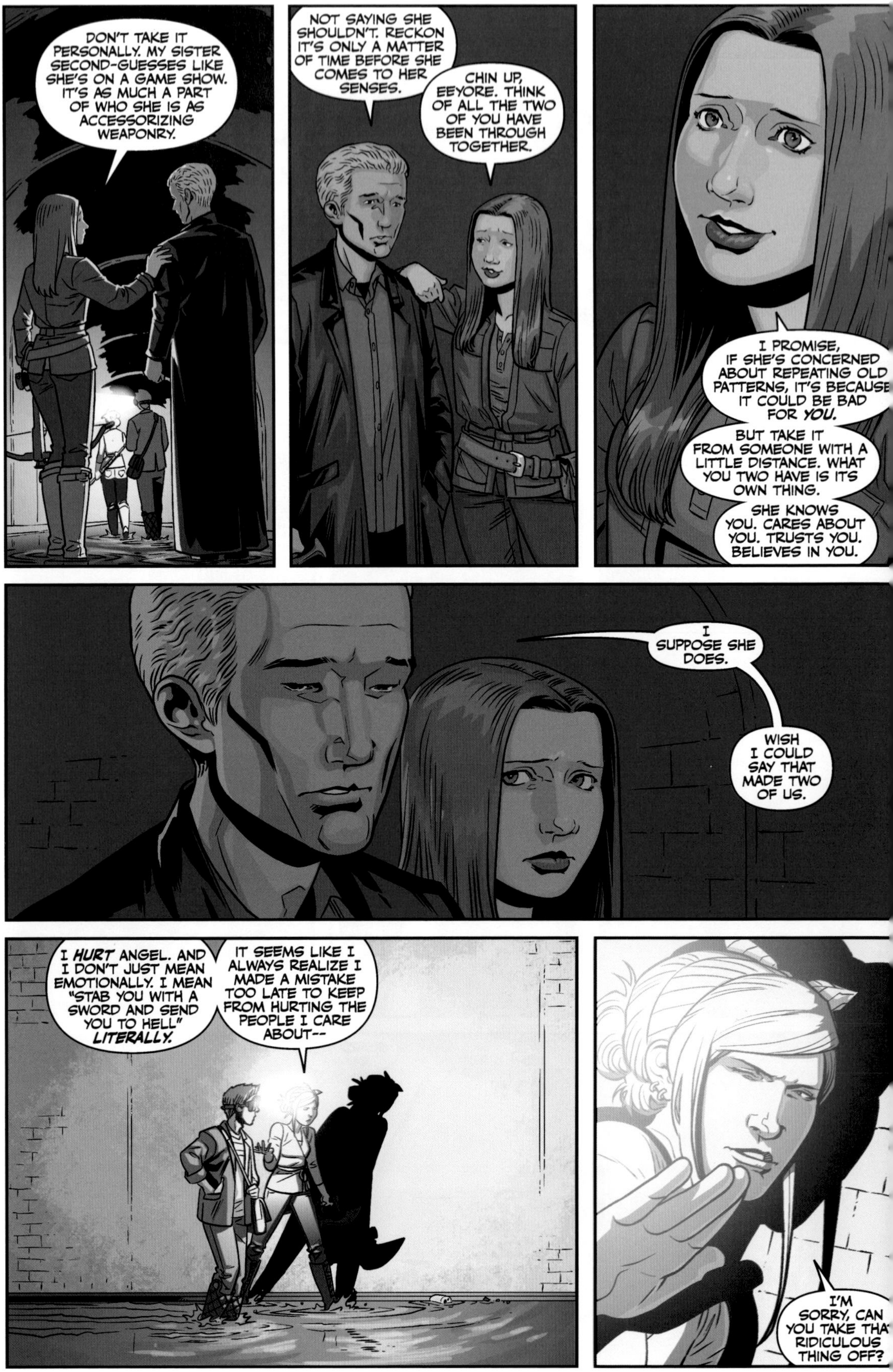
DON'T TAKE IT PERSONALLY. MY SISTER SECOND-GUESSES LIKE SHE'S ON A GAME SHOW. IT'S AS MUCH A PART OF WHO SHE IS AS ACCESSORIZING WEAPONRY.
NOT SAYING SHE SHOULDN'T. RECKON IT'S ONLY A MATTER OF TIME BEFORE SHE COMES TO HER SENSES.
CHIN UP, EEYORE. THINK OF ALL THE TWO OF YOU HAVE BEEN THROUGH TOGETHER.
I PROMISE, IF SHE'S CONCERNED ABOUT REPEATING OLD PATTERNS, IT'S BECAUSE IT COULD BE BAD FOR *YOU.*
BUT TAKE IT FROM SOMEONE WITH A LITTLE DISTANCE. WHAT YOU TWO HAVE IS ITS OWN THING.
SHE KNOWS YOU. CARES ABOUT YOU. TRUSTS YOU. BELIEVES IN YOU.
I SUPPOSE SHE DOES.
WISH I COULD SAY THAT MADE TWO OF US.
I *HURT* ANGEL. AND I DON'T JUST MEAN EMOTIONALLY. I MEAN "STAB YOU WITH A SWORD AND SEND YOU TO HELL" *LITERALLY.*
IT SEEMS LIKE I ALWAYS REALIZE I MADE A MISTAKE TOO LATE TO KEEP FROM HURTING THE PEOPLE I CARE ABOUT--
I'M SORRY, CAN YOU TAKE THA RIDICULOUS THING OFF?

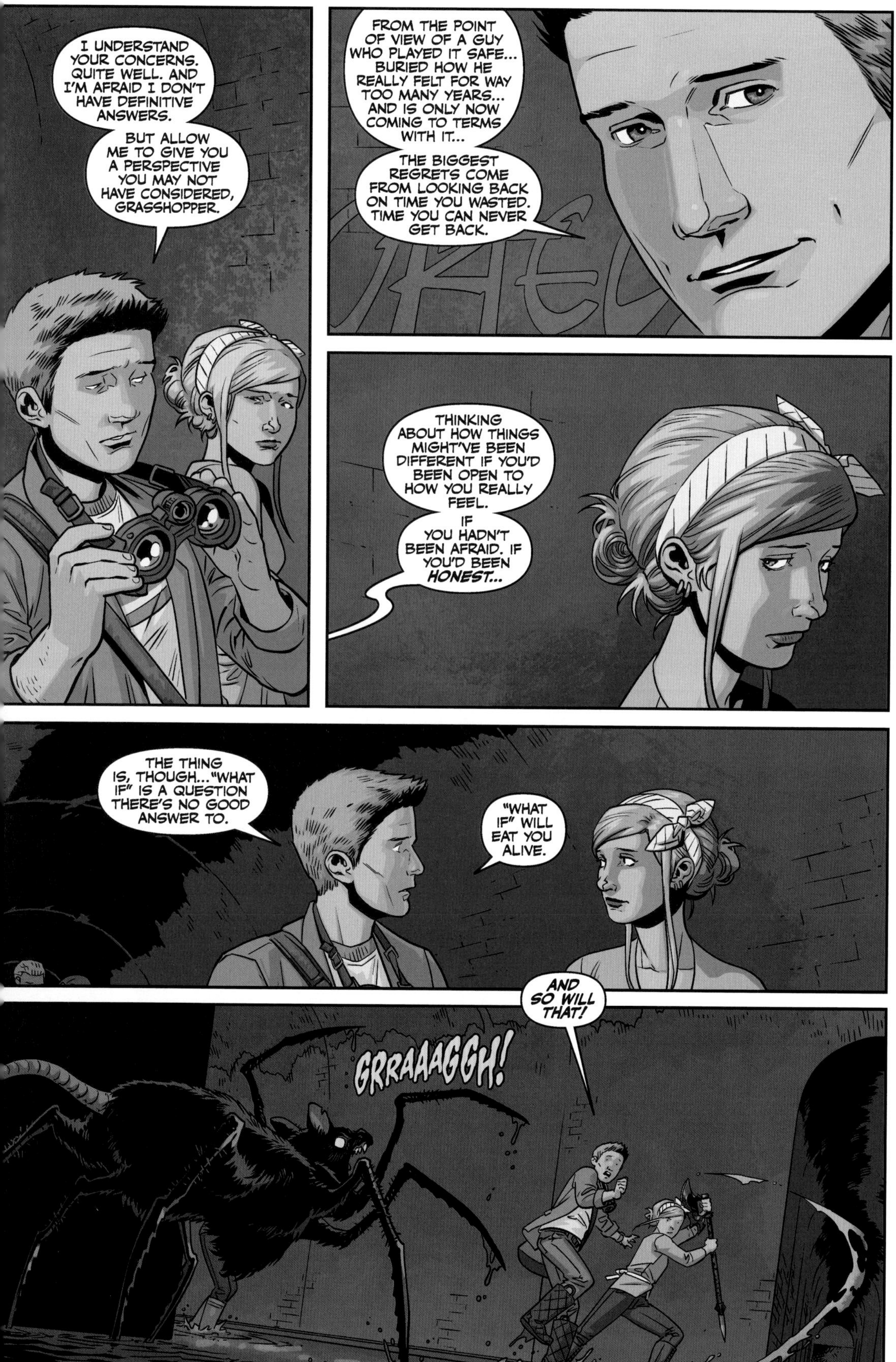
I UNDERSTAND YOUR CONCERNS. QUITE WELL. AND I'M AFRAID I DON'T HAVE DEFINITIVE ANSWERS.
BUT ALLOW ME TO GIVE YOU A PERSPECTIVE YOU MAY NOT HAVE CONSIDERED, GRASSHOPPER.
FROM THE POINT OF VIEW OF A GUY WHO PLAYED IT SAFE... BURIED HOW HE REALLY FELT FOR WAY TOO MANY YEARS... AND IS ONLY NOW COMING TO TERMS WITH IT...
THE BIGGEST REGRETS COME FROM LOOKING BACK ON TIME YOU WASTED. TIME YOU CAN NEVER GET BACK.
THINKING ABOUT HOW THINGS MIGHT'VE BEEN DIFFERENT IF YOU'D BEEN OPEN TO HOW YOU REALLY FEEL.
IF YOU HADN'T BEEN AFRAID. IF YOU'D BEEN *HONEST...*
THE THING IS, THOUGH..."WHAT IF" IS A QUESTION THERE'S NO GOOD ANSWER TO.
"WHAT IF" WILL EAT YOU ALIVE.
AND SO WILL THAT!
GRRAAAGGH!

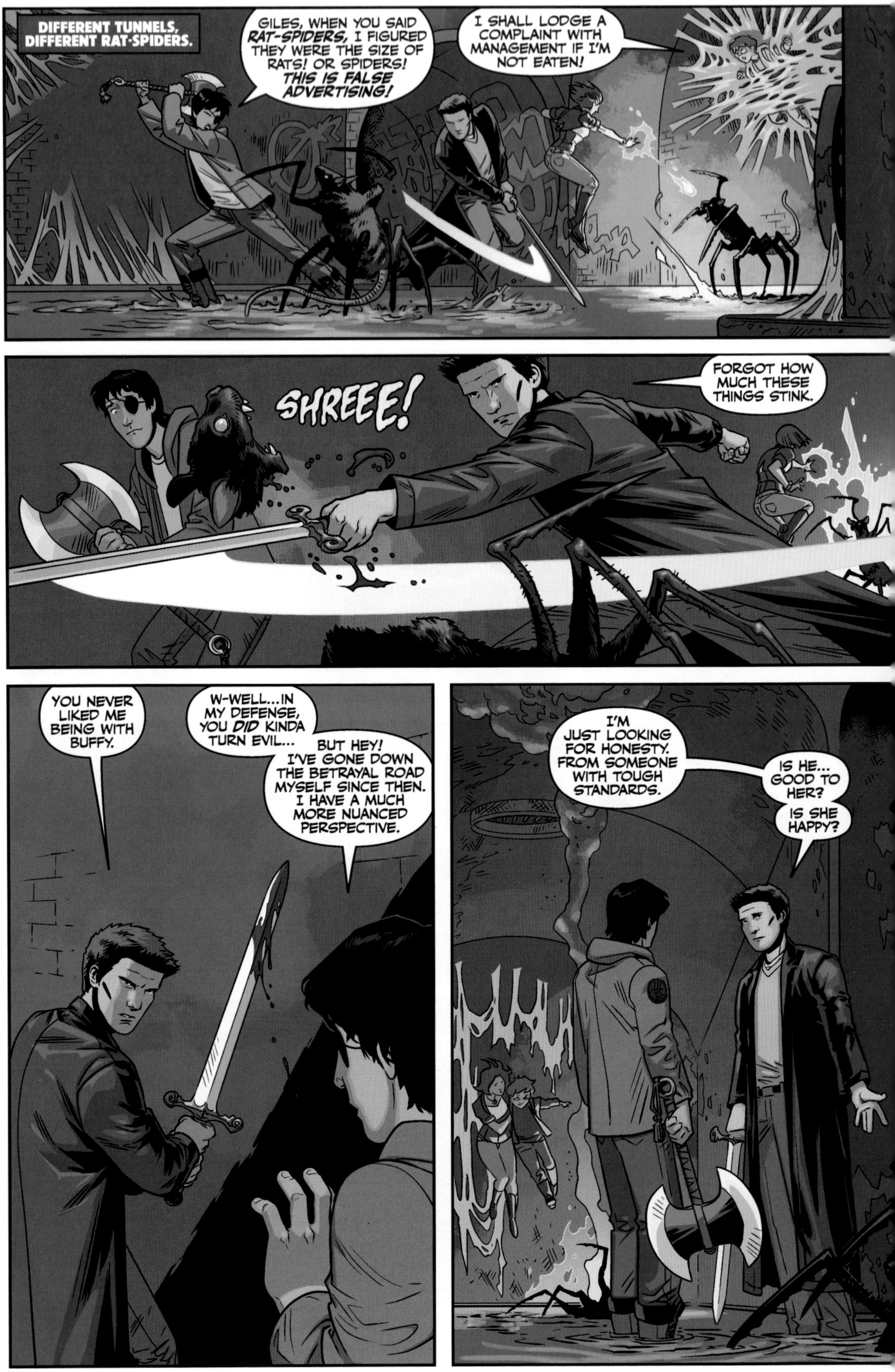
DIFFERENT TUNNELS, DIFFERENT RAT-SPIDERS.
GILES, WHEN YOU SAID RAT-SPIDERS, I FIGURED THEY WERE THE SIZE OF RATS! OR SPIDERS! THIS IS FALSE ADVERTISING!
I SHALL LODGE A COMPLAINT WITH MANAGEMENT IF I'M NOT EATEN!
SHREEE!
FORGOT HOW MUCH THESE THINGS STINK.
YOU NEVER LIKED ME BEING WITH BUFFY.
W-WELL...IN MY DEFENSE, YOU DID KINDA TURN EVIL...
BUT HEY! I'VE GONE DOWN THE BETRAYAL ROAD MYSELF SINCE THEN. I HAVE A MUCH MORE NUANCED PERSPECTIVE.
I'M JUST LOOKING FOR HONESTY. FROM SOMEONE WITH TOUGH STANDARDS.
IS HE... GOOD TO HER?
IS SHE HAPPY?

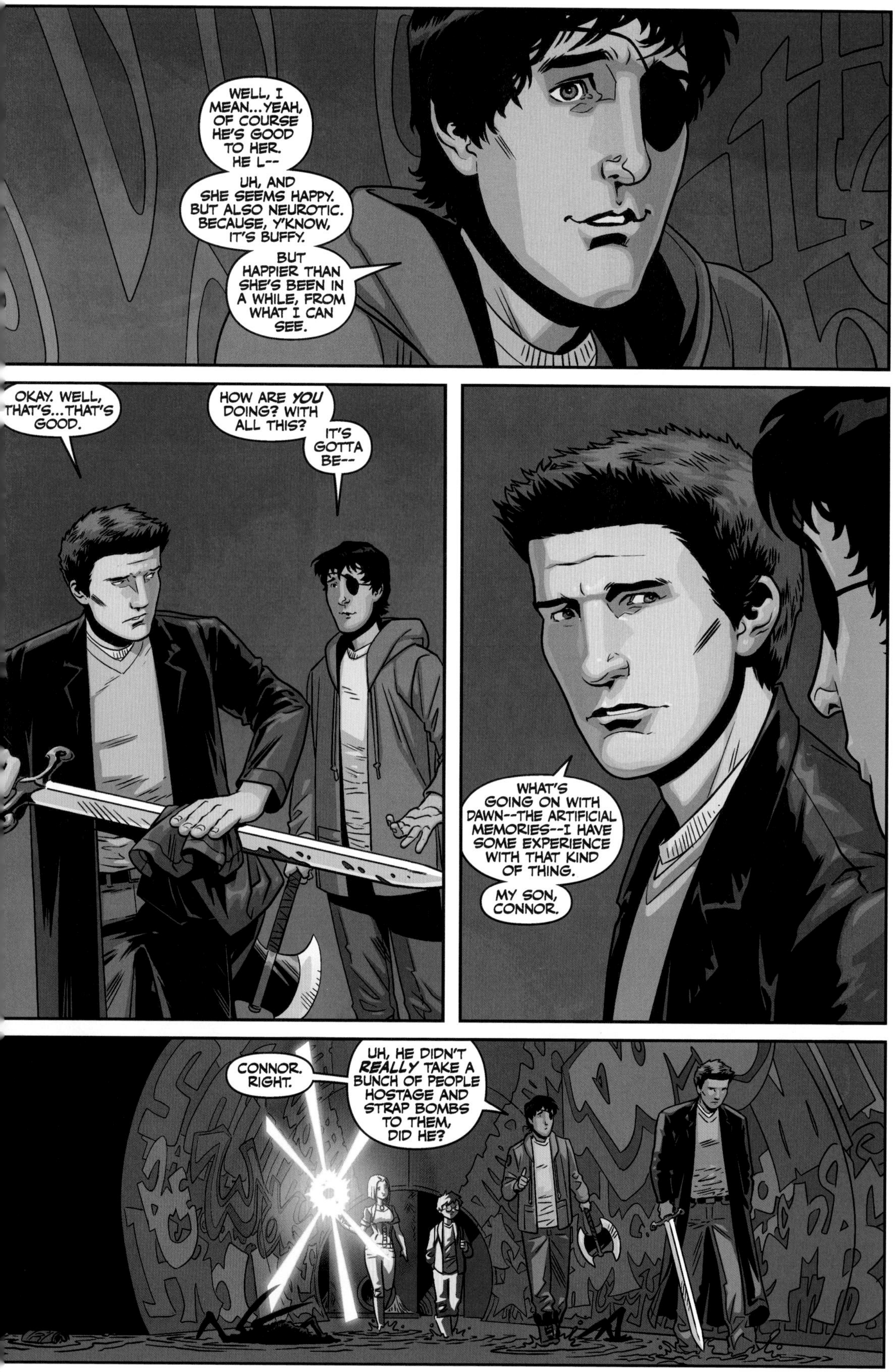
WELL, I MEAN...YEAH, OF COURSE HE'S GOOD TO HER. HE L--
UH, AND SHE SEEMS HAPPY. BUT ALSO NEUROTIC. BECAUSE, Y'KNOW, IT'S BUFFY.
BUT HAPPIER THAN SHE'S BEEN IN A WHILE, FROM WHAT I CAN SEE.
OKAY. WELL, THAT'S...THAT'S GOOD.
HOW ARE *YOU* DOING? WITH ALL THIS?
IT'S GOTTA BE--
WHAT'S GOING ON WITH DAWN--THE ARTIFICIAL MEMORIES--I HAVE SOME EXPERIENCE WITH THAT KIND OF THING.
MY SON, CONNOR.
CONNOR. RIGHT.
UH, HE DIDN'T *REALLY* TAKE A BUNCH OF PEOPLE HOSTAGE AND STRAP BOMBS TO THEM, DID HE?

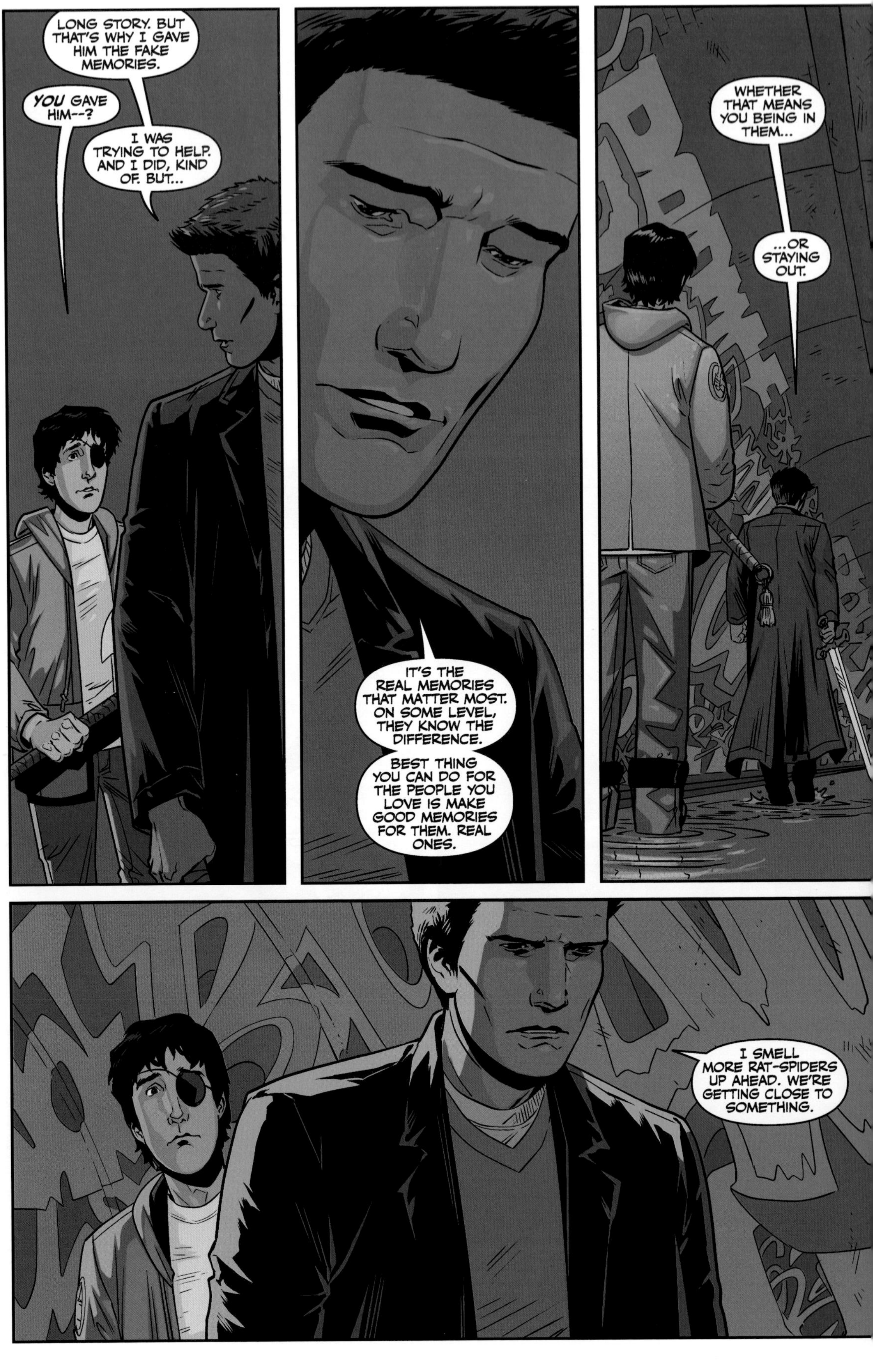
LONG STORY. BUT THAT'S WHY I GAVE HIM THE FAKE MEMORIES.
YOU GAVE HIM--?
I WAS TRYING TO HELP. AND I DID, KIND OF. BUT...
IT'S THE REAL MEMORIES THAT MATTER MOST. ON SOME LEVEL, THEY KNOW THE DIFFERENCE.
BEST THING YOU CAN DO FOR THE PEOPLE YOU LOVE IS MAKE GOOD MEMORIES FOR THEM. REAL ONES.
WHETHER THAT MEANS YOU BEING IN THEM...
...OR STAYING OUT.
I SMELL MORE RAT-SPIDERS UP AHEAD. WE'RE GETTING CLOSE TO SOMETHING.

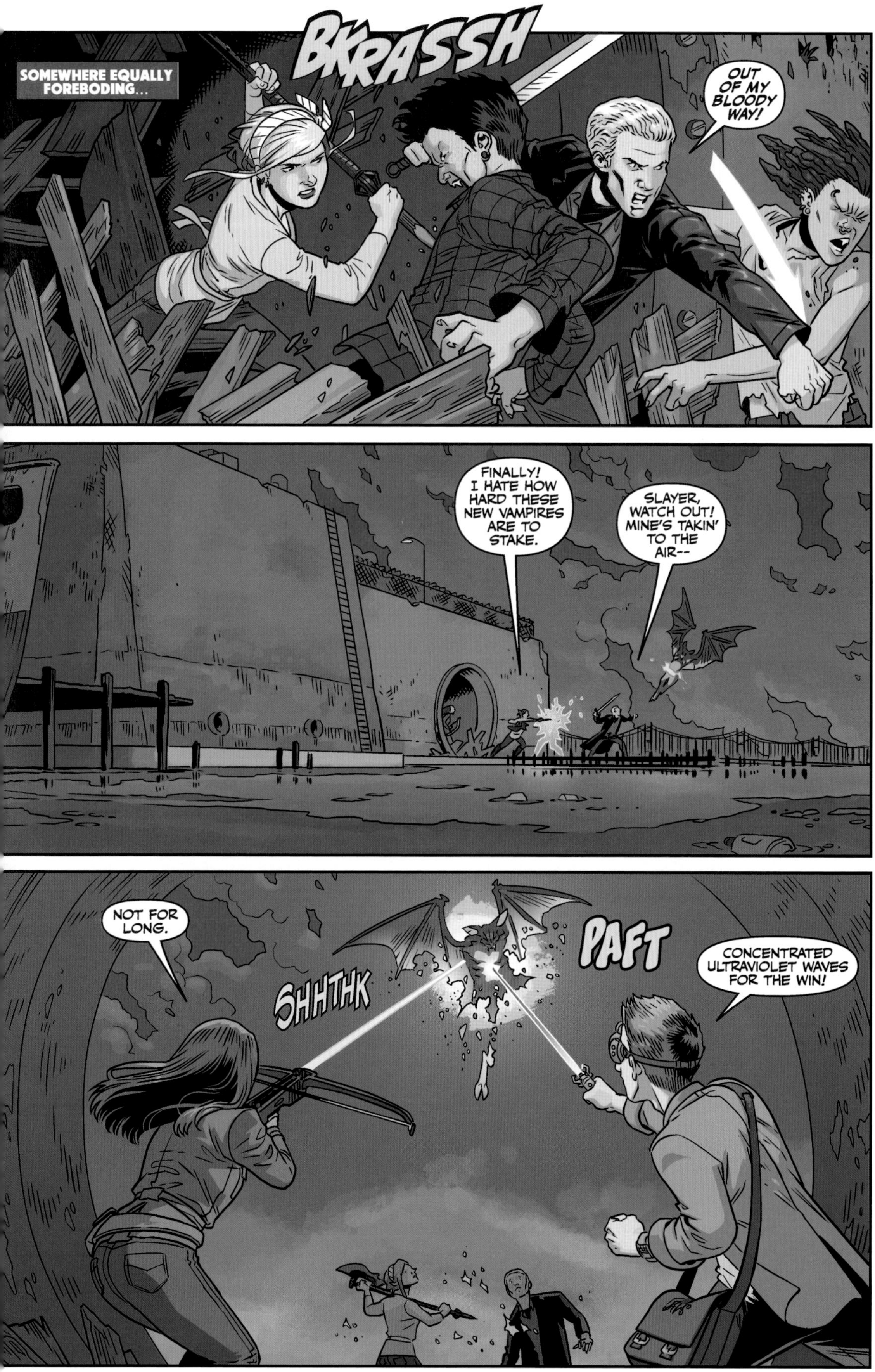
BKRASSH
SOMEWHERE EQUALLY FOREBODING...
OUT OF MY BLOODY WAY!
FINALLY! I HATE HOW HARD THESE NEW VAMPIRES ARE TO STAKE.
SLAYER, WATCH OUT! MINE'S TAKIN' TO THE AIR--
NOT FOR LONG.
SHHTHK
PAFT
CONCENTRATED ULTRAVIOLET WAVES FOR THE WIN!

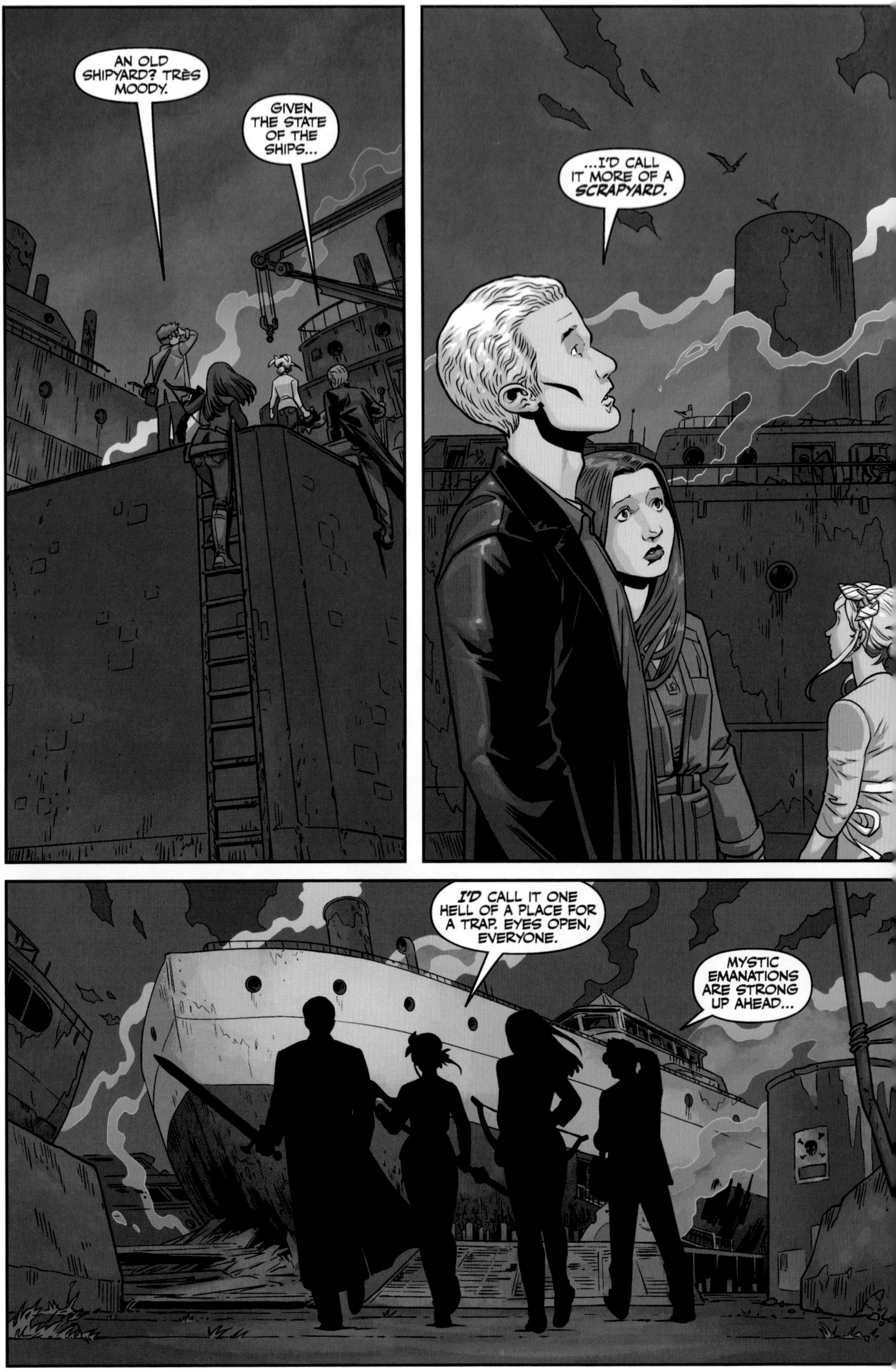
AN OLD SHIPYARD? TRÈS MOODY.
GIVEN THE STATE OF THE SHIPS...
...I'D CALL IT MORE OF A *SCRAPYARD.*
I'D CALL IT ONE HELL OF A PLACE FOR A TRAP. EYES OPEN, EVERYONE.
MYSTIC EMANATIONS ARE STRONG UP AHEAD...

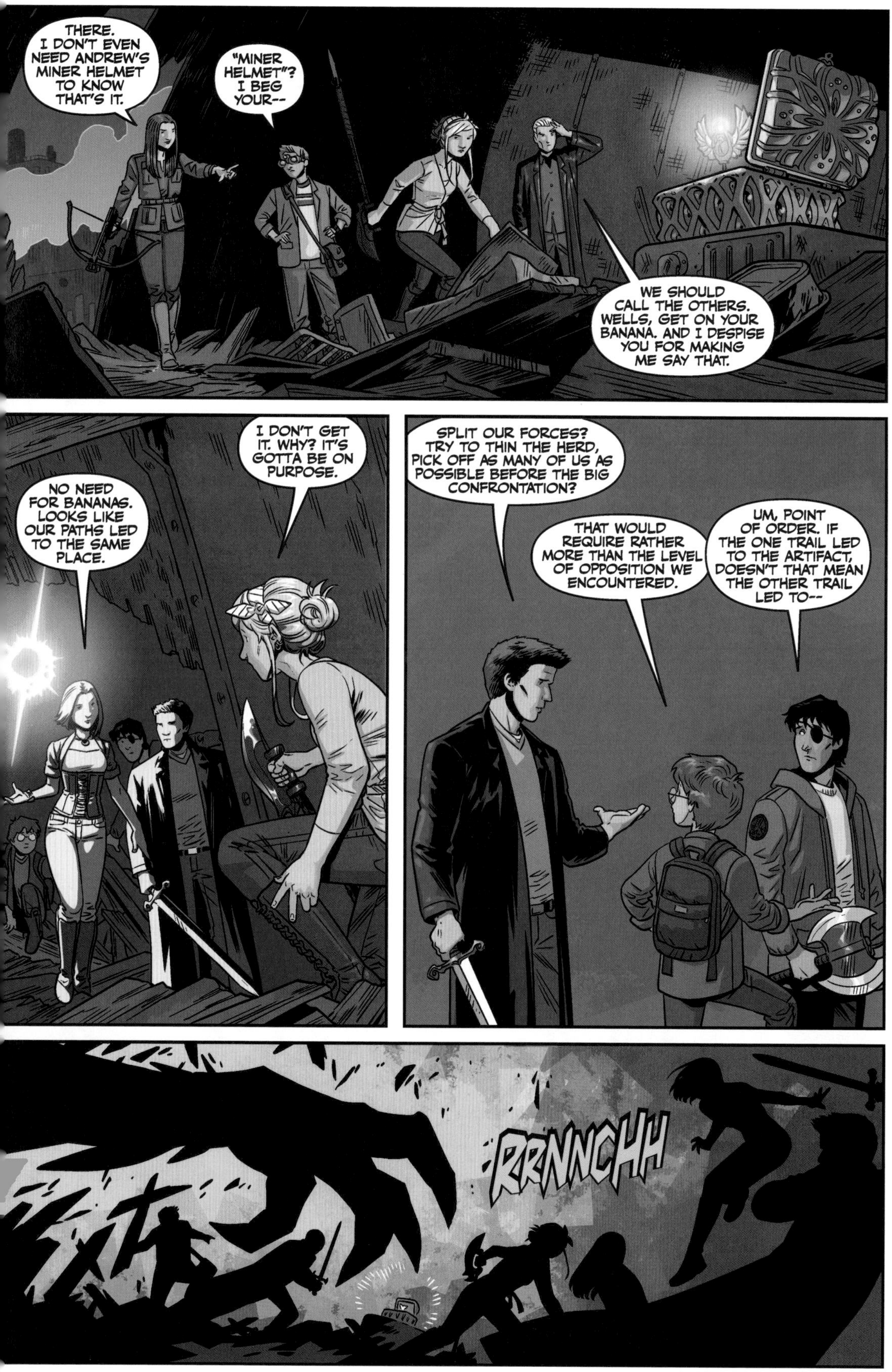
THERE. I DON'T EVEN NEED ANDREW'S MINER HELMET TO KNOW THAT'S IT.
"MINER HELMET"? I BEG YOUR--
WE SHOULD CALL THE OTHERS. WELLS, GET ON YOUR BANANA. AND I DESPISE YOU FOR MAKING ME SAY THAT.
NO NEED FOR BANANAS. LOOKS LIKE OUR PATHS LED TO THE SAME PLACE.
I DON'T GET IT. WHY? IT'S GOTTA BE ON PURPOSE.
SPLIT OUR FORCES? TRY TO THIN THE HERD, PICK OFF AS MANY OF US AS POSSIBLE BEFORE THE BIG CONFRONTATION?
THAT WOULD REQUIRE RATHER MORE THAN THE LEVEL OF OPPOSITION WE ENCOUNTERED.
UM, POINT OF ORDER. IF THE ONE TRAIL LED TO THE ARTIFACT, DOESN'T THAT MEAN THE OTHER TRAIL LED TO--
RRNNCHH

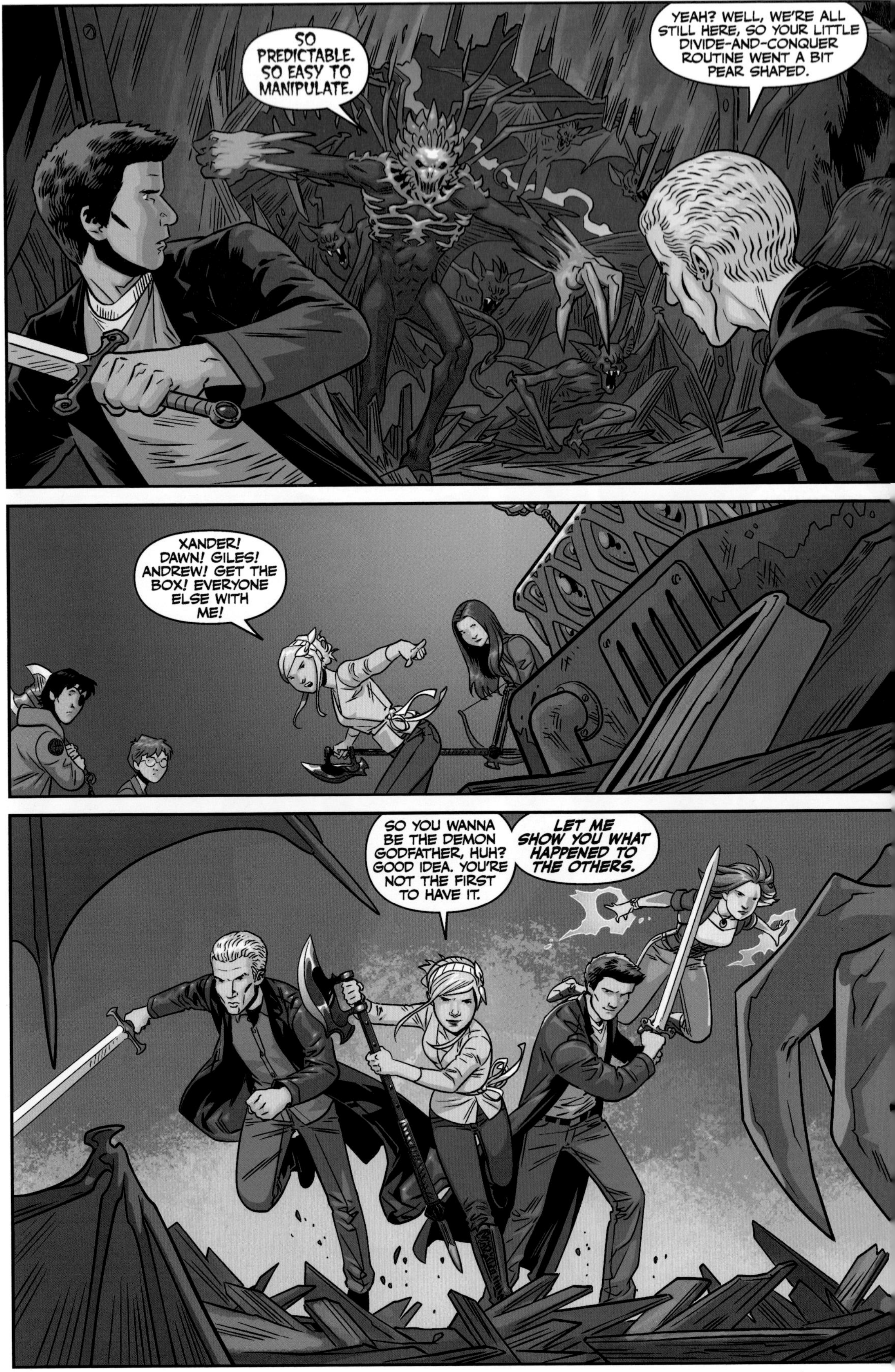
SO PREDICTABLE. SO EASY TO MANIPULATE.
YEAH? WELL, WE'RE ALL STILL HERE, SO YOUR LITTLE DIVIDE-AND-CONQUER ROUTINE WENT A BIT PEAR SHAPED.
XANDER! DAWN! GILES! ANDREW! GET THE BOX! EVERYONE ELSE WITH ME!
SO YOU WANNA BE THE DEMON GODFATHER, HUH? GOOD IDEA. YOU'RE NOT THE FIRST TO HAVE IT.
LET ME SHOW YOU WHAT HAPPENED TO THE OTHERS.

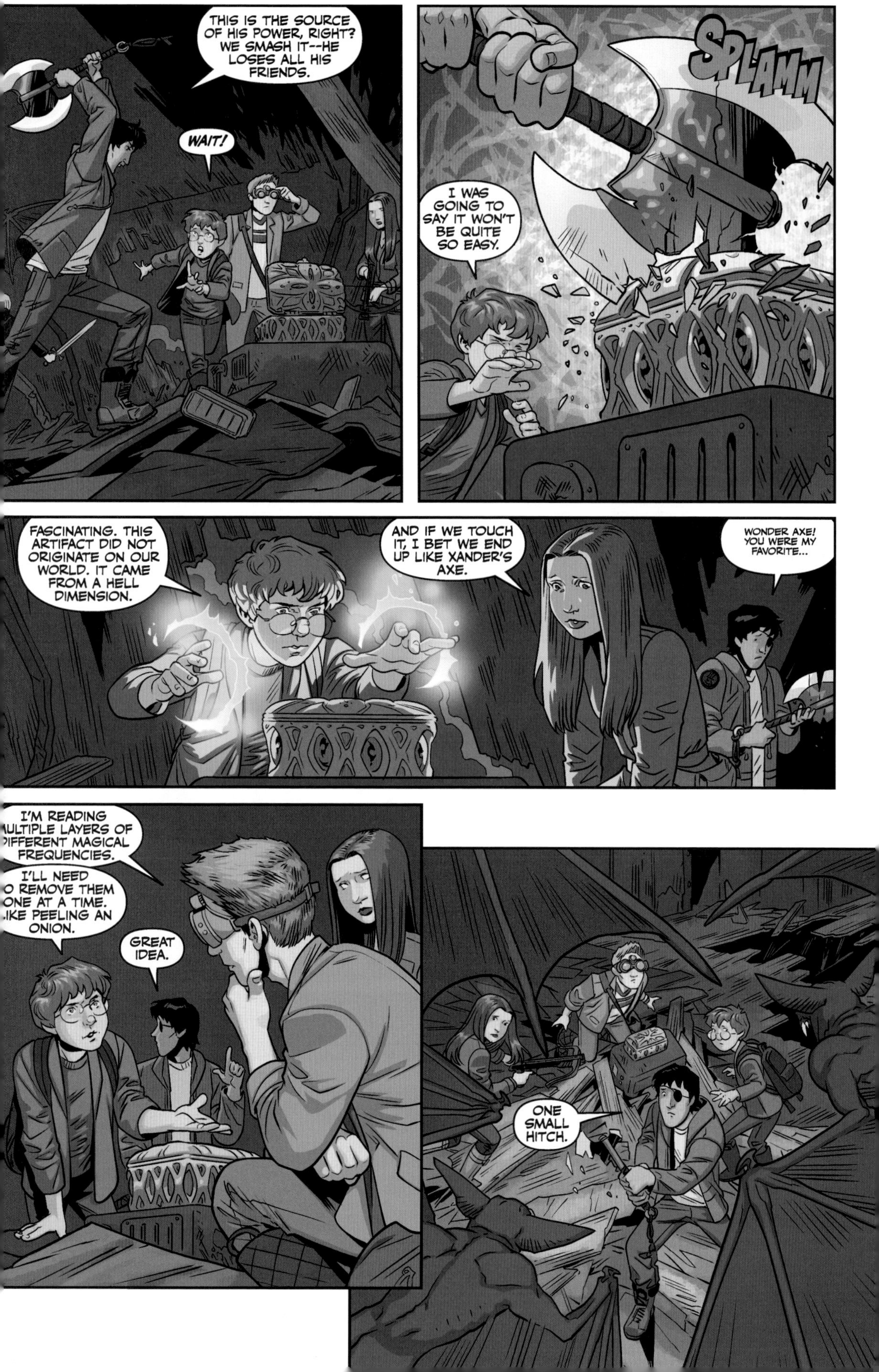
THIS IS THE SOURCE OF HIS POWER, RIGHT? WE SMASH IT--HE LOSES ALL HIS FRIENDS.
WAIT!
SPLAMM
I WAS GOING TO SAY IT WON'T BE QUITE SO EASY.
FASCINATING. THIS ARTIFACT DID NOT ORIGINATE ON OUR WORLD. IT CAME FROM A HELL DIMENSION.
AND IF WE TOUCH IT, I BET WE END UP LIKE XANDER'S AXE.
WONDER AXE! YOU WERE MY FAVORITE...
I'M READING ULTIPLE LAYERS OF DIFFERENT MAGICAL FREQUENCIES.
I'LL NEED O REMOVE THEM ONE AT A TIME. LIKE PEELING AN ONION.
GREAT IDEA.
ONE SMALL HITCH.

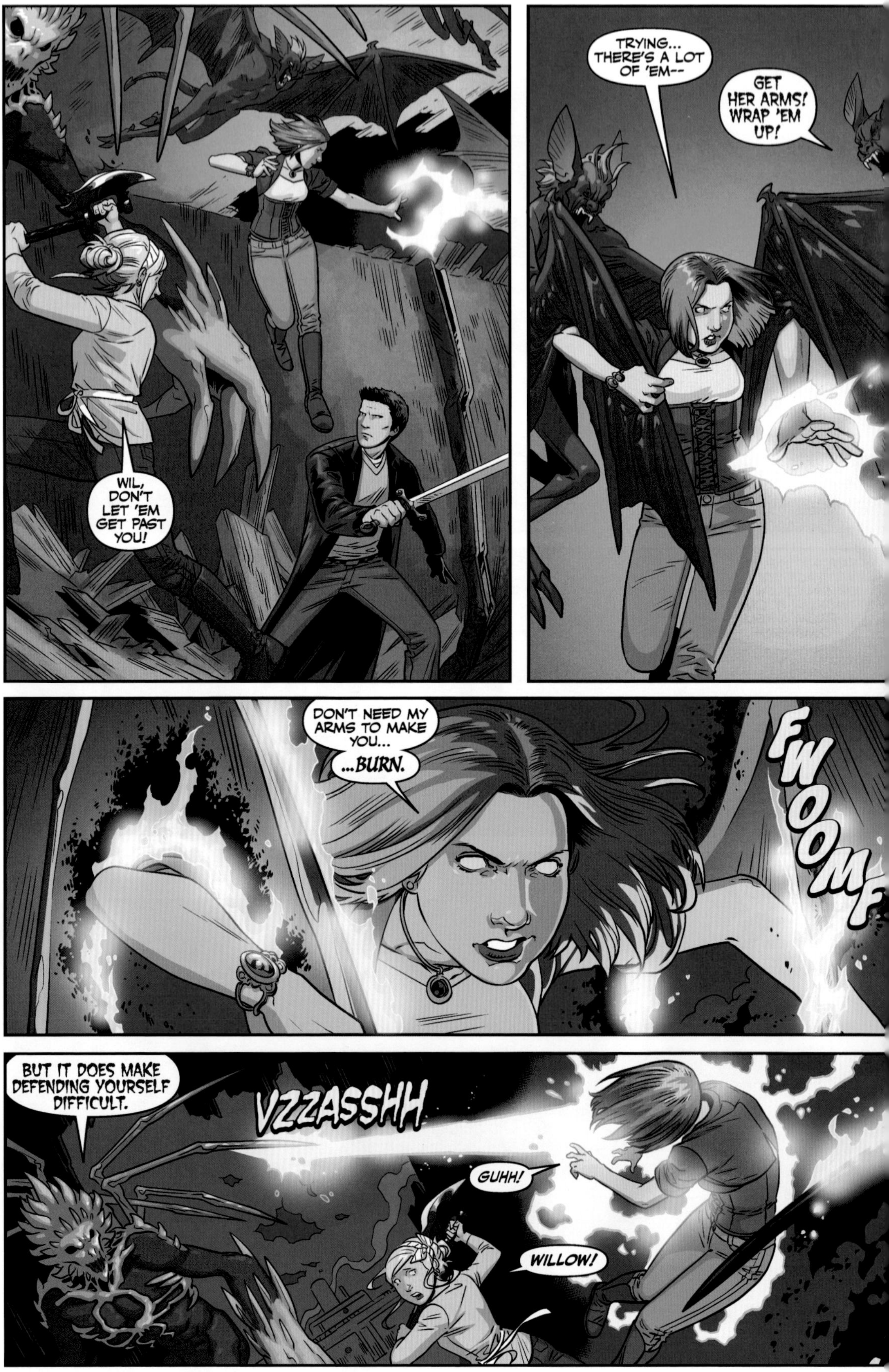
WIL, DON'T LET 'EM GET PAST YOU!
TRYING... THERE'S A LOT OF 'EM--
GET HER ARMS! WRAP 'EM UP!
DON'T NEED MY ARMS TO MAKE YOU...
...BURN.
FWOOMF
BUT IT DOES MAKE DEFENDING YOURSELF DIFFICULT.
VZZASSHH
GUHH!
WILLOW!

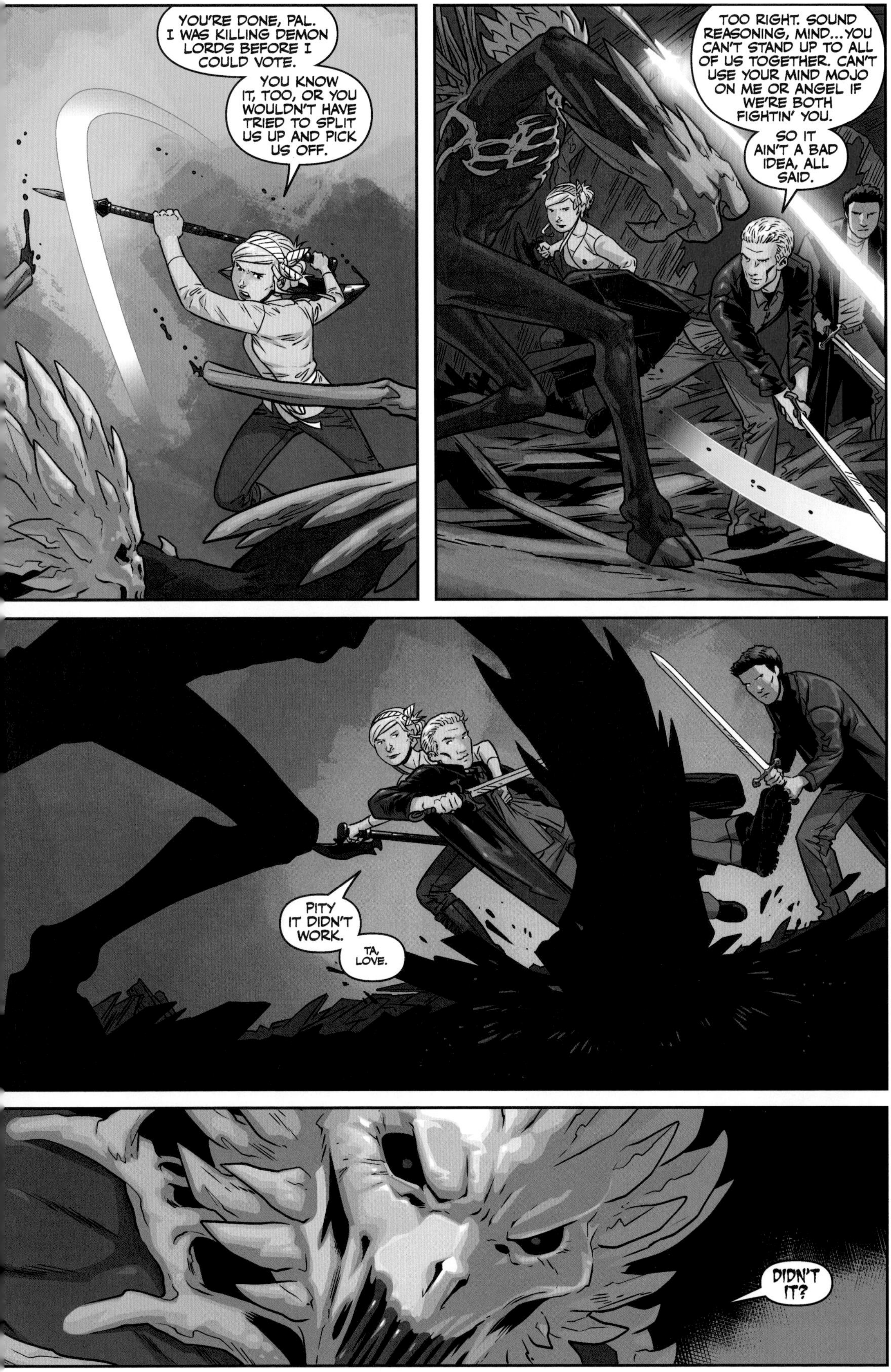
YOU'RE DONE, PAL. I WAS KILLING DEMON LORDS BEFORE I COULD VOTE.
YOU KNOW IT, TOO, OR YOU WOULDN'T HAVE TRIED TO SPLIT US UP AND PICK US OFF.
TOO RIGHT. SOUND REASONING, MIND...YOU CAN'T STAND UP TO ALL OF US TOGETHER. CAN'T USE YOUR MIND MOJO ON ME OR ANGEL IF WE'RE BOTH FIGHTIN' YOU.
SO IT AIN'T A BAD IDEA, ALL SAID.
PITY IT DIDN'T WORK.
TA, LOVE.
DIDN'T IT?

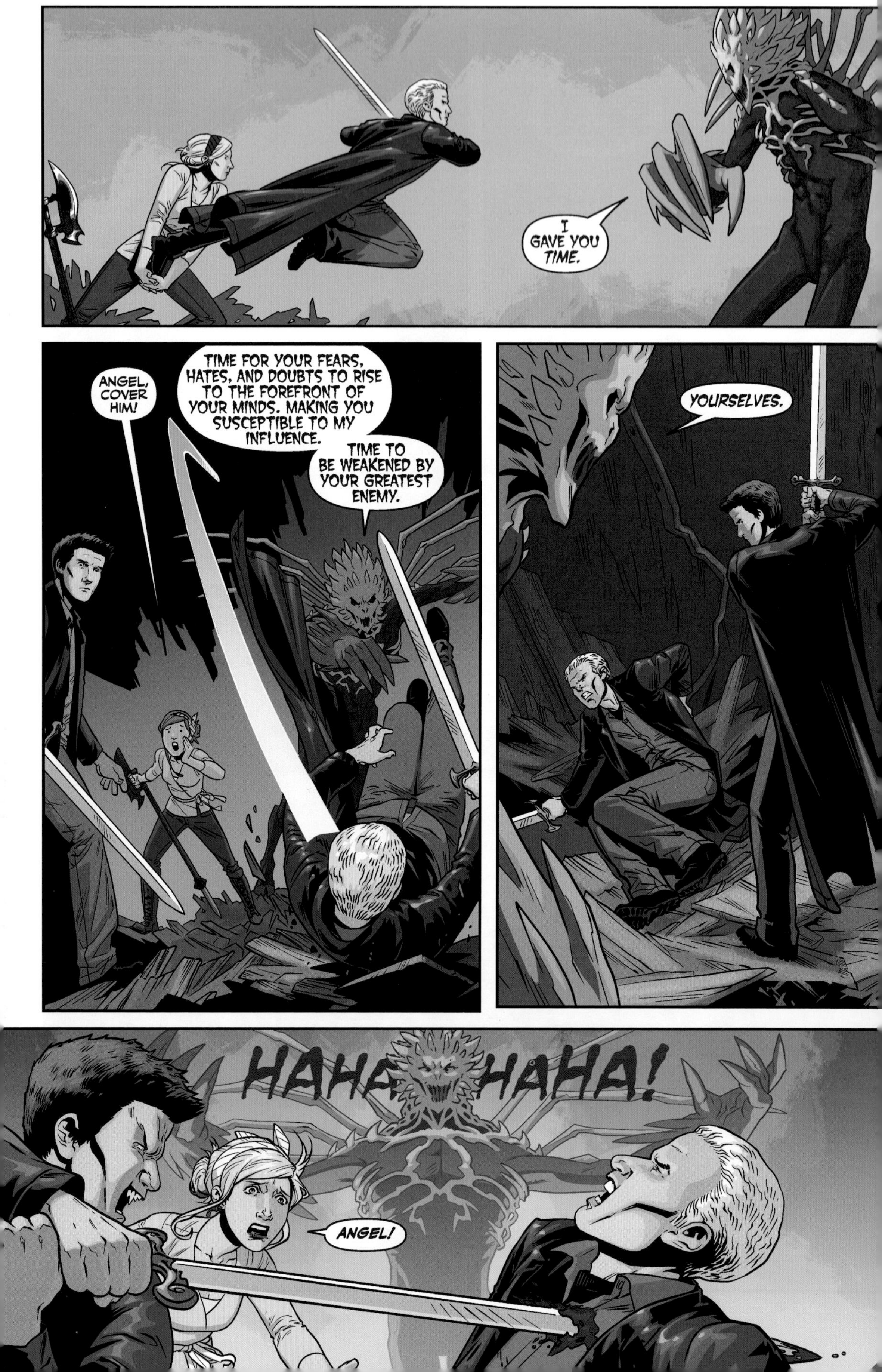

I GAVE YOU TIME.
ANGEL, COVER HIM!
TIME FOR YOUR FEARS, HATES, AND DOUBTS TO RISE TO THE FOREFRONT OF YOUR MINDS. MAKING YOU SUSCEPTIBLE TO MY INFLUENCE.
TIME TO BE WEAKENED BY YOUR GREATEST ENEMY.
YOURSELVES.
HAHA HAHA!
ANGEL!

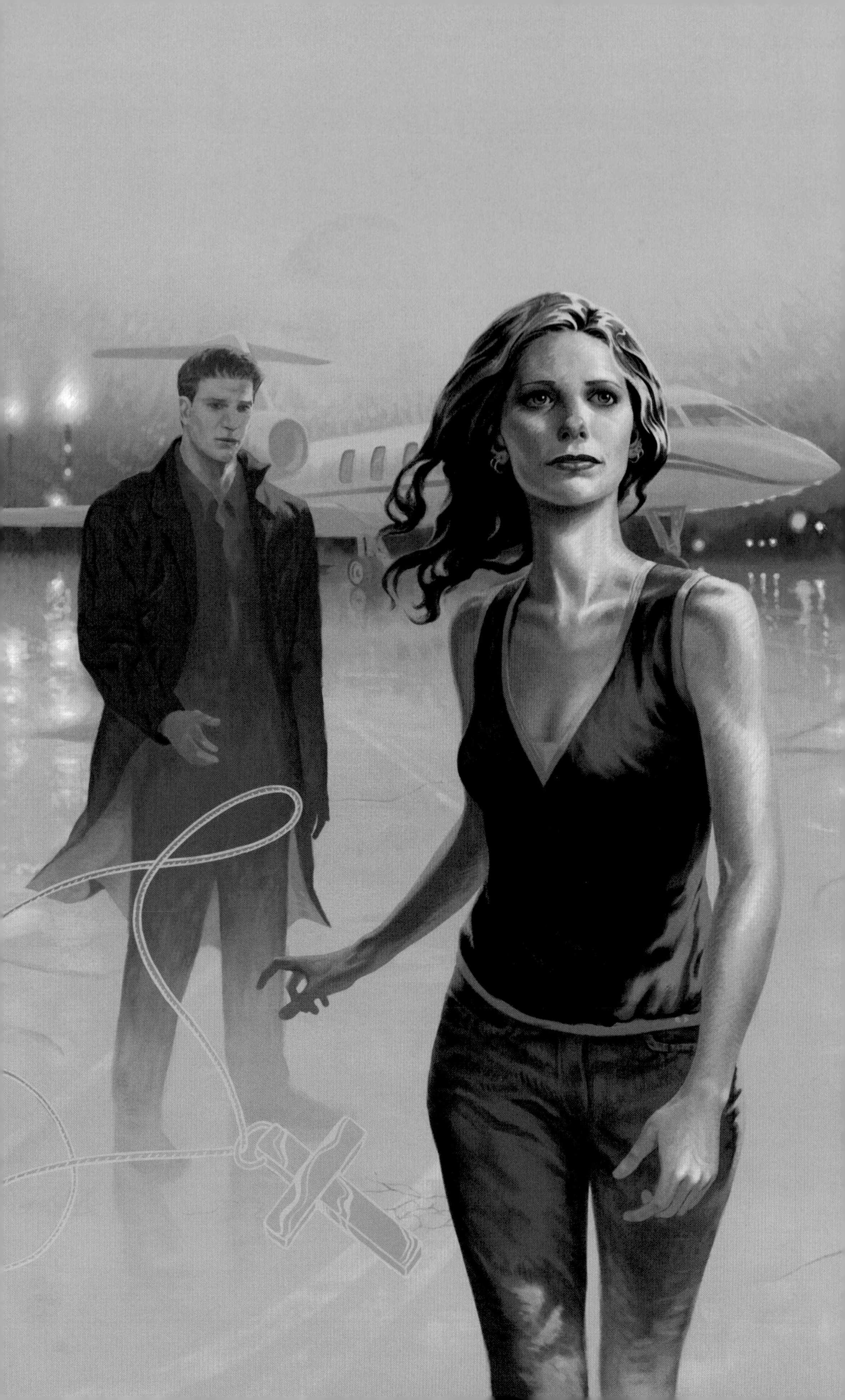

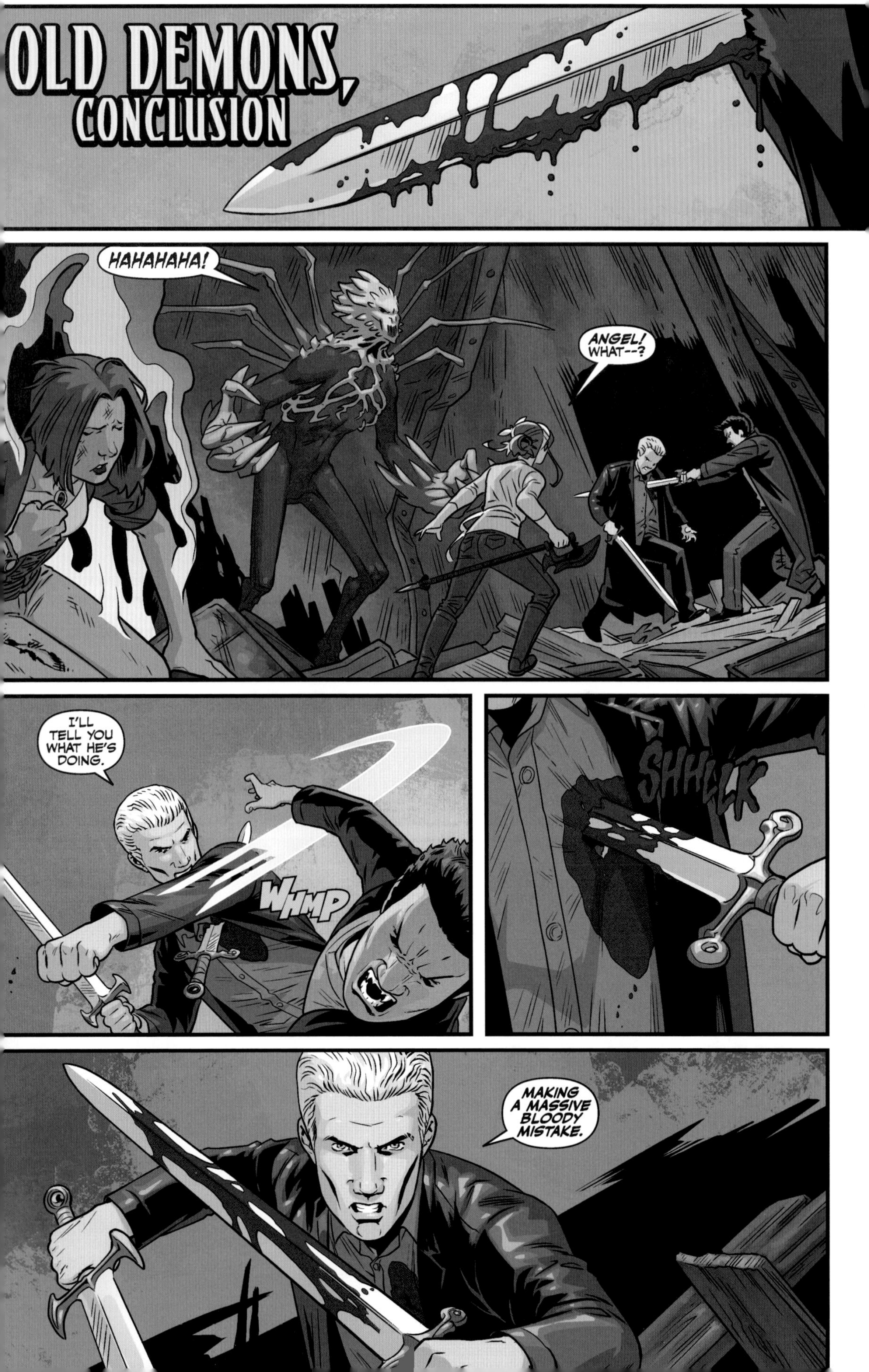
OLD DEMONS,
CONCLUSION
HAHAHAHA!
ANGEL! WHAT--?
I'LL TELL YOU WHAT HE'S DOING.
WHMP
SHHLLK
MAKING A MASSIVE BLOODY MISTAKE.

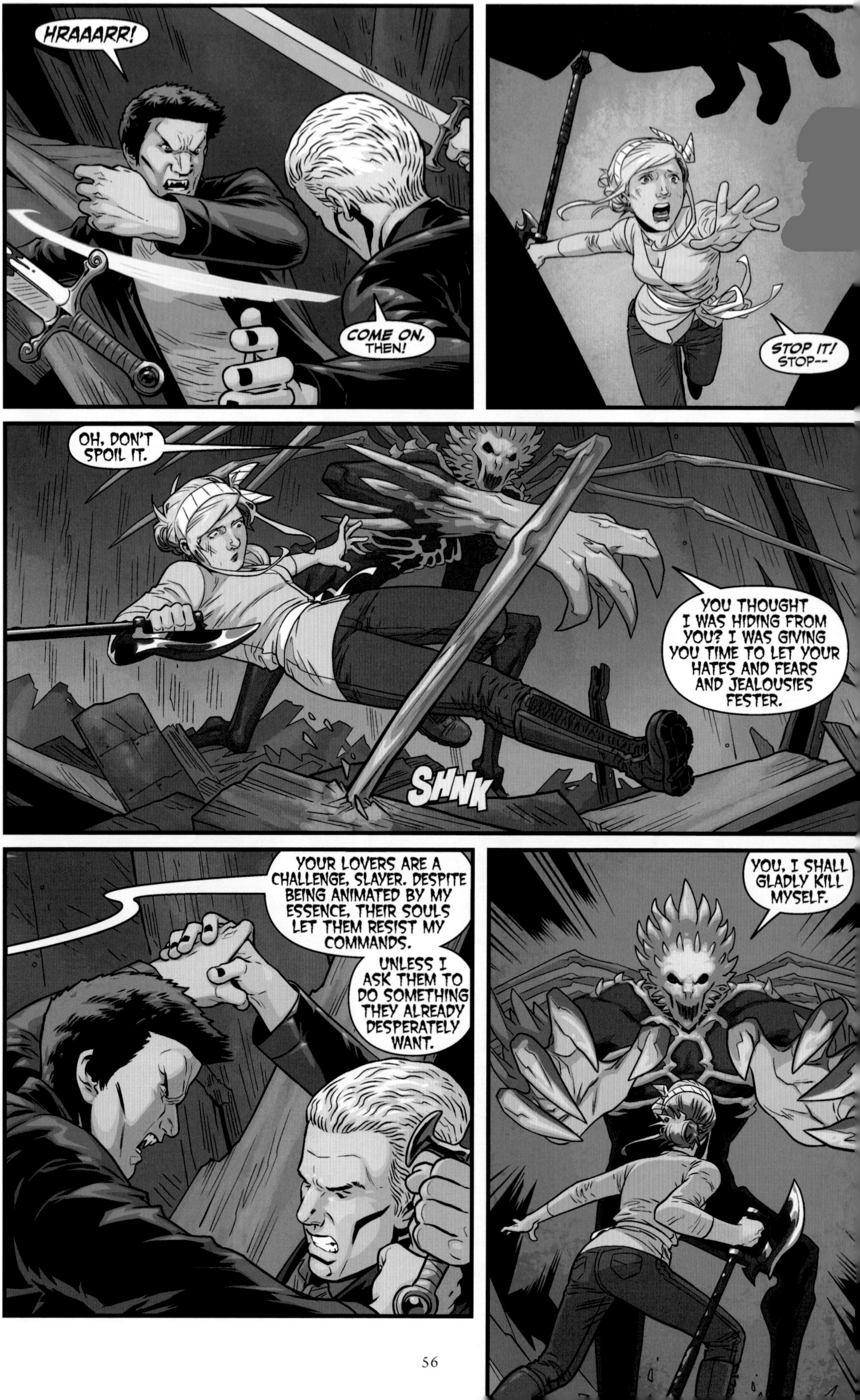
HRAAARR!
COME ON, THEN!
STOP IT! STOP--
OH, DON'T SPOIL IT.
YOU THOUGHT I WAS HIDING FROM YOU? I WAS GIVING YOU TIME TO LET YOUR HATES AND FEARS AND JEALOUSIES FESTER.
SHNK
YOUR LOVERS ARE A CHALLENGE, SLAYER. DESPITE BEING ANIMATED BY MY ESSENCE, THEIR SOULS LET THEM RESIST MY COMMANDS.
UNLESS I ASK THEM TO DO SOMETHING THEY ALREADY DESPERATELY WANT.
YOU, I SHALL GLADLY KILL MYSELF.

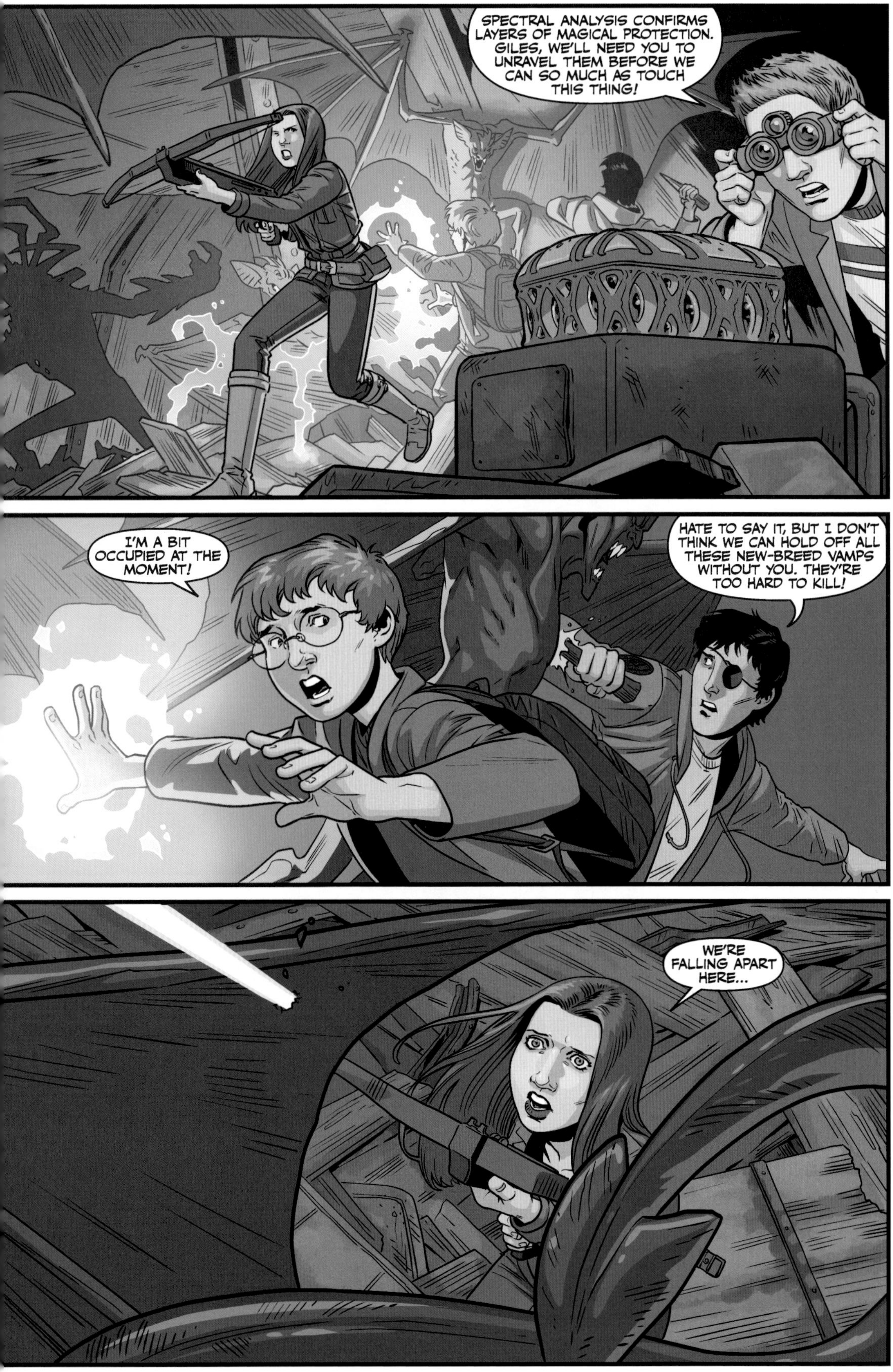
SPECTRAL ANALYSIS CONFIRMS LAYERS OF MAGICAL PROTECTION. GILES, WE'LL NEED YOU TO UNRAVEL THEM BEFORE WE CAN SO MUCH AS TOUCH THIS THING!
I'M A BIT OCCUPIED AT THE MOMENT!
HATE TO SAY IT, BUT I DON'T THINK WE CAN HOLD OFF ALL THESE NEW-BREED VAMPS WITHOUT YOU. THEY'RE TOO HARD TO KILL!
WE'RE FALLING APART HERE...

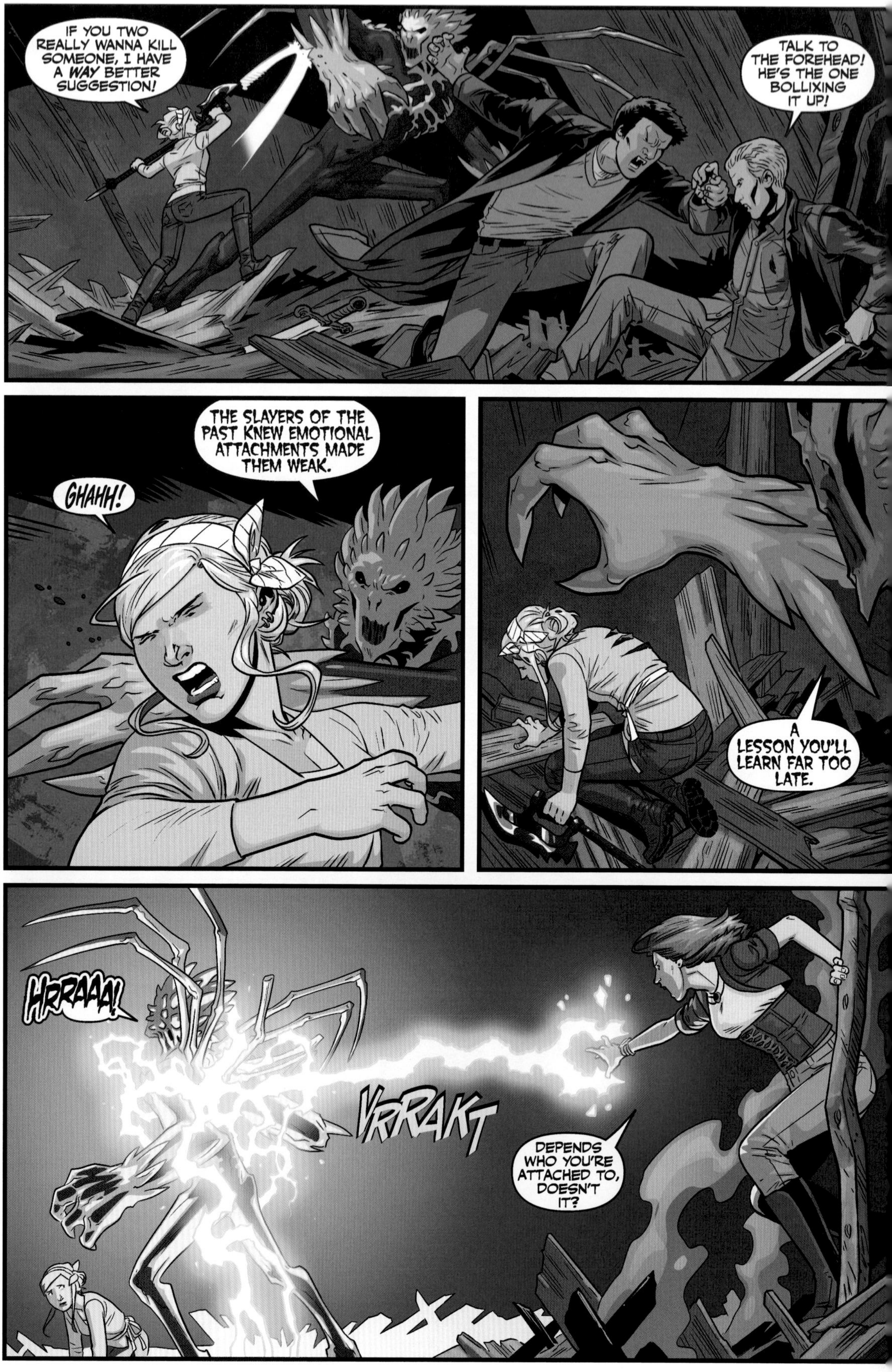
IF YOU TWO REALLY WANNA KILL SOMEONE, I HAVE A WAY BETTER SUGGESTION!
TALK TO THE FOREHEAD! HE'S THE ONE BOLLIXING IT UP!
THE SLAYERS OF THE PAST KNEW EMOTIONAL ATTACHMENTS MADE THEM WEAK.
GHAHH!
A LESSON YOU'LL LEARN FAR TOO LATE.
HRRAAA!
VRRAKT
DEPENDS WHO YOU'RE ATTACHED TO, DOESN'T IT?

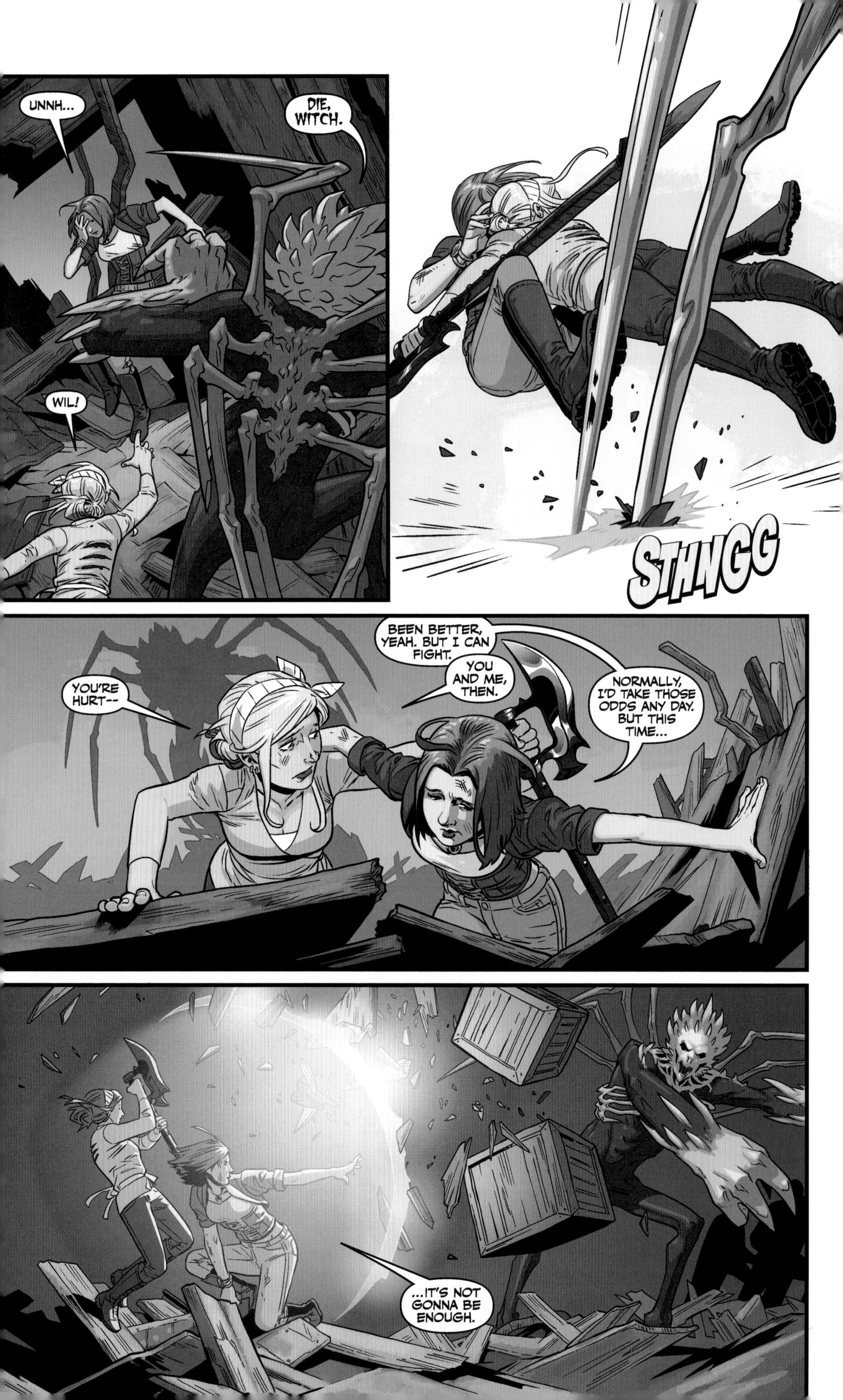
UNNH...
DIE, WITCH.
WIL!
STHNGG
YOU'RE HURT--
BEEN BETTER, YEAH. BUT I CAN FIGHT.
YOU AND ME, THEN.
NORMALLY, I'D TAKE THOSE ODDS ANY DAY. BUT THIS TIME...
...IT'S NOT GONNA BE ENOUGH.

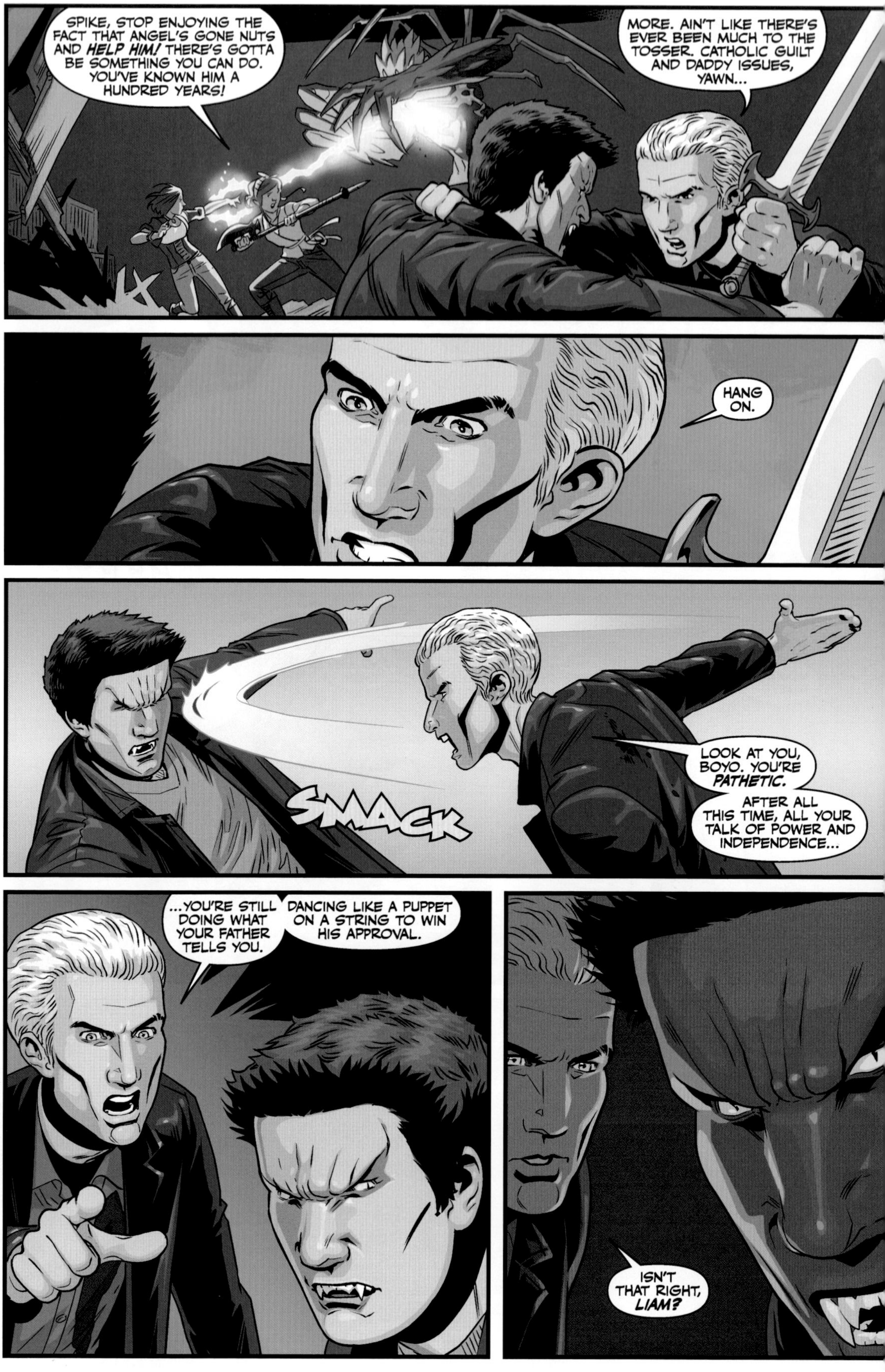
SPIKE, STOP ENJOYING THE FACT THAT ANGEL'S GONE NUTS AND ***HELP HIM!*** THERE'S GOTTA BE SOMETHING YOU CAN DO. YOU'VE KNOWN HIM A HUNDRED YEARS!
MORE. AIN'T LIKE THERE'S EVER BEEN MUCH TO THE TOSSER. CATHOLIC GUILT AND DADDY ISSUES, YAWN...
HANG ON.
LOOK AT YOU, BOYO. YOU'RE ***PATHETIC.***
AFTER ALL THIS TIME, ALL YOUR TALK OF POWER AND INDEPENDENCE...
SMACK
...YOU'RE STILL DOING WHAT YOUR FATHER TELLS YOU.
DANCING LIKE A PUPPET ON A STRING TO WIN HIS APPROVAL.
ISN'T THAT RIGHT, ***LIAM?***

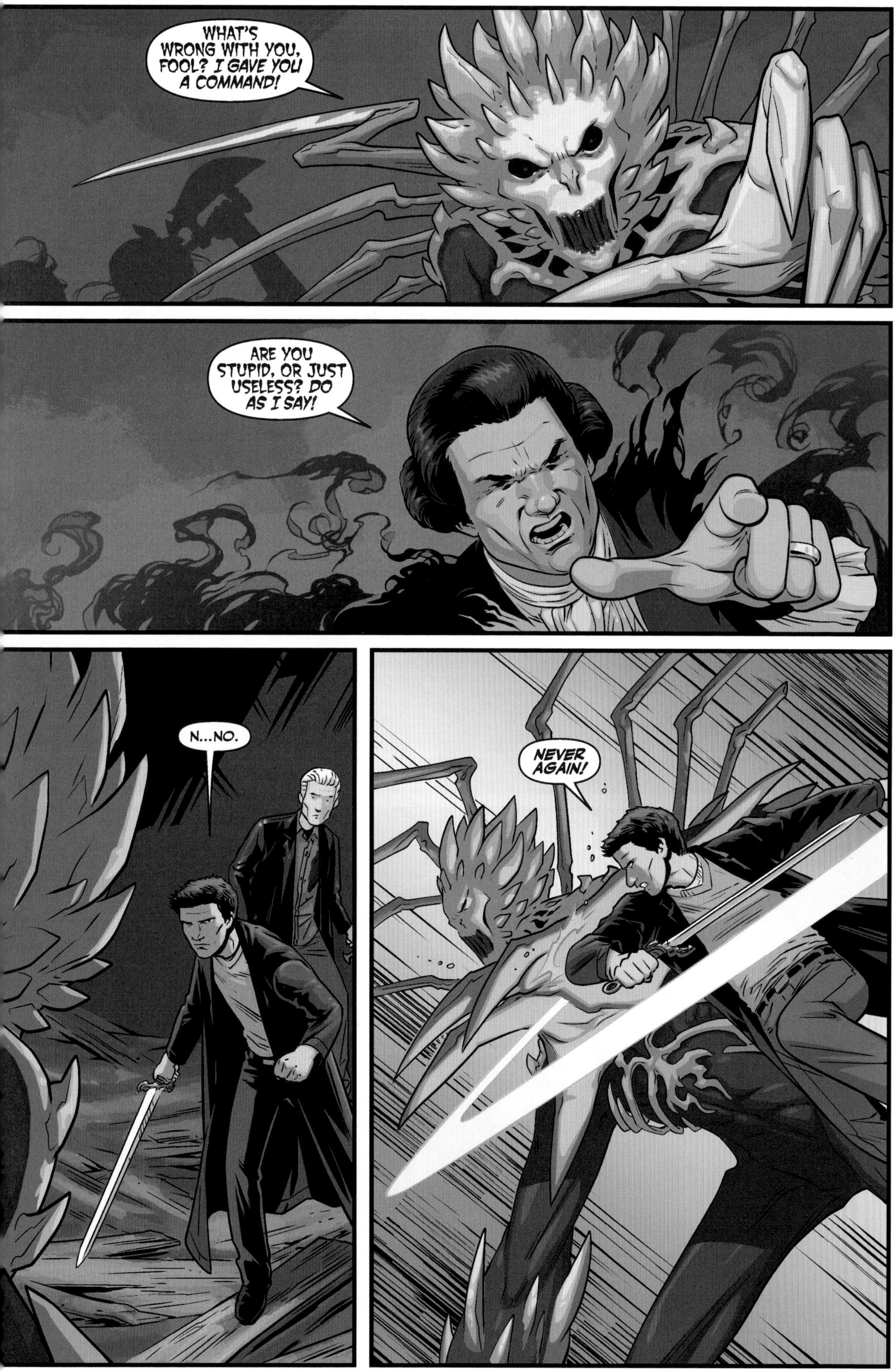
WHAT'S WRONG WITH YOU, FOOL? I GAVE YOU A COMMAND!
ARE YOU STUPID, OR JUST USELESS? DO AS I SAY!
N...NO.
NEVER AGAIN!

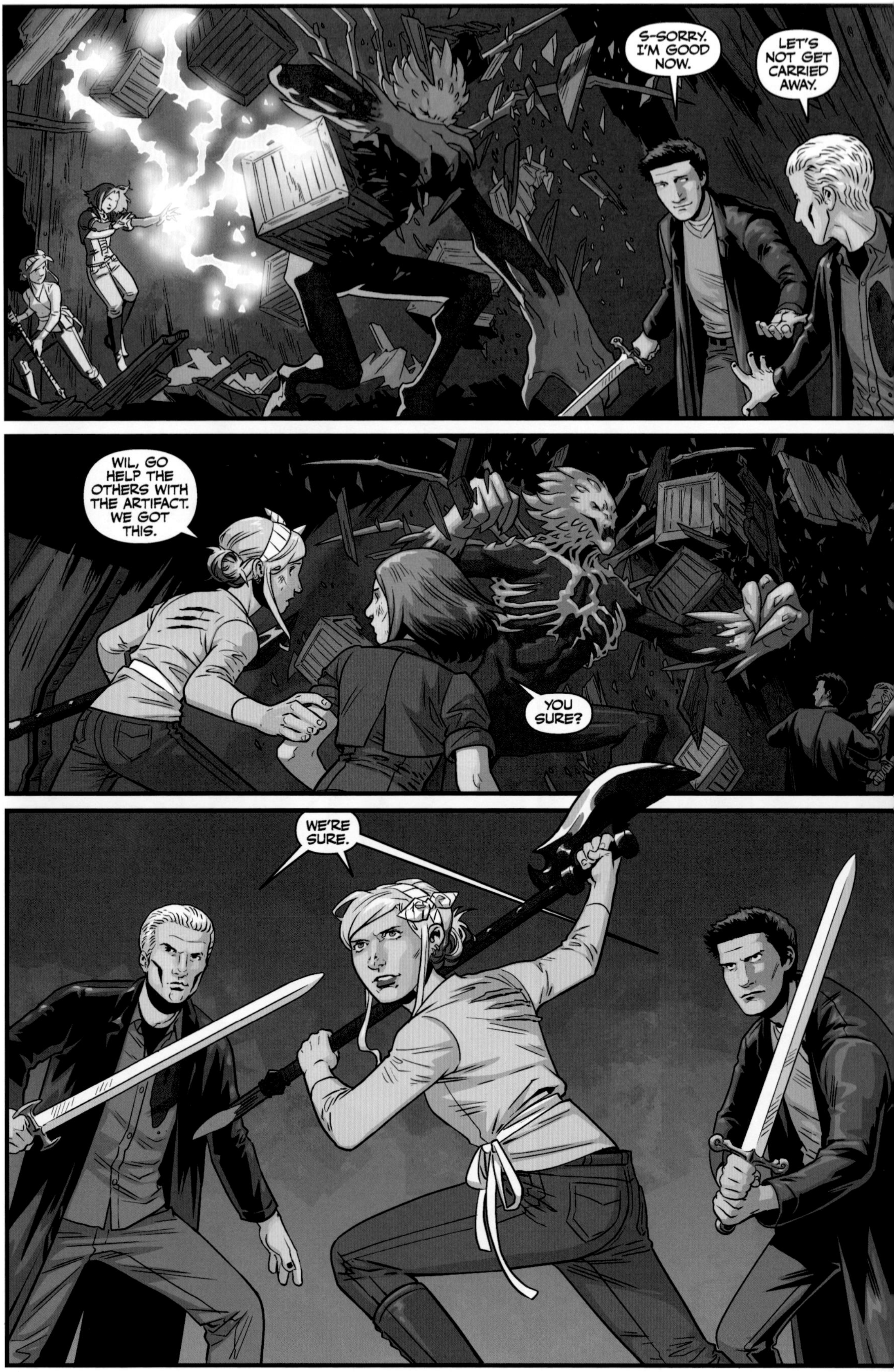
S-SORRY. I'M GOOD NOW.
LET'S NOT GET CARRIED AWAY.
WIL, GO HELP THE OTHERS WITH THE ARTIFACT. WE GOT THIS.
YOU SURE?
WE'RE SURE.

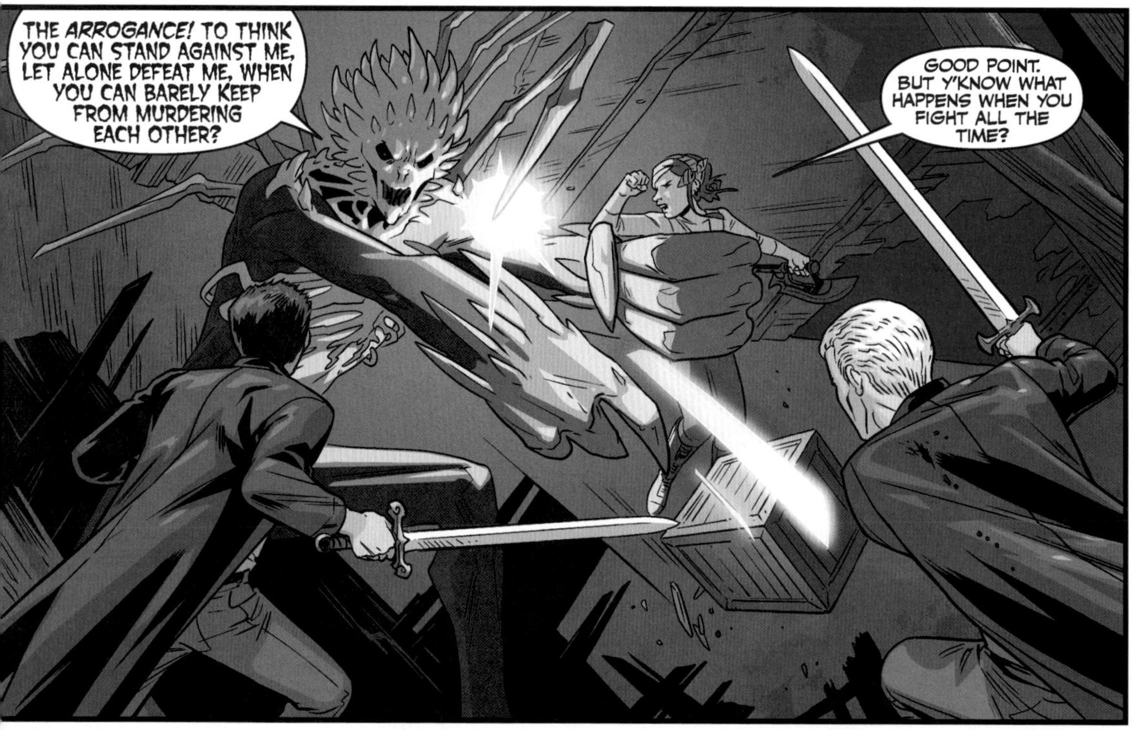
THE ARROGANCE! TO THINK YOU CAN STAND AGAINST ME, LET ALONE DEFEAT ME, WHEN YOU CAN BARELY KEEP FROM MURDERING EACH OTHER?
GOOD POINT. BUT Y'KNOW WHAT HAPPENS WHEN YOU FIGHT ALL THE TIME?

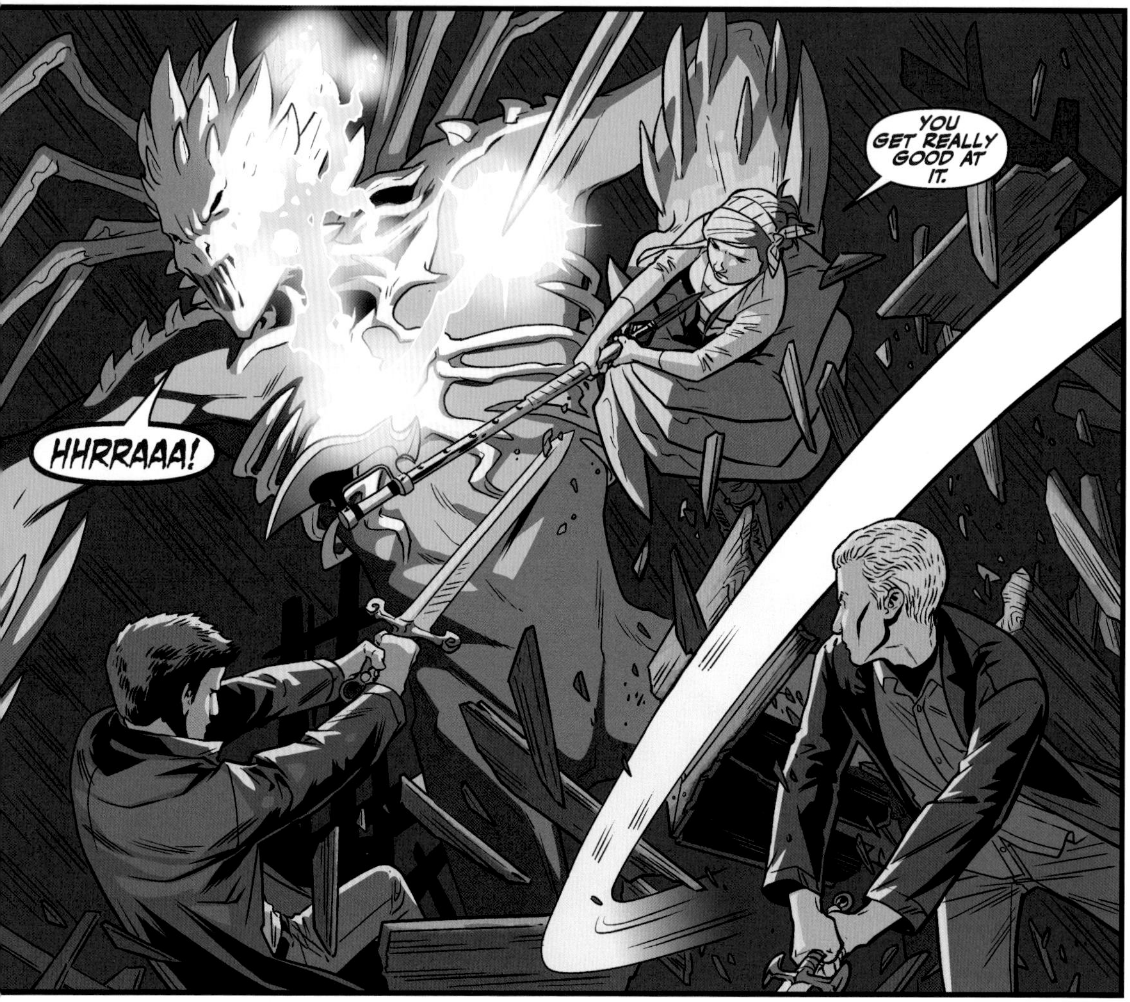
YOU GET REALLY GOOD AT IT.
HHRRAAA!

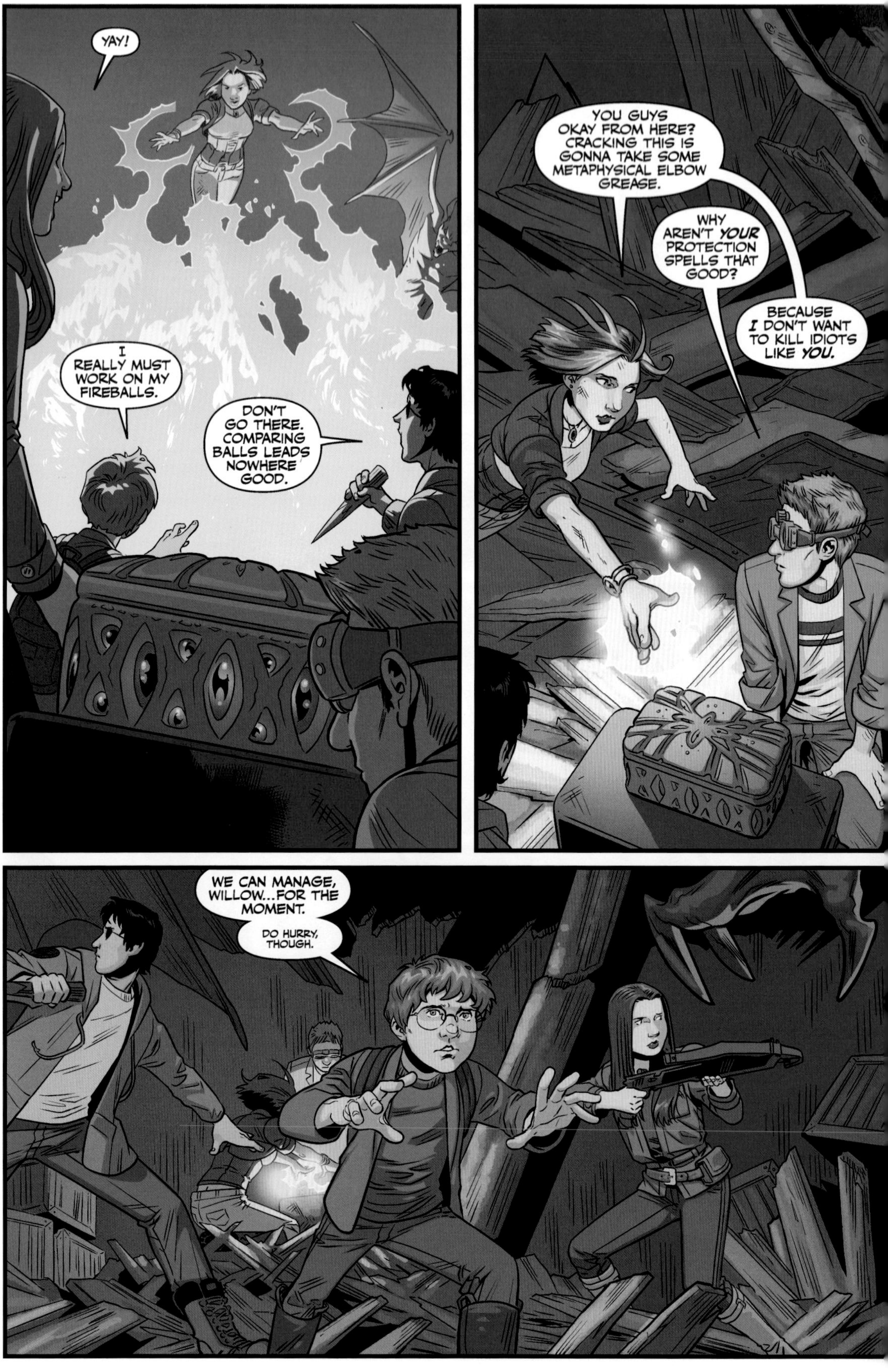
YAY!
I REALLY MUST WORK ON MY FIREBALLS.
DON'T GO THERE. COMPARING BALLS LEADS NOWHERE GOOD.
YOU GUYS OKAY FROM HERE? CRACKING THIS IS GONNA TAKE SOME METAPHYSICAL ELBOW GREASE.
WHY AREN'T *YOUR* PROTECTION SPELLS THAT GOOD?
BECAUSE *I* DON'T WANT TO KILL IDIOTS LIKE *YOU.*
WE CAN MANAGE, WILLOW...FOR THE MOMENT.
DO HURRY, THOUGH.

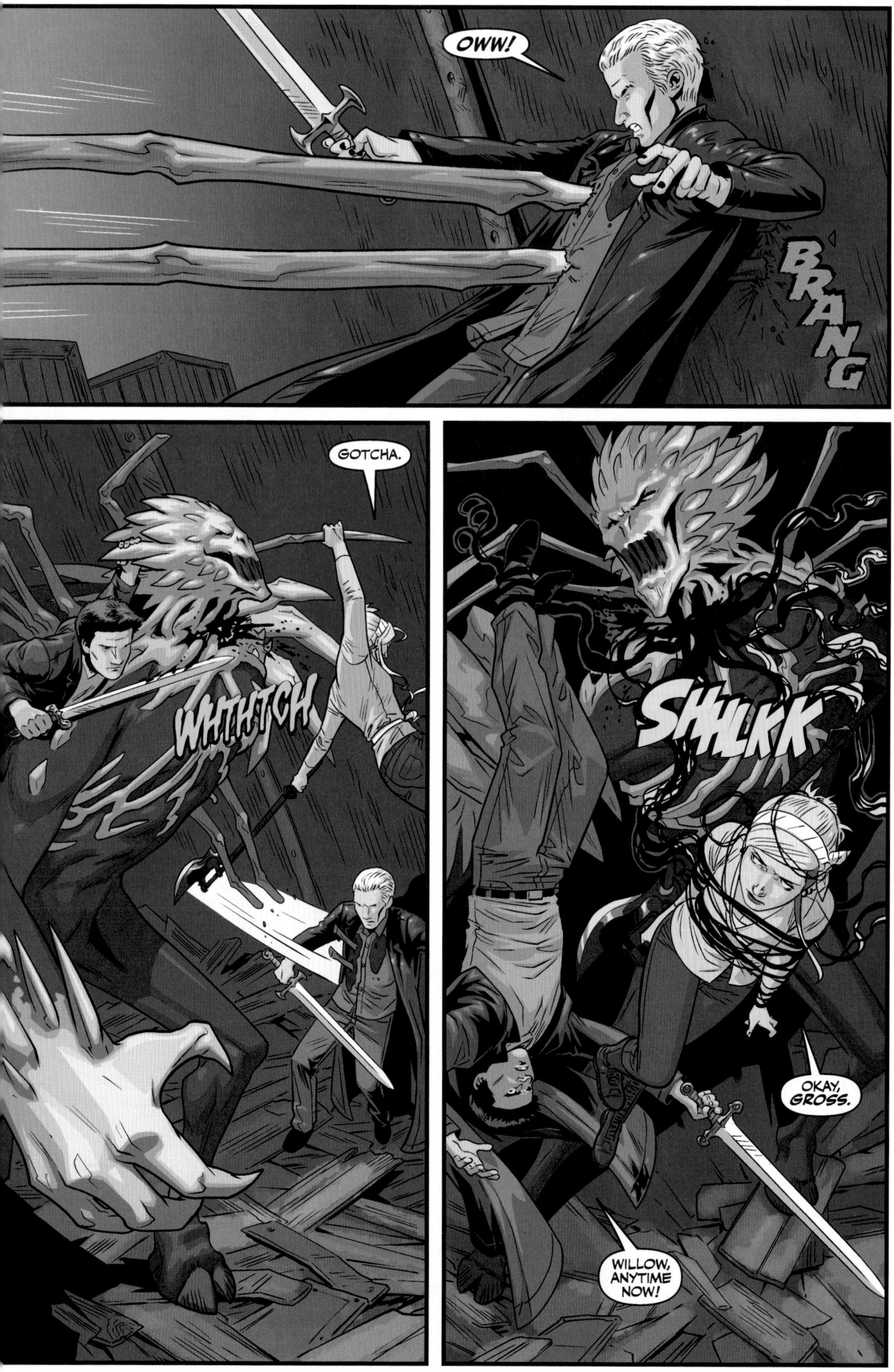
OWW!
BRANG
GOTCHA.
WHTHTCH
SHLKK
OKAY, GROSS.
WILLOW, ANYTIME NOW!

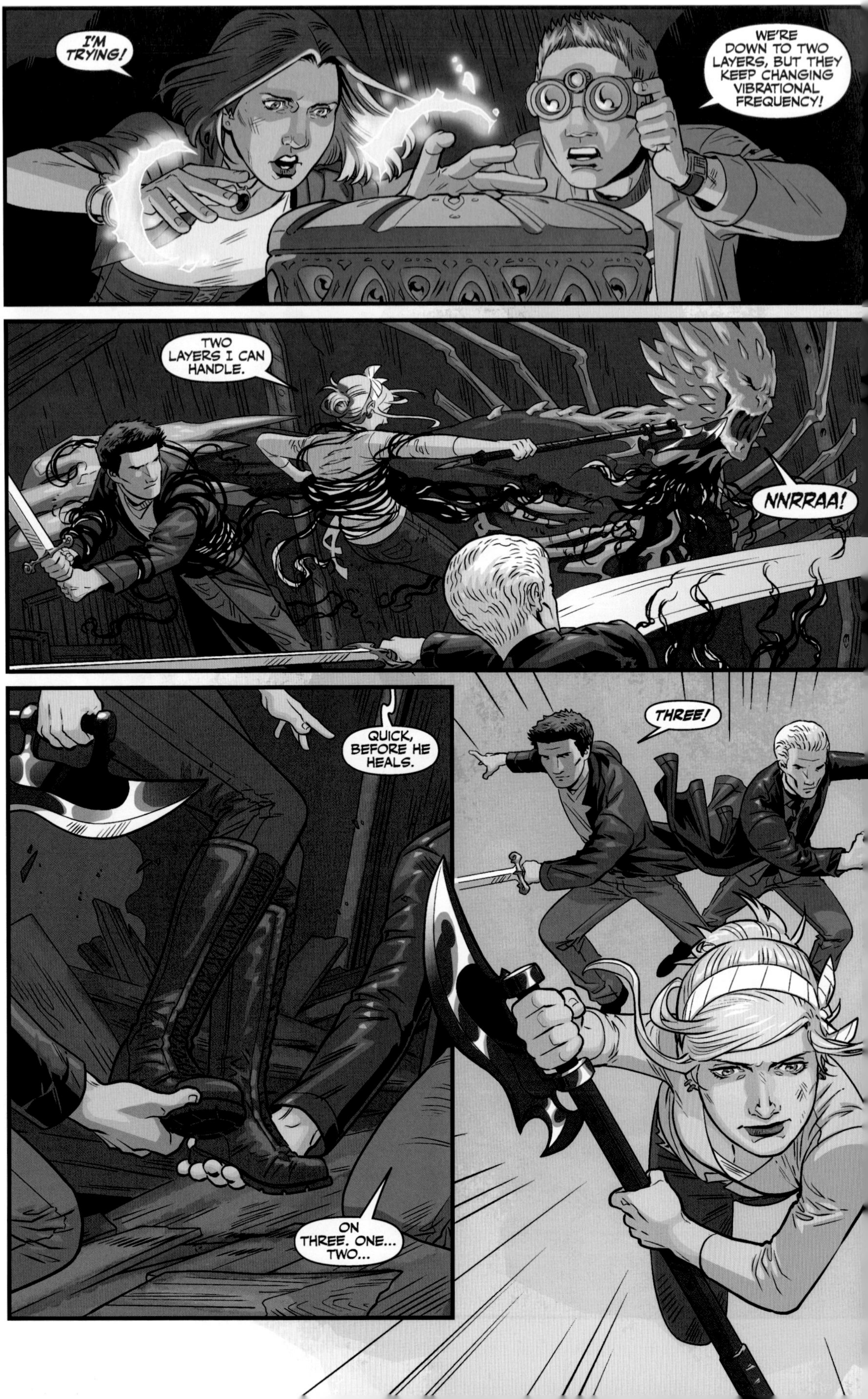
I'M TRYING!
WE'RE DOWN TO TWO LAYERS, BUT THEY KEEP CHANGING VIBRATIONAL FREQUENCY!
TWO LAYERS I CAN HANDLE.
NNRRAA!
QUICK, BEFORE HE HEALS.
ON THREE. ONE... TWO...
THREE!

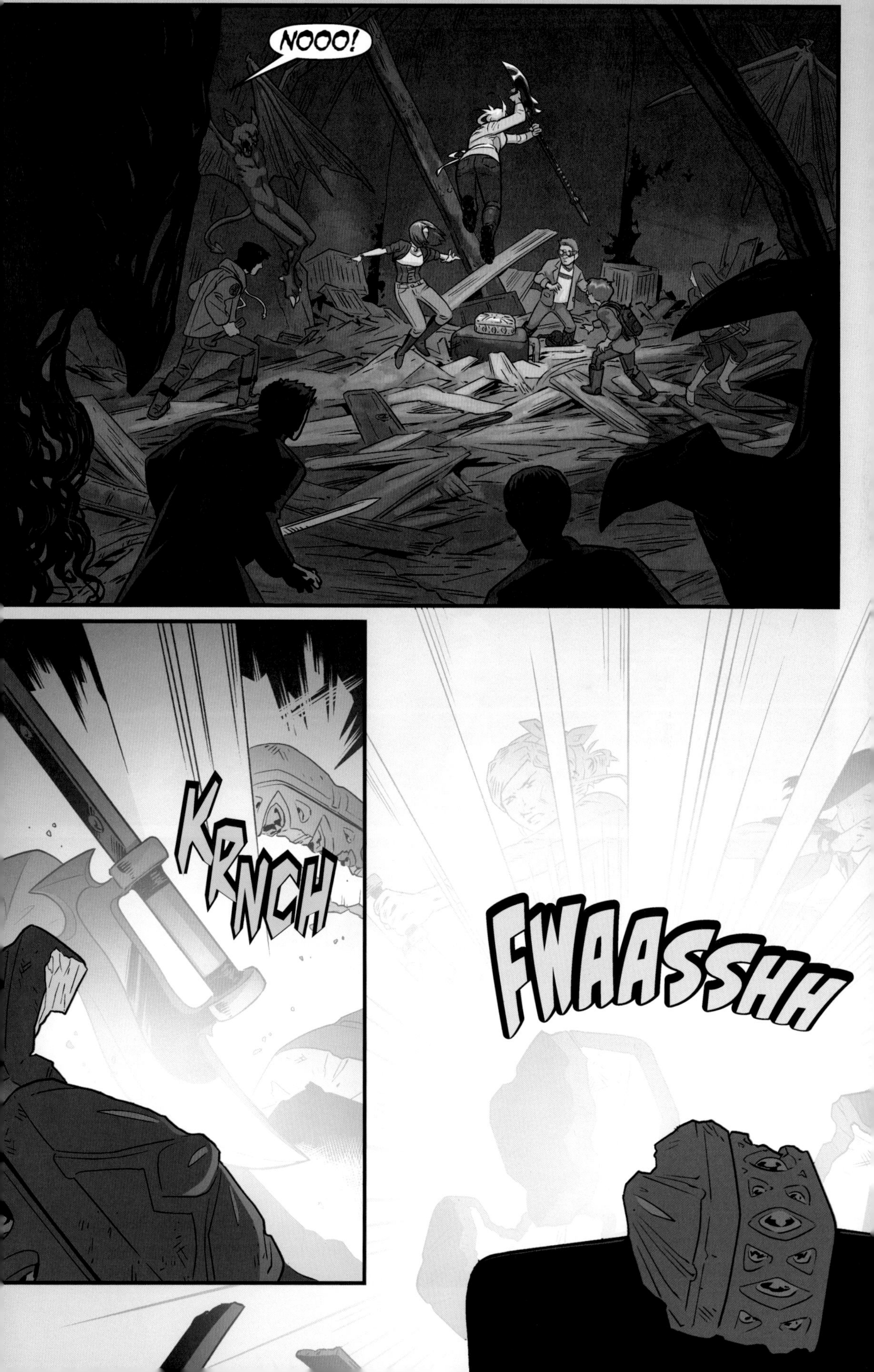
NOOO!
KRNCH
FWAASSHH

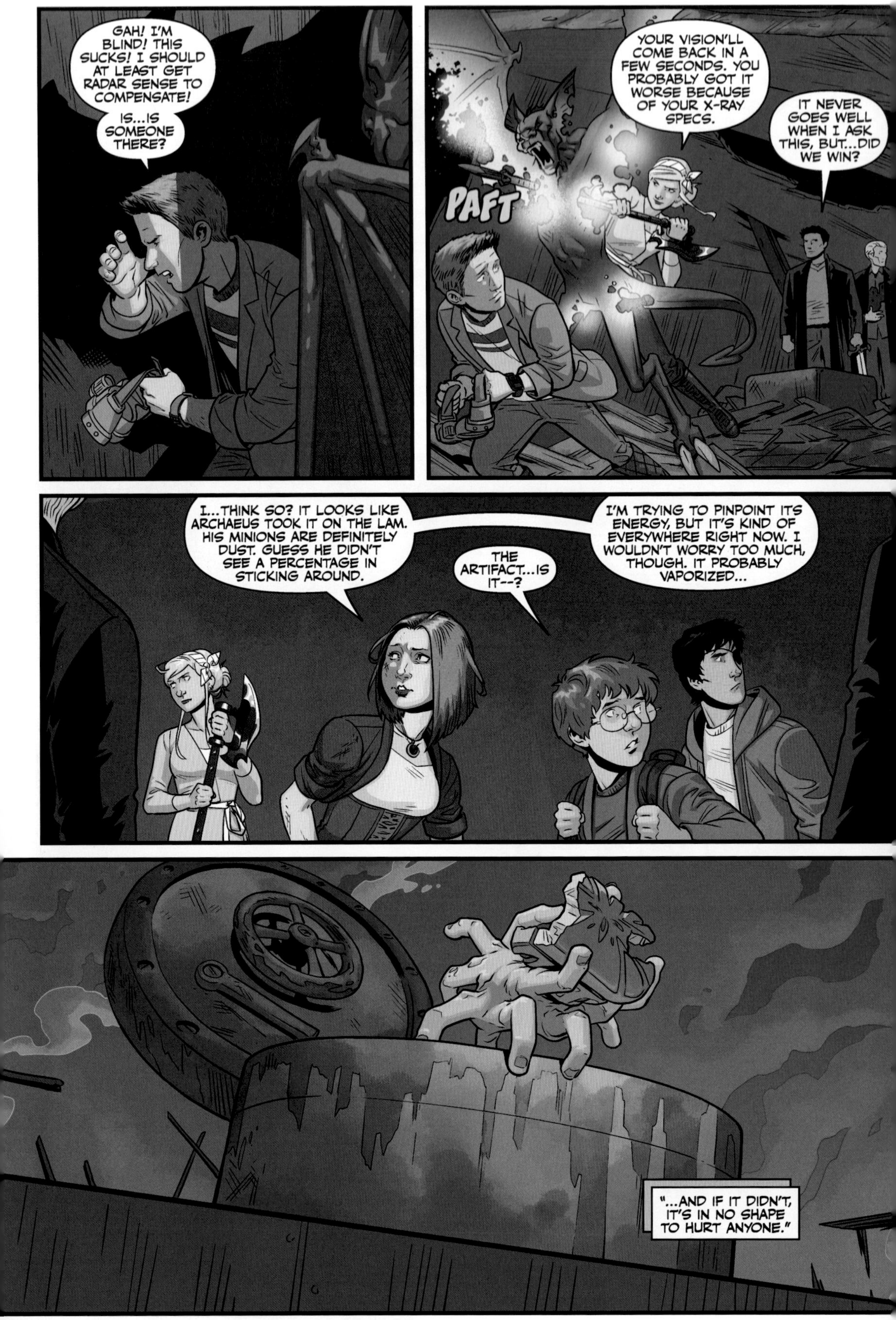
GAH! I'M BLIND! THIS SUCKS! I SHOULD AT LEAST GET RADAR SENSE TO COMPENSATE!
IS...IS SOMEONE THERE?
YOUR VISION'LL COME BACK IN A FEW SECONDS. YOU PROBABLY GOT IT WORSE BECAUSE OF YOUR X-RAY SPECS.
PAFT
IT NEVER GOES WELL WHEN I ASK THIS, BUT...DID WE WIN?
I...THINK SO? IT LOOKS LIKE ARCHAEUS TOOK IT ON THE LAM. HIS MINIONS ARE DEFINITELY DUST. GUESS HE DIDN'T SEE A PERCENTAGE IN STICKING AROUND.
THE ARTIFACT...IS IT--?
I'M TRYING TO PINPOINT ITS ENERGY, BUT IT'S KIND OF EVERYWHERE RIGHT NOW. I WOULDN'T WORRY TOO MUCH, THOUGH. IT PROBABLY VAPORIZED...
"...AND IF IT DIDN'T, IT'S IN NO SHAPE TO HURT ANYONE."

YOU'VE WON *NOTHING!*

AN ARTIFACT LIKE THE *RESTLESS DOOR* CANNOT BE DESTROYED SO EASILY.

DO YOU REALIZE WHAT HAPPENED WHILE YOU STOOD AROUND CONGRATULATING EACH OTHER ON YOUR "VICTORY"? ITS FRAGMENTS WERE *STOLEN.*

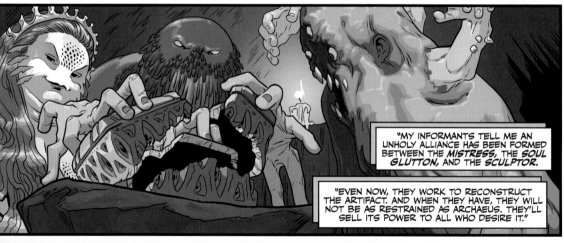

"MY INFORMANTS TELL ME AN UNHOLY ALLIANCE HAS BEEN FORMED BETWEEN THE *MISTRESS,* THE *SOUL GLUTTON,* AND THE *SCULPTOR.*

"EVEN NOW, THEY WORK TO RECONSTRUCT THE ARTIFACT. AND WHEN THEY HAVE, THEY WILL NOT BE AS RESTRAINED AS ARCHAEUS. THEY'LL SELL ITS POWER TO ALL WHO DESIRE IT."

AFTER ALL THE WORK WE'VE DONE TO PROTECT THIS WORLD, YOU'VE MADE IT AN INFINITELY MORE DANGEROUS PLACE! A *HUNTING GROUND* FOR DEMON KIND!

WHO IS THIS GUY AGAIN?

D'HOFFRYN. HEADS THE MYSTIC COUNCIL. KIND OF A YELLER.

LOOK, WE HAVE THE MAGIC RULE BOOK. CAN'T WE JUST WRITE IN IT THAT THE RESTLESS DOOR DOESN'T WORK ANYMORE?

SADLY, NO. THE BOOK SHAPES THE LAWS OF MAGIC ON *THIS* WORLD. THE RESTLESS DOOR ORIGINATED IN A HELL DIMENSION. WE HAVE NO CLAIM OVER IT.

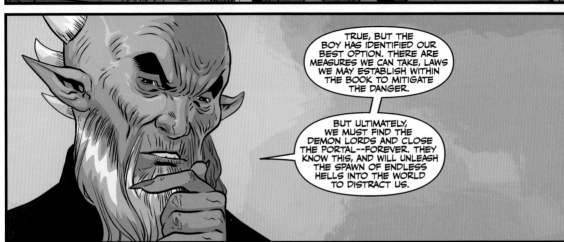

TRUE, BUT THE BOY HAS IDENTIFIED OUR BEST OPTION. THERE ARE MEASURES WE CAN TAKE, LAWS WE MAY ESTABLISH WITHIN THE BOOK TO MITIGATE THE DANGER.

BUT ULTIMATELY, WE MUST FIND THE DEMON LORDS AND CLOSE THE PORTAL--FOREVER. THEY KNOW THIS, AND WILL UNLEASH THE SPAWN OF ENDLESS HELLS INTO THE WORLD TO DISTRACT US.

THERE ARE FOLKS WE CAN CALL. PUT 'EM ON HIGH ALERT. RILEY, BILLY, KENNEDY...THERE'S NOT MUCH THEY CAN'T HANDLE WHILE WE GO AFTER THE BOSSES.

WE MUST ALSO BE VIGILANT FOR ARCHAEUS. LOSING HIS SOURCE OF POWER DIMINISHES HIS THREAT, BUT HARDLY ELIMINATES IT.

I'VE BEEN TRYING TO TRACK HIM EVER SINCE HE BAILED, BUT HE'S NOT AROUND HERE.

I'VE GOT SOME PRETTY GOOD CONTACTS BACK IN LONDON. I'LL PUT THE WORD OUT. SEE IF I CAN FIGURE OUT WHERE HE'S HIDING.

AND GIVE FAITH AND THE OTHERS THE HEADS-UP THAT THINGS ARE ABOUT TO GET WORSE.

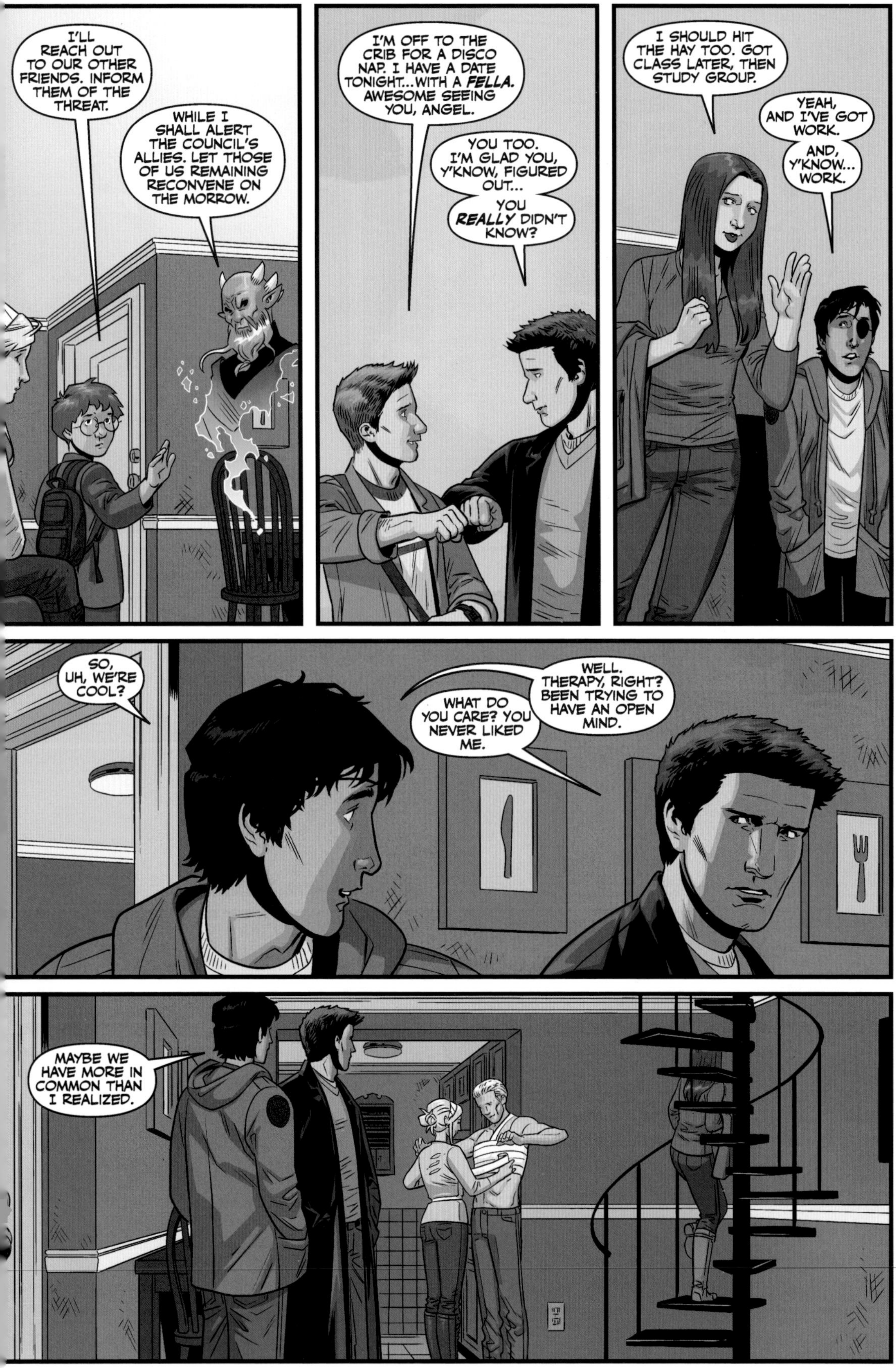
I'LL REACH OUT TO OUR OTHER FRIENDS. INFORM THEM OF THE THREAT.
WHILE I SHALL ALERT THE COUNCIL'S ALLIES. LET THOSE OF US REMAINING RECONVENE ON THE MORROW.
I'M OFF TO THE CRIB FOR A DISCO NAP. I HAVE A DATE TONIGHT...WITH A *FELLA.* AWESOME SEEING YOU, ANGEL.
YOU TOO. I'M GLAD YOU, Y'KNOW, FIGURED OUT...
YOU *REALLY* DIDN'T KNOW?
I SHOULD HIT THE HAY TOO. GOT CLASS LATER, THEN STUDY GROUP.
YEAH, AND I'VE GOT WORK.
AND, Y'KNOW... WORK.
SO, UH, WE'RE COOL?
WELL. THERAPY, RIGHT? BEEN TRYING TO HAVE AN OPEN MIND.
WHAT DO YOU CARE? YOU NEVER LIKED ME.
MAYBE WE HAVE MORE IN COMMON THAN I REALIZED.

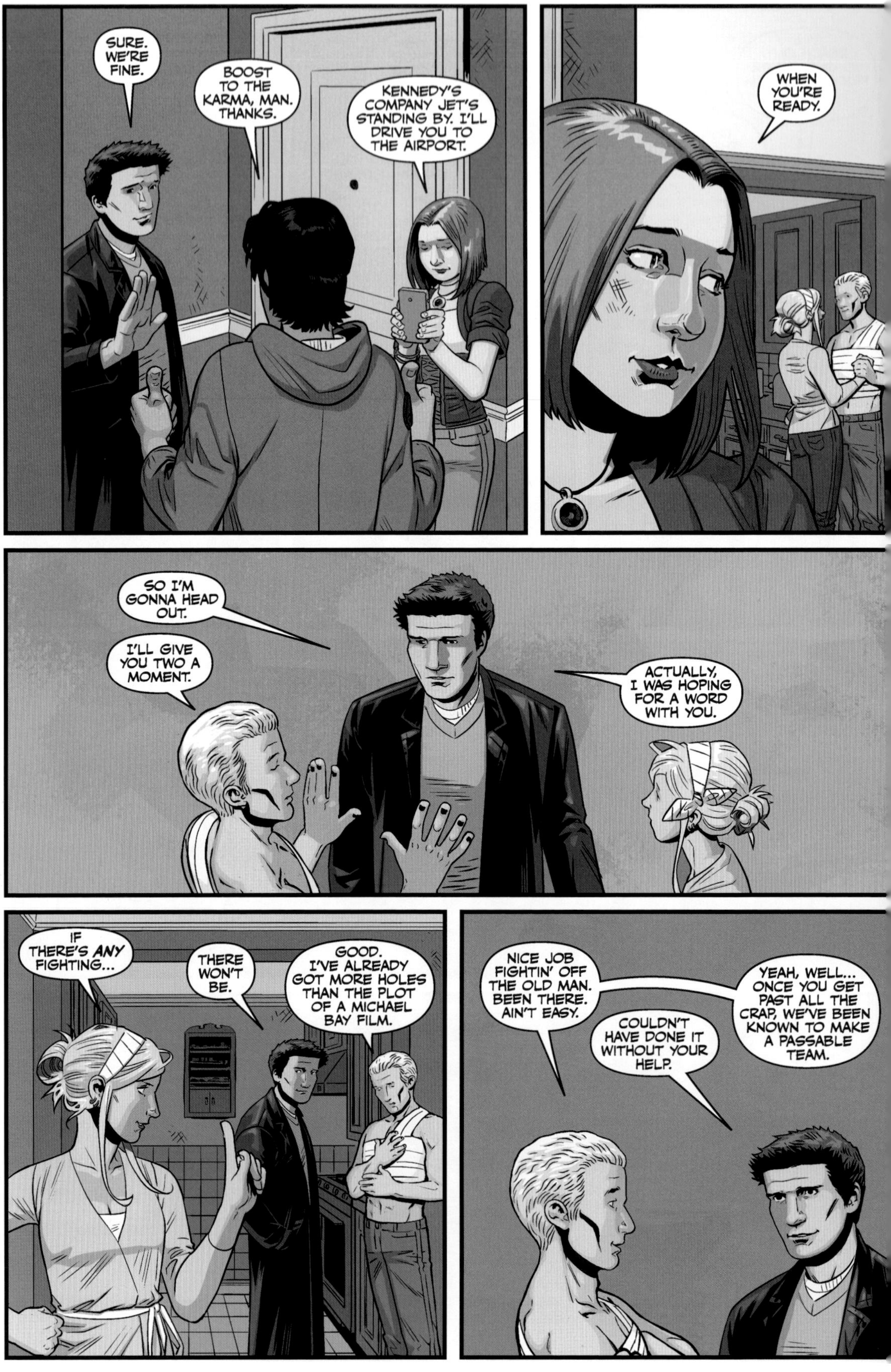
SURE. WE'RE FINE.
BOOST TO THE KARMA, MAN. THANKS.
KENNEDY'S COMPANY JET'S STANDING BY. I'LL DRIVE YOU TO THE AIRPORT.
WHEN YOU'RE READY.
SO I'M GONNA HEAD OUT.
I'LL GIVE YOU TWO A MOMENT.
ACTUALLY, I WAS HOPING FOR A WORD WITH YOU.
IF THERE'S *ANY* FIGHTING...
THERE WON'T BE.
GOOD. I'VE ALREADY GOT MORE HOLES THAN THE PLOT OF A MICHAEL BAY FILM.
NICE JOB FIGHTIN' OFF THE OLD MAN. BEEN THERE. AIN'T EASY.
COULDN'T HAVE DONE IT WITHOUT YOUR HELP.
YEAH, WELL... ONCE YOU GET PAST ALL THE CRAP, WE'VE BEEN KNOWN TO MAKE A PASSABLE TEAM.

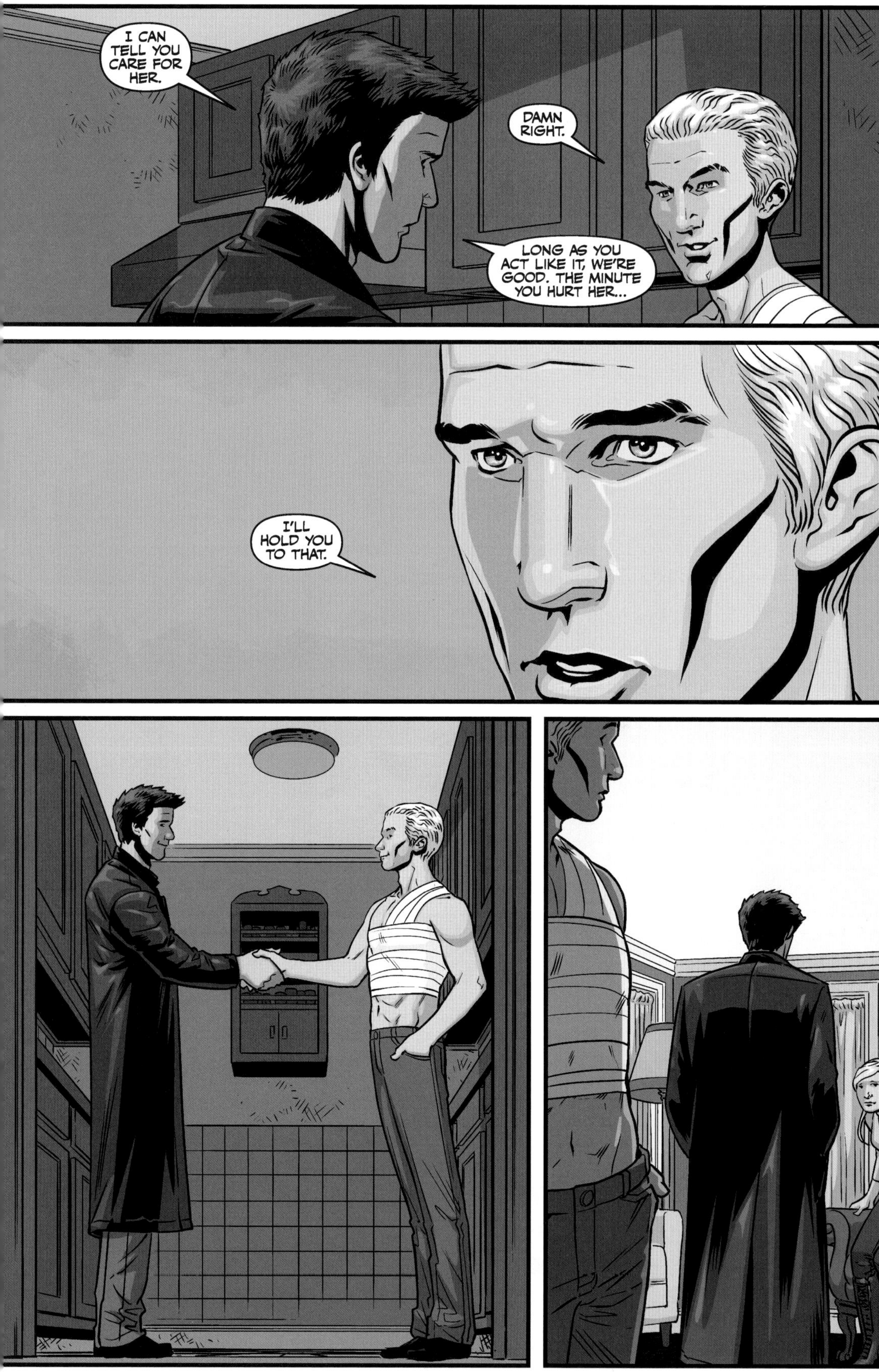
I CAN TELL YOU CARE FOR HER.
DAMN RIGHT.
LONG AS YOU ACT LIKE IT, WE'RE GOOD. THE MINUTE YOU HURT HER...
I'LL HOLD YOU TO THAT.

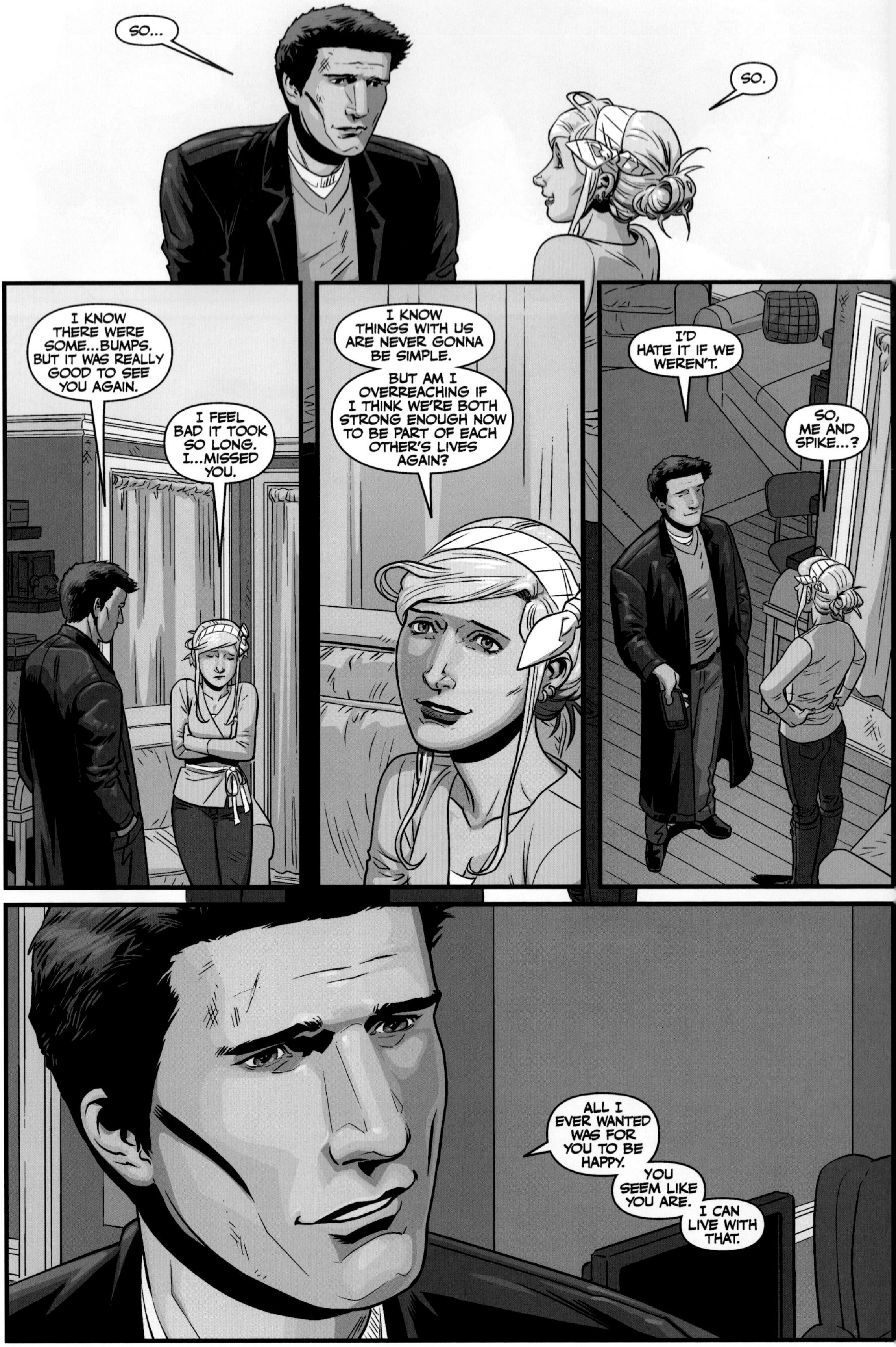
SO...
SO.
I KNOW THERE WERE SOME...BUMPS. BUT IT WAS REALLY GOOD TO SEE YOU AGAIN.
I FEEL BAD IT TOOK SO LONG. I...MISSED YOU.
I KNOW THINGS WITH US ARE NEVER GONNA BE SIMPLE.
BUT AM I OVERREACHING IF I THINK WE'RE BOTH STRONG ENOUGH NOW TO BE PART OF EACH OTHER'S LIVES AGAIN?
I'D HATE IT IF WE WEREN'T.
SO, ME AND SPIKE...?
ALL I EVER WANTED WAS FOR YOU TO BE HAPPY.
YOU SEEM LIKE YOU ARE.
I CAN LIVE WITH THAT.

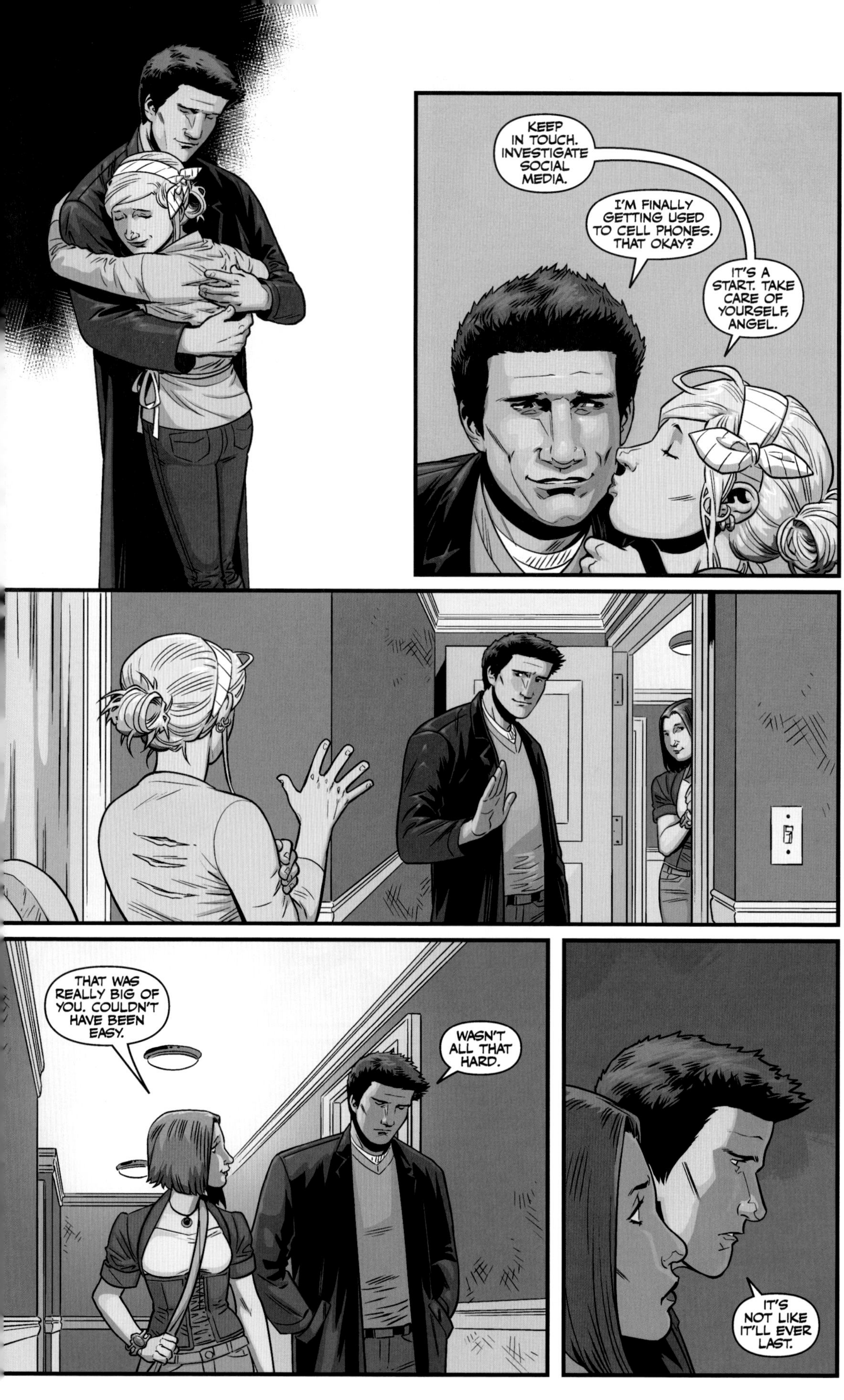
KEEP IN TOUCH. INVESTIGATE SOCIAL MEDIA.
I'M FINALLY GETTING USED TO CELL PHONES. THAT OKAY?
IT'S A START. TAKE CARE OF YOURSELF, ANGEL.
THAT WAS REALLY BIG OF YOU. COULDN'T HAVE BEEN EASY.
WASN'T ALL THAT HARD.
IT'S NOT LIKE IT'LL EVER LAST.

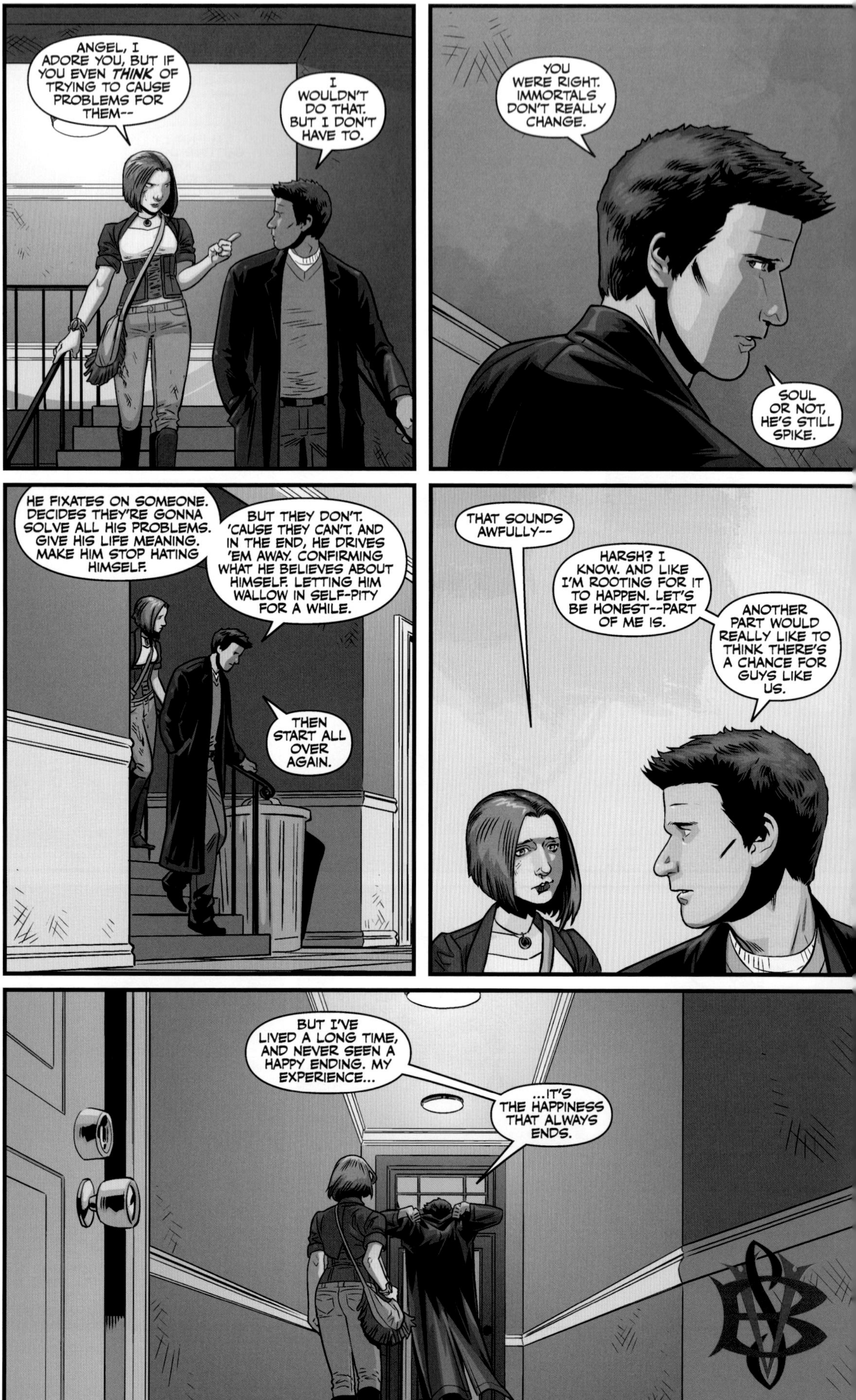
ANGEL, I ADORE YOU, BUT IF YOU EVEN *THINK* OF TRYING TO CAUSE PROBLEMS FOR THEM--
I WOULDN'T DO THAT. BUT I DON'T HAVE TO.
YOU WERE RIGHT. IMMORTALS DON'T REALLY CHANGE.
SOUL OR NOT, HE'S STILL SPIKE.
HE FIXATES ON SOMEONE. DECIDES THEY'RE GONNA SOLVE ALL HIS PROBLEMS. GIVE HIS LIFE MEANING. MAKE HIM STOP HATING HIMSELF.
BUT THEY DON'T. 'CAUSE THEY CAN'T. AND IN THE END, HE DRIVES 'EM AWAY. CONFIRMING WHAT HE BELIEVES ABOUT HIMSELF. LETTING HIM WALLOW IN SELF-PITY FOR A WHILE.
THEN START ALL OVER AGAIN.
THAT SOUNDS AWFULLY--
HARSH? I KNOW. AND LIKE I'M ROOTING FOR IT TO HAPPEN. LET'S BE HONEST--PART OF ME IS.
ANOTHER PART WOULD REALLY LIKE TO THINK THERE'S A CHANCE FOR GUYS LIKE US.
BUT I'VE LIVED A LONG TIME, AND NEVER SEEN A HAPPY ENDING. MY EXPERIENCE...
...IT'S THE HAPPINESS THAT ALWAYS ENDS.

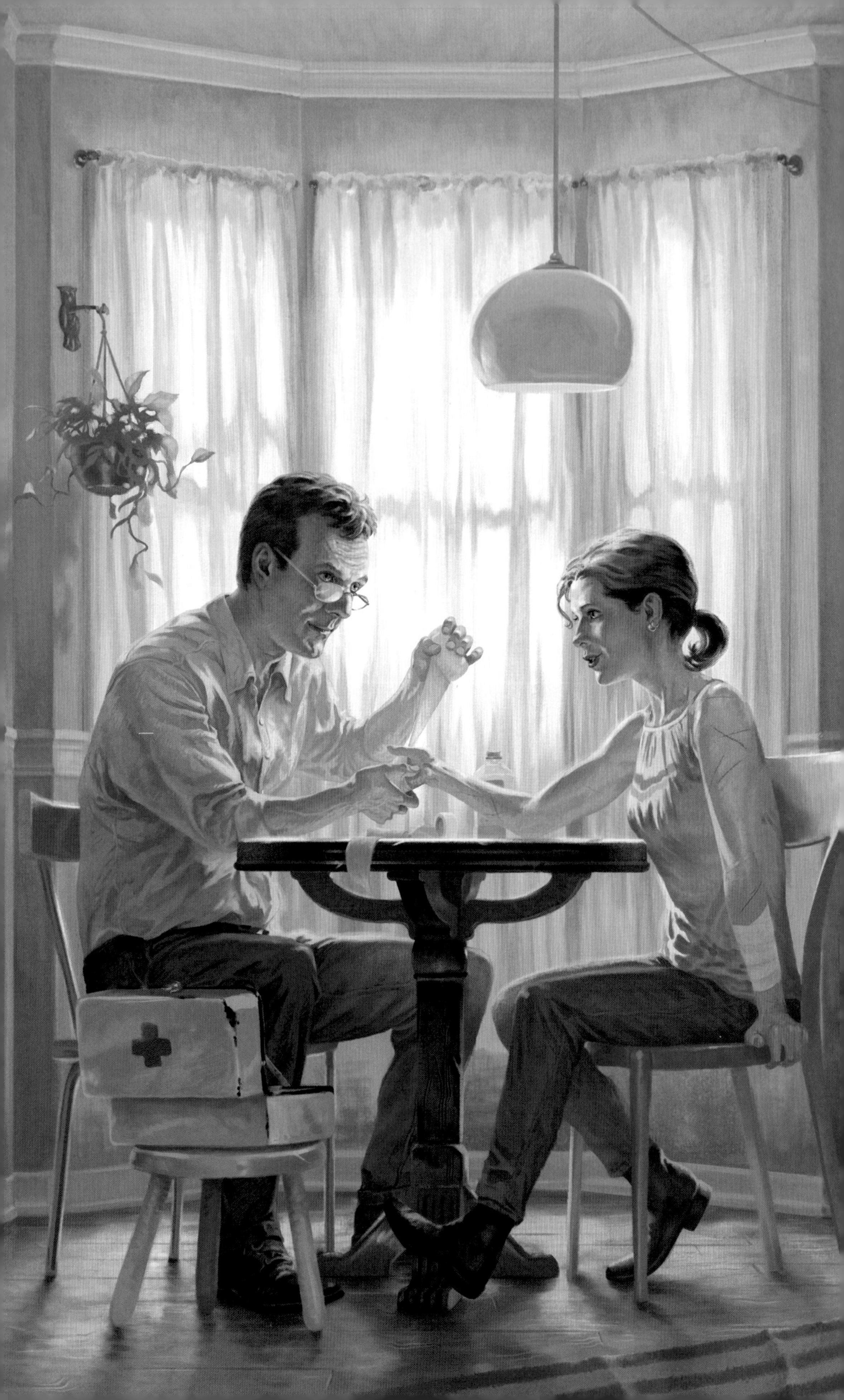

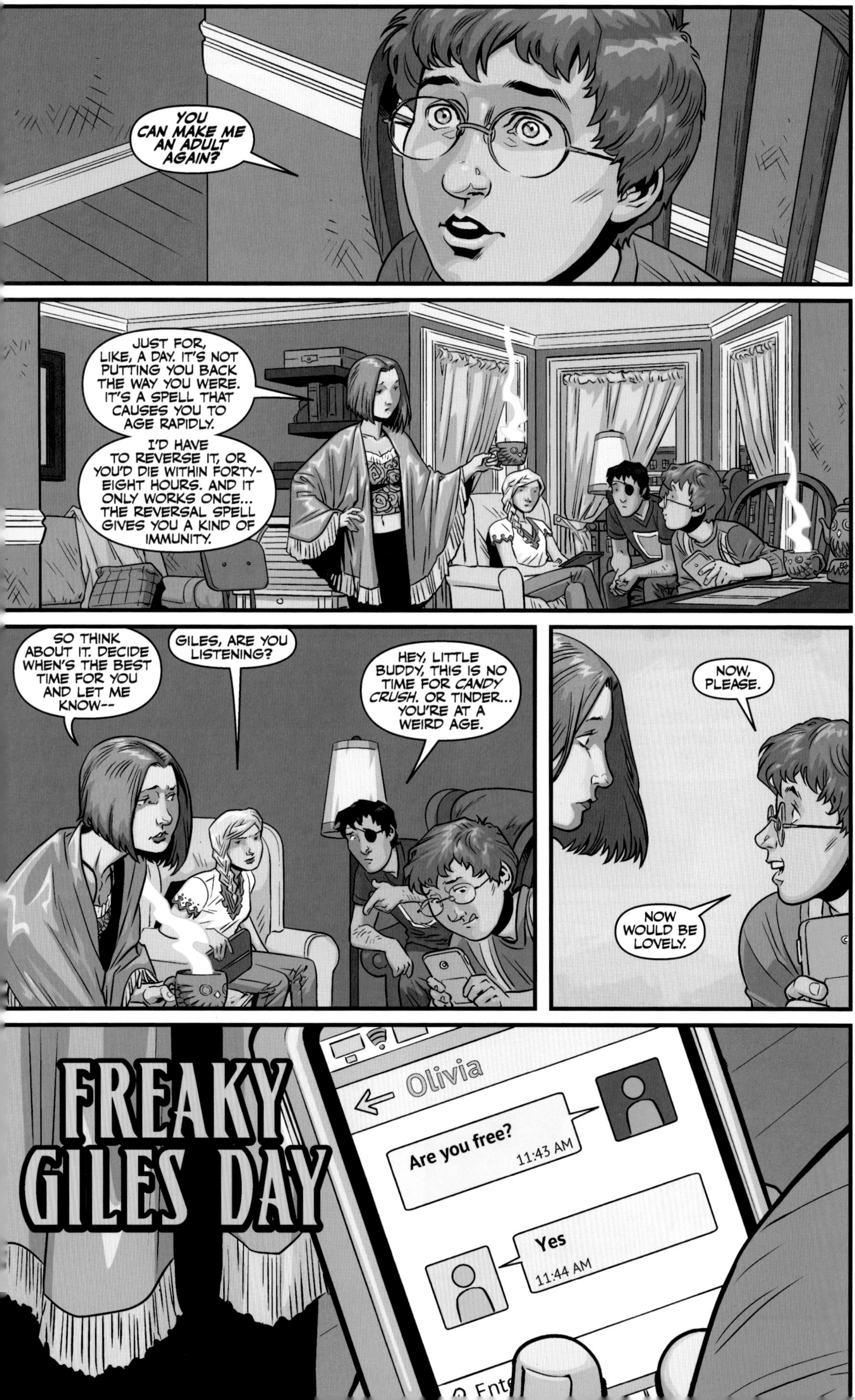
YOU CAN MAKE ME AN ADULT AGAIN?
JUST FOR, LIKE, A DAY. IT'S NOT PUTTING YOU BACK THE WAY YOU WERE. IT'S A SPELL THAT CAUSES YOU TO AGE RAPIDLY.
I'D HAVE TO REVERSE IT, OR YOU'D DIE WITHIN FORTY-EIGHT HOURS. AND IT ONLY WORKS ONCE... THE REVERSAL SPELL GIVES YOU A KIND OF IMMUNITY.
SO THINK ABOUT IT. DECIDE WHEN'S THE BEST TIME FOR YOU AND LET ME KNOW--
GILES, ARE YOU LISTENING?
HEY, LITTLE BUDDY, THIS IS NO TIME FOR *CANDY CRUSH*. OR TINDER... YOU'RE AT A WEIRD AGE.
NOW, PLEASE.
NOW WOULD BE LOVELY.
FREAKY GILES DAY
Olivia
Are you free?
11:43 AM
Yes
11:44 AM

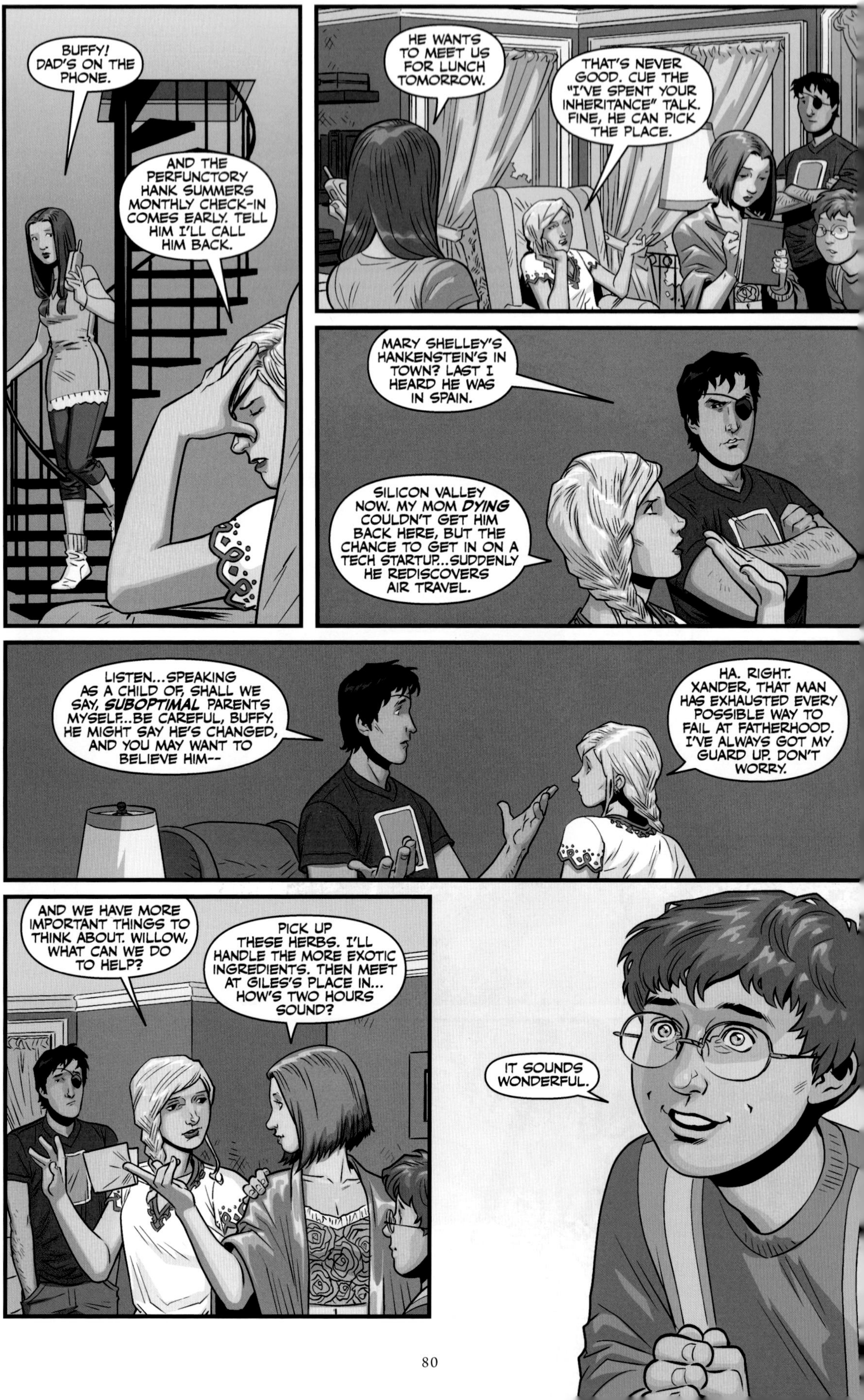
BUFFY! DAD'S ON THE PHONE.
AND THE PERFUNCTORY HANK SUMMERS MONTHLY CHECK-IN COMES EARLY. TELL HIM I'LL CALL HIM BACK.
HE WANTS TO MEET US FOR LUNCH TOMORROW.
THAT'S NEVER GOOD. CUE THE "I'VE SPENT YOUR INHERITANCE" TALK. FINE, HE CAN PICK THE PLACE.
MARY SHELLEY'S HANKENSTEIN'S IN TOWN? LAST I HEARD HE WAS IN SPAIN.
SILICON VALLEY NOW. MY MOM *DYING* COULDN'T GET HIM BACK HERE, BUT THE CHANCE TO GET IN ON A TECH STARTUP...SUDDENLY HE REDISCOVERS AIR TRAVEL.
LISTEN...SPEAKING AS A CHILD OF, SHALL WE SAY, *SUBOPTIMAL* PARENTS MYSELF...BE CAREFUL, BUFFY. HE MIGHT SAY HE'S CHANGED, AND YOU MAY WANT TO BELIEVE HIM--
HA. RIGHT. XANDER, THAT MAN HAS EXHAUSTED EVERY POSSIBLE WAY TO FAIL AT FATHERHOOD. I'VE ALWAYS GOT MY GUARD UP. DON'T WORRY.
AND WE HAVE MORE IMPORTANT THINGS TO THINK ABOUT. WILLOW, WHAT CAN WE DO TO HELP?
PICK UP THESE HERBS. I'LL HANDLE THE MORE EXOTIC INGREDIENTS. THEN MEET AT GILES'S PLACE IN... HOW'S TWO HOURS SOUND?
IT SOUNDS WONDERFUL.

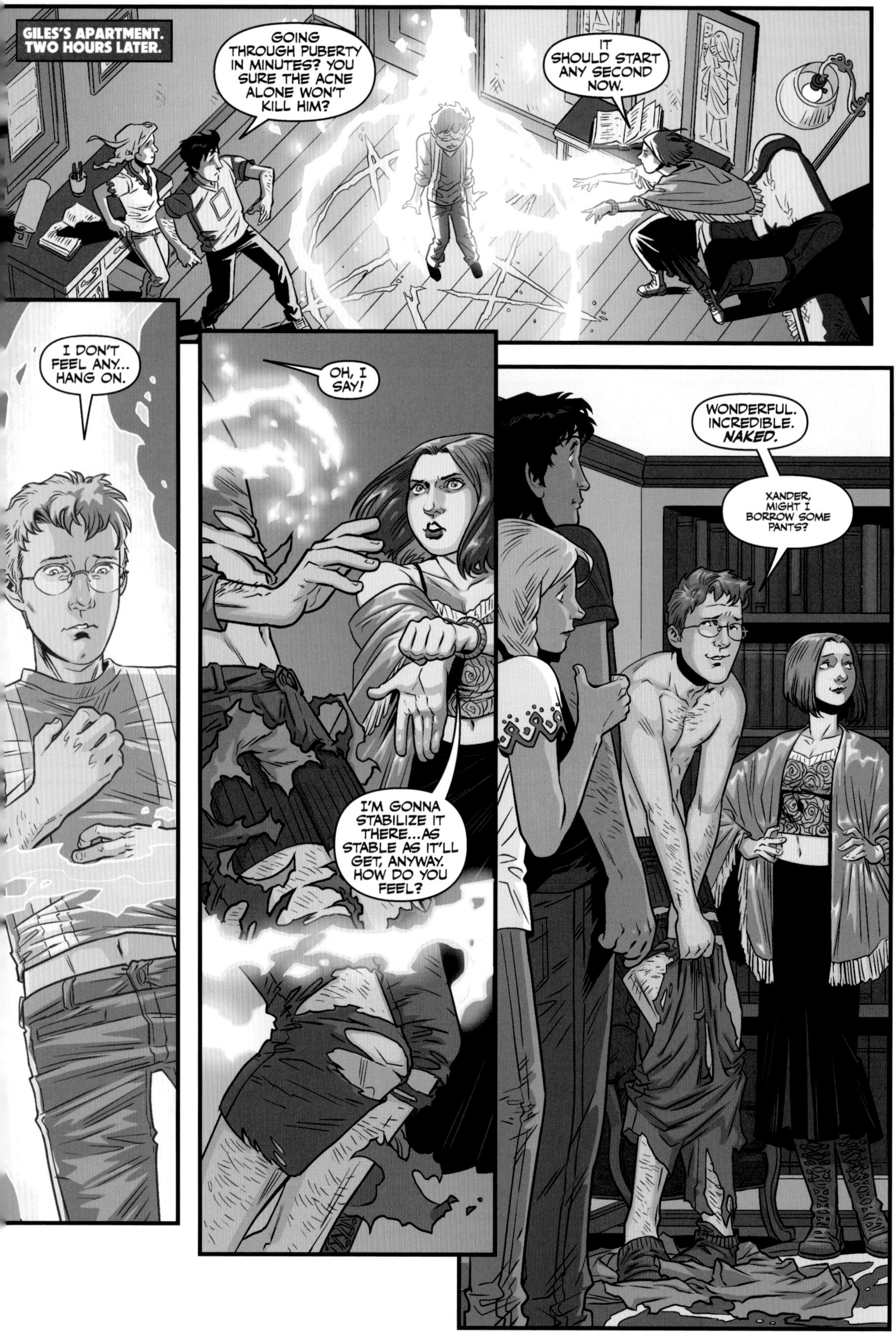
GILES'S APARTMENT. TWO HOURS LATER.
GOING THROUGH PUBERTY IN MINUTES? YOU SURE THE ACNE ALONE WON'T KILL HIM?
IT SHOULD START ANY SECOND NOW.
I DON'T FEEL ANY... HANG ON.
OH, I SAY!
I'M GONNA STABILIZE IT THERE...AS STABLE AS IT'LL GET, ANYWAY. HOW DO YOU FEEL?
WONDERFUL. INCREDIBLE. *NAKED.*
XANDER, MIGHT I BORROW SOME PANTS?

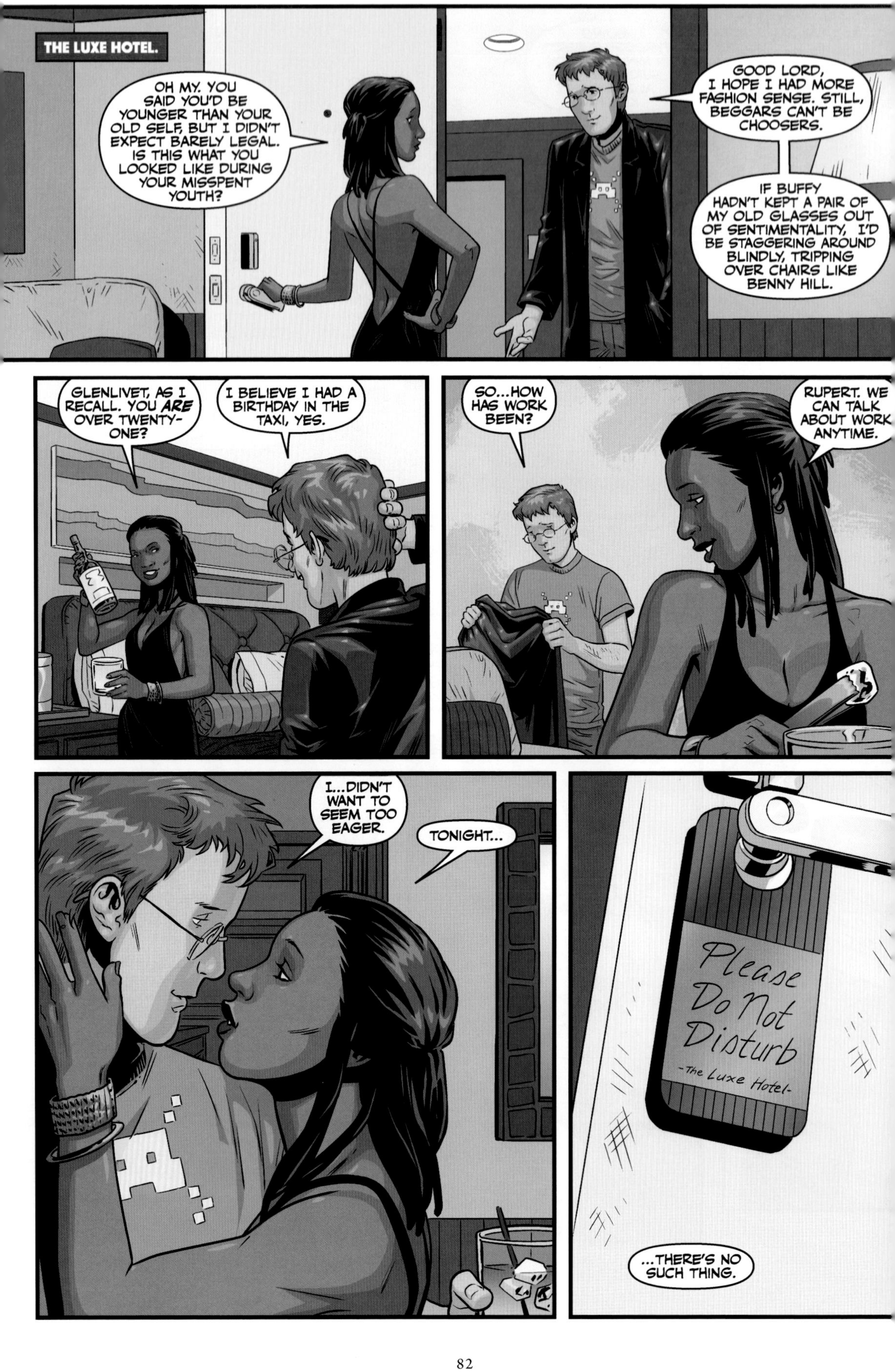
THE LUXE HOTEL.
OH MY. YOU SAID YOU'D BE YOUNGER THAN YOUR OLD SELF, BUT I DIDN'T EXPECT BARELY LEGAL. IS THIS WHAT YOU LOOKED LIKE DURING YOUR MISSPENT YOUTH?
GOOD LORD, I HOPE I HAD MORE FASHION SENSE. STILL, BEGGARS CAN'T BE CHOOSERS.
IF BUFFY HADN'T KEPT A PAIR OF MY OLD GLASSES OUT OF SENTIMENTALITY, I'D BE STAGGERING AROUND BLINDLY, TRIPPING OVER CHAIRS LIKE BENNY HILL.
GLENLIVET, AS I RECALL. YOU ARE OVER TWENTY-ONE?
I BELIEVE I HAD A BIRTHDAY IN THE TAXI, YES.
SO...HOW HAS WORK BEEN?
RUPERT. WE CAN TALK ABOUT WORK ANYTIME.
I...DIDN'T WANT TO SEEM TOO EAGER.
TONIGHT...
Please Do Not Disturb
-The Luxe Hotel-
...THERE'S NO SUCH THING.

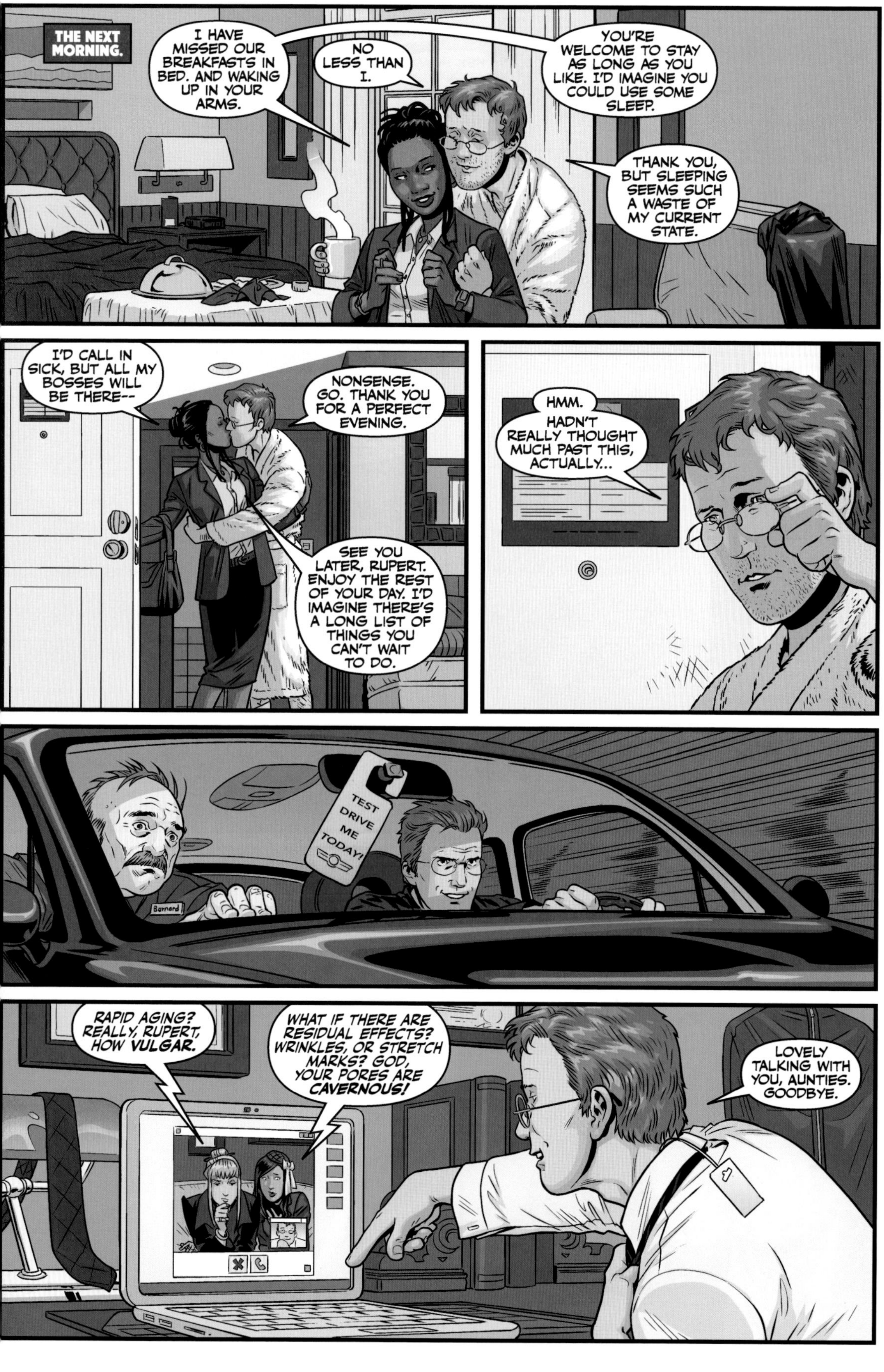
THE NEXT MORNING.
I HAVE MISSED OUR BREAKFASTS IN BED. AND WAKING UP IN YOUR ARMS.
NO LESS THAN I.
YOU'RE WELCOME TO STAY AS LONG AS YOU LIKE. I'D IMAGINE YOU COULD USE SOME SLEEP.
THANK YOU, BUT SLEEPING SEEMS SUCH A WASTE OF MY CURRENT STATE.
I'D CALL IN SICK, BUT ALL MY BOSSES WILL BE THERE--
NONSENSE. GO. THANK YOU FOR A PERFECT EVENING.
SEE YOU LATER, RUPERT. ENJOY THE REST OF YOUR DAY. I'D IMAGINE THERE'S A LONG LIST OF THINGS YOU CAN'T WAIT TO DO.
HMM. HADN'T REALLY THOUGHT MUCH PAST THIS, ACTUALLY...
TEST DRIVE ME TODAY!
Barnard
RAPID AGING? REALLY, RUPERT, HOW VULGAR.
WHAT IF THERE ARE RESIDUAL EFFECTS? WRINKLES, OR STRETCH MARKS? GOD, YOUR PORES ARE CAVERNOUS!
LOVELY TALKING WITH YOU, AUNTIES. GOODBYE.

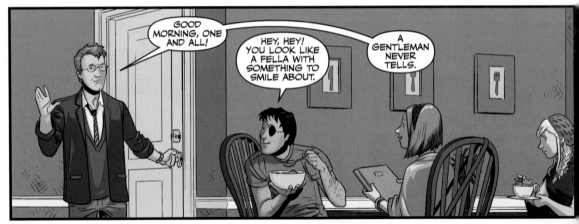

GOOD MORNING, ONE AND ALL!

HEY, HEY! YOU LOOK LIKE A FELLA WITH SOMETHING TO SMILE ABOUT.

A GENTLEMAN NEVER TELLS.

WHAT ARE YOU DOING BACK?

OH... OLIVIA HAD TO GO TO WORK.

LOT OF THAT GOING AROUND. SPIKE'S ON A POLICE CASE, AND I'VE GOT MY FINAL INTERVIEW WITH THEO DANIELS TODAY. IF THIS WORKS, I AM ONCE AGAIN GAINFULLY EMPLOYED.

AH! WELL, I MIGHT SUGGEST SOMETHING A BIT MORE... BUSINESSLIKE. A SKIRT, PERHAPS. SUIT JACKET, DEFINITELY.

ONE MUST CONSTANTLY PRESENT THE IMPRESSION OF A SERIOUS, DEDICATED PROFESSIONAL WHO WILL FOCUS ENTIRELY ON THE JOB AT HAND.

THIS ISN'T WALL STREET. THEY HAVE NERF GUNS IN THE OFFICE, YOGA BREAKS... A BALL PIT.

NO SET HOURS, WORK AT YOUR OWN PACE, WHATEVER IT TAKES TO SPARK THE MUSE. THEY WANT YOU TO LOOK CREATIVE, UNIQUE, OUT OF THE BOX. THEY'RE BIG ON THAT.

APPRECIATE THE THOUGHT. BUT I GOT IT COVERED.

YES, I SEE.

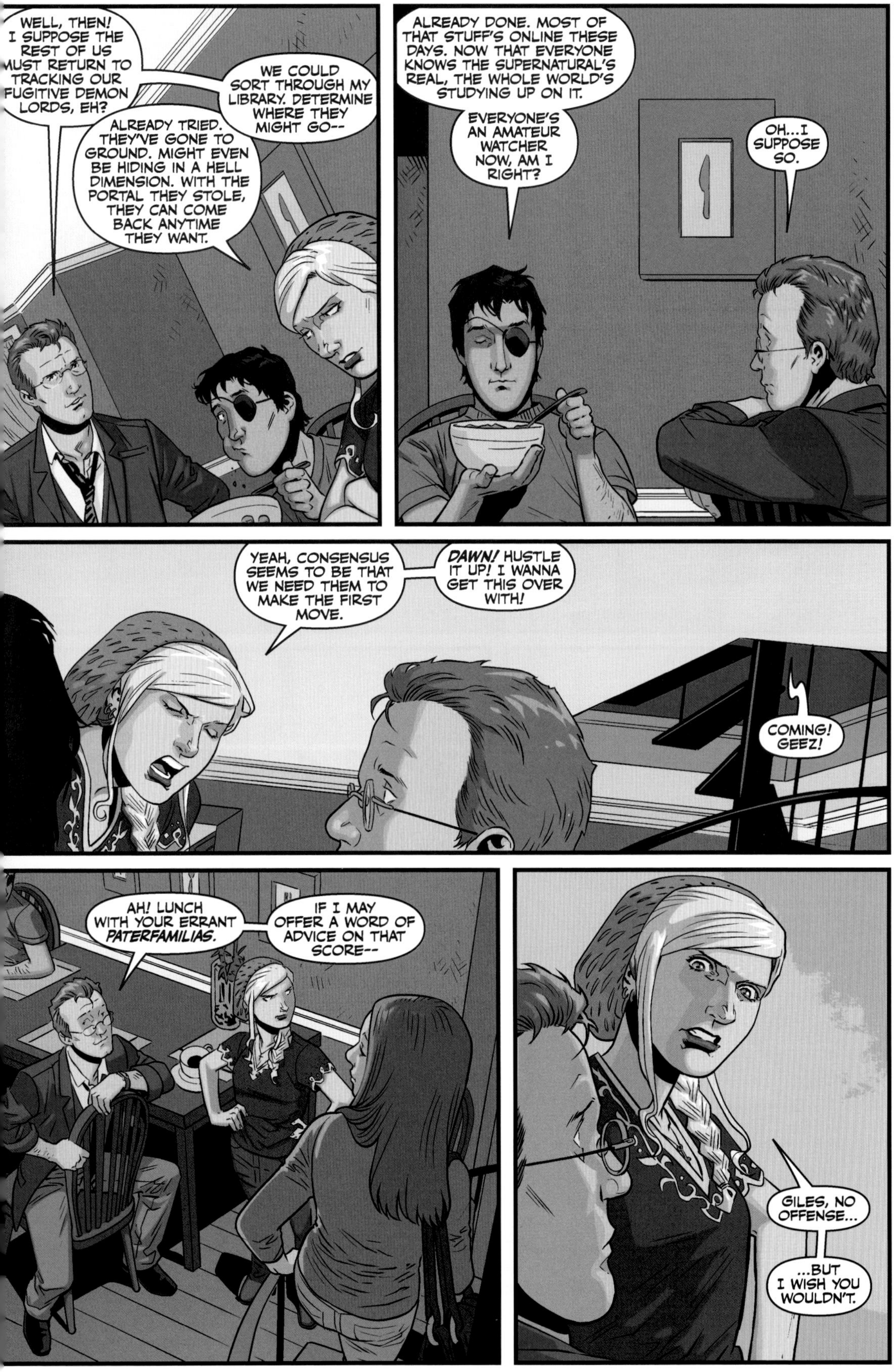

WELL, THEN! I SUPPOSE THE REST OF US MUST RETURN TO TRACKING OUR FUGITIVE DEMON LORDS, EH?
WE COULD SORT THROUGH MY LIBRARY. DETERMINE WHERE THEY MIGHT GO--
ALREADY TRIED. THEY'VE GONE TO GROUND. MIGHT EVEN BE HIDING IN A HELL DIMENSION. WITH THE PORTAL THEY STOLE, THEY CAN COME BACK ANYTIME THEY WANT.
ALREADY DONE. MOST OF THAT STUFF'S ONLINE THESE DAYS. NOW THAT EVERYONE KNOWS THE SUPERNATURAL'S REAL, THE WHOLE WORLD'S STUDYING UP ON IT.
EVERYONE'S AN AMATEUR WATCHER NOW, AM I RIGHT?
OH...I SUPPOSE SO.
YEAH, CONSENSUS SEEMS TO BE THAT WE NEED THEM TO MAKE THE FIRST MOVE.
DAWN! HUSTLE IT UP! I WANNA GET THIS OVER WITH!
COMING! GEEZ!
AH! LUNCH WITH YOUR ERRANT PATERFAMILIAS.
IF I MAY OFFER A WORD OF ADVICE ON THAT SCORE--
GILES, NO OFFENSE...
...BUT I WISH YOU WOULDN'T.

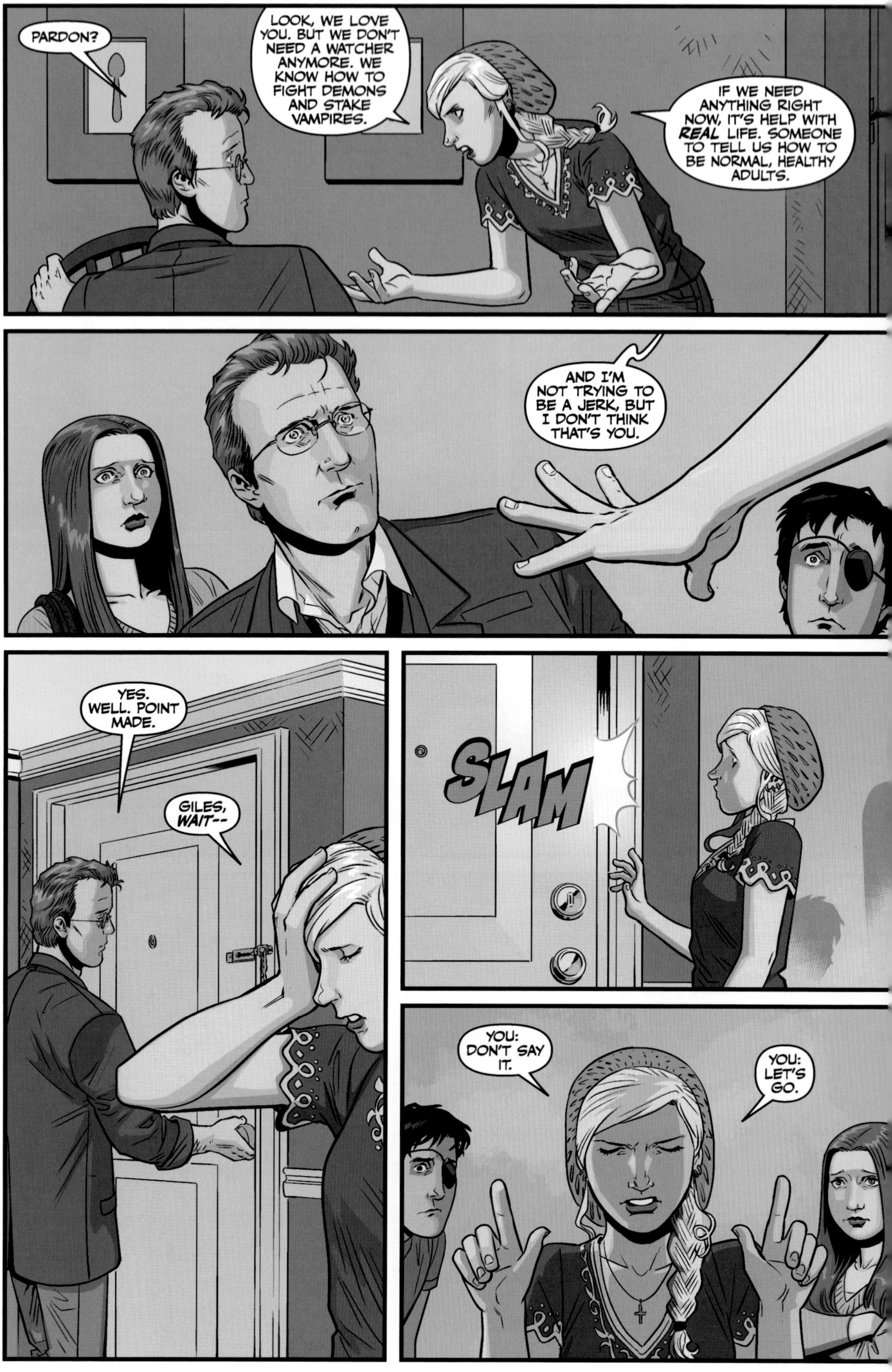
PARDON?
LOOK, WE LOVE YOU. BUT WE DON'T NEED A WATCHER ANYMORE. WE KNOW HOW TO FIGHT DEMONS AND STAKE VAMPIRES.
IF WE NEED ANYTHING RIGHT NOW, IT'S HELP WITH *REAL* LIFE. SOMEONE TO TELL US HOW TO BE NORMAL, HEALTHY ADULTS.
AND I'M NOT TRYING TO BE A JERK, BUT I DON'T THINK THAT'S YOU.
YES. WELL. POINT MADE.
GILES, *WAIT--*
SLAM
YOU: DON'T SAY IT.
YOU: LET'S GO.

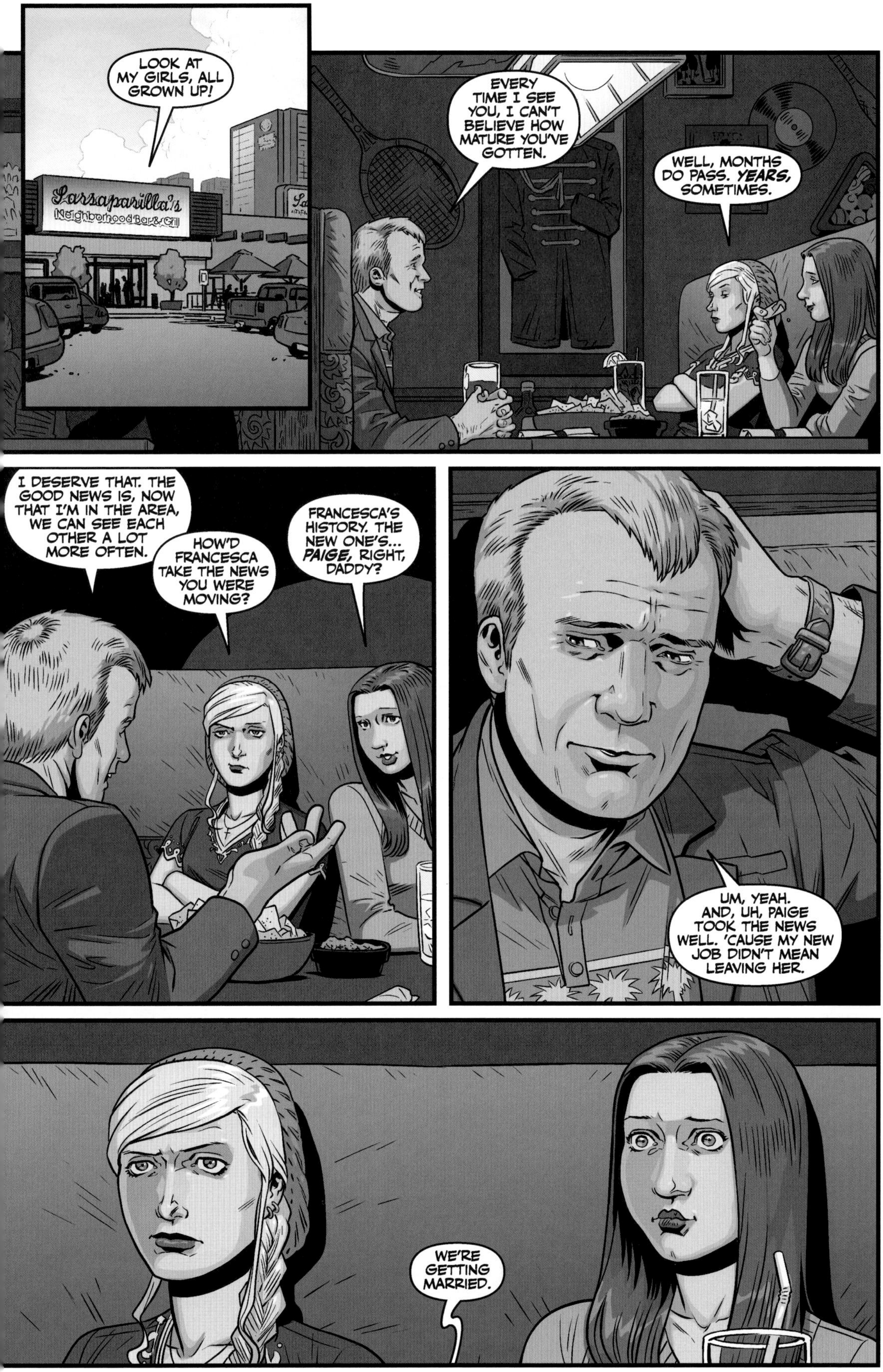
LOOK AT MY GIRLS, ALL GROWN UP!
Sarsaparilla's Neighborhood Bar & Grill
EVERY TIME I SEE YOU, I CAN'T BELIEVE HOW MATURE YOU'VE GOTTEN.
WELL, MONTHS DO PASS. YEARS, SOMETIMES.
I DESERVE THAT. THE GOOD NEWS IS, NOW THAT I'M IN THE AREA, WE CAN SEE EACH OTHER A LOT MORE OFTEN.
HOW'D FRANCESCA TAKE THE NEWS YOU WERE MOVING?
FRANCESCA'S HISTORY. THE NEW ONE'S... PAIGE, RIGHT, DADDY?
UM, YEAH. AND, UH, PAIGE TOOK THE NEWS WELL. 'CAUSE MY NEW JOB DIDN'T MEAN LEAVING HER.
WE'RE GETTING MARRIED.

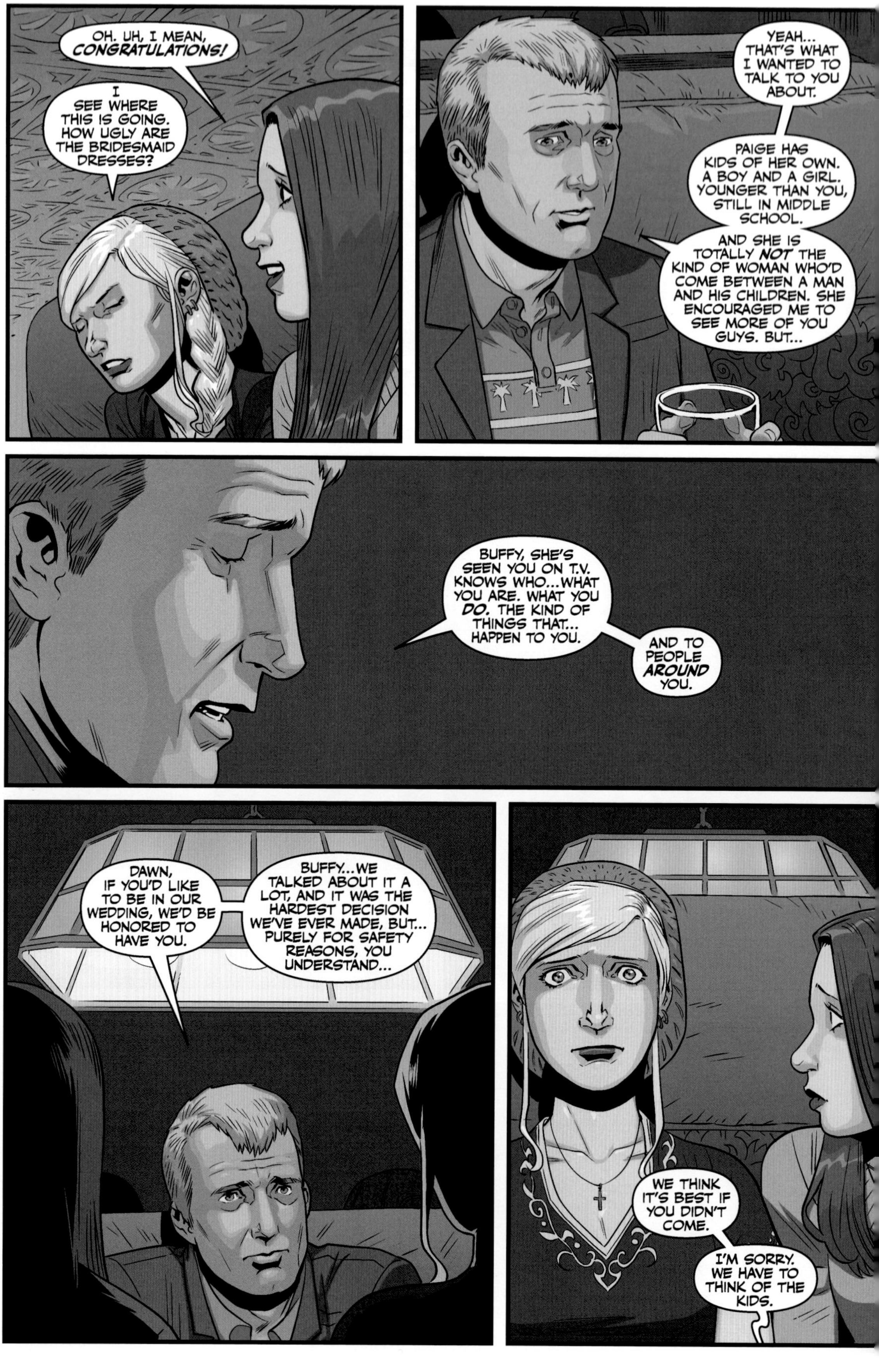
OH. UH, I MEAN, CONGRATULATIONS!
I SEE WHERE THIS IS GOING. HOW UGLY ARE THE BRIDESMAID DRESSES?
YEAH... THAT'S WHAT I WANTED TO TALK TO YOU ABOUT.
PAIGE HAS KIDS OF HER OWN. A BOY AND A GIRL. YOUNGER THAN YOU, STILL IN MIDDLE SCHOOL.
AND SHE IS TOTALLY NOT THE KIND OF WOMAN WHO'D COME BETWEEN A MAN AND HIS CHILDREN. SHE ENCOURAGED ME TO SEE MORE OF YOU GUYS. BUT...
BUFFY, SHE'S SEEN YOU ON T.V. KNOWS WHO...WHAT YOU ARE. WHAT YOU DO. THE KIND OF THINGS THAT... HAPPEN TO YOU.
AND TO PEOPLE AROUND YOU.
DAWN, IF YOU'D LIKE TO BE IN OUR WEDDING, WE'D BE HONORED TO HAVE YOU.
BUFFY...WE TALKED ABOUT IT A LOT, AND IT WAS THE HARDEST DECISION WE'VE EVER MADE, BUT... PURELY FOR SAFETY REASONS, YOU UNDERSTAND...
WE THINK IT'S BEST IF YOU DIDN'T COME.
I'M SORRY. WE HAVE TO THINK OF THE KIDS.

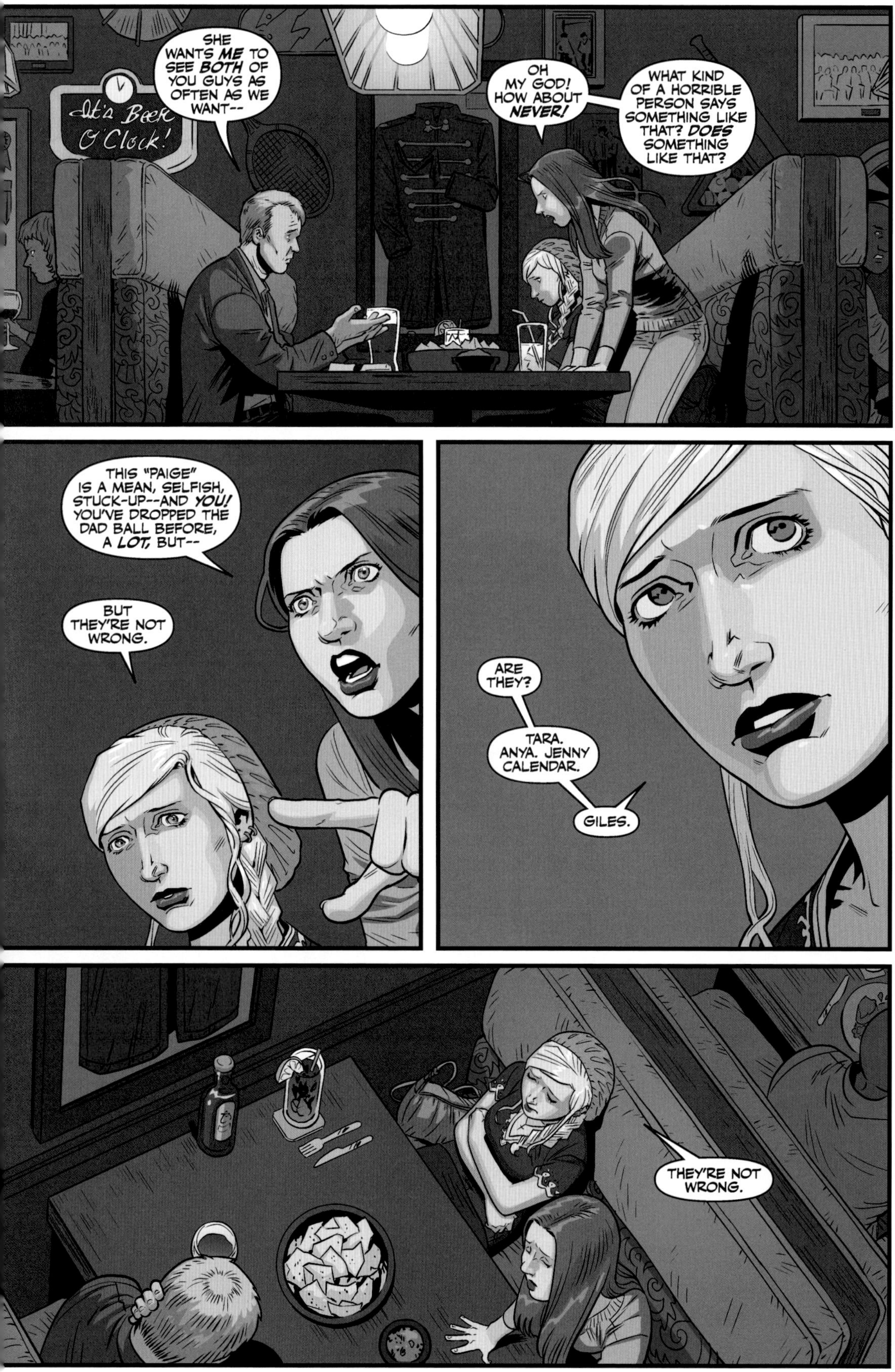
SHE WANTS ME TO SEE BOTH OF YOU GUYS AS OFTEN AS WE WANT--
It's Beer O'Clock!
OH MY GOD! HOW ABOUT NEVER!
WHAT KIND OF A HORRIBLE PERSON SAYS SOMETHING LIKE THAT? DOES SOMETHING LIKE THAT?
THIS "PAIGE" IS A MEAN, SELFISH, STUCK-UP--AND YOU! YOU'VE DROPPED THE DAD BALL BEFORE, A LOT, BUT--
BUT THEY'RE NOT WRONG.
ARE THEY?
TARA. ANYA. JENNY CALENDAR.
GILES.
THEY'RE NOT WRONG.

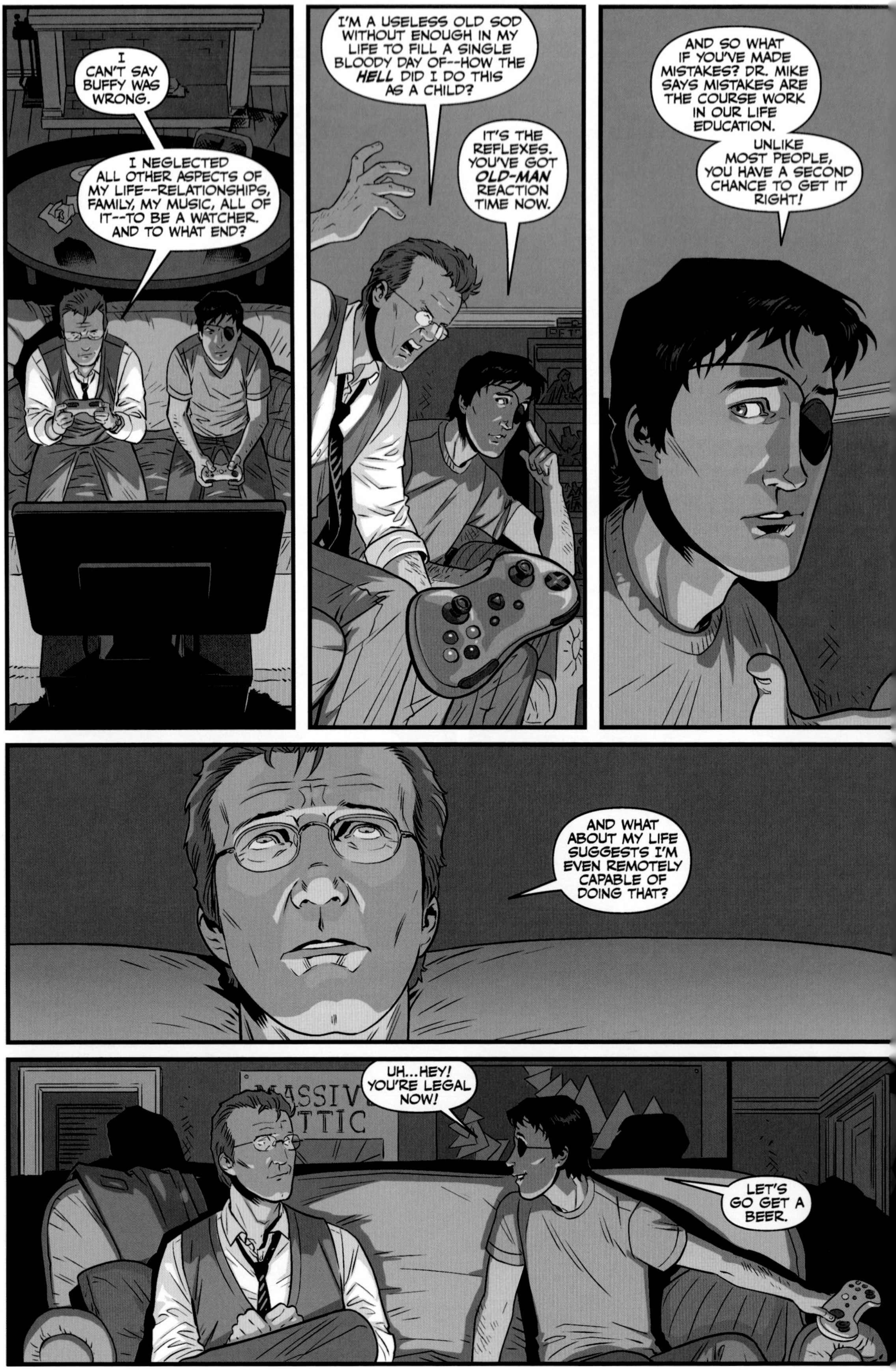
I CAN'T SAY BUFFY WAS WRONG.
I NEGLECTED ALL OTHER ASPECTS OF MY LIFE--RELATIONSHIPS, FAMILY, MY MUSIC, ALL OF IT--TO BE A WATCHER. AND TO WHAT END?
I'M A USELESS OLD SOD WITHOUT ENOUGH IN MY LIFE TO FILL A SINGLE BLOODY DAY OF--HOW THE HELL DID I DO THIS AS A CHILD?
IT'S THE REFLEXES. YOU'VE GOT OLD-MAN REACTION TIME NOW.
AND SO WHAT IF YOU'VE MADE MISTAKES? DR. MIKE SAYS MISTAKES ARE THE COURSE WORK IN OUR LIFE EDUCATION.
UNLIKE MOST PEOPLE, YOU HAVE A SECOND CHANCE TO GET IT RIGHT!
AND WHAT ABOUT MY LIFE SUGGESTS I'M EVEN REMOTELY CAPABLE OF DOING THAT?
UH...HEY! YOU'RE LEGAL NOW!
LET'S GO GET A BEER.

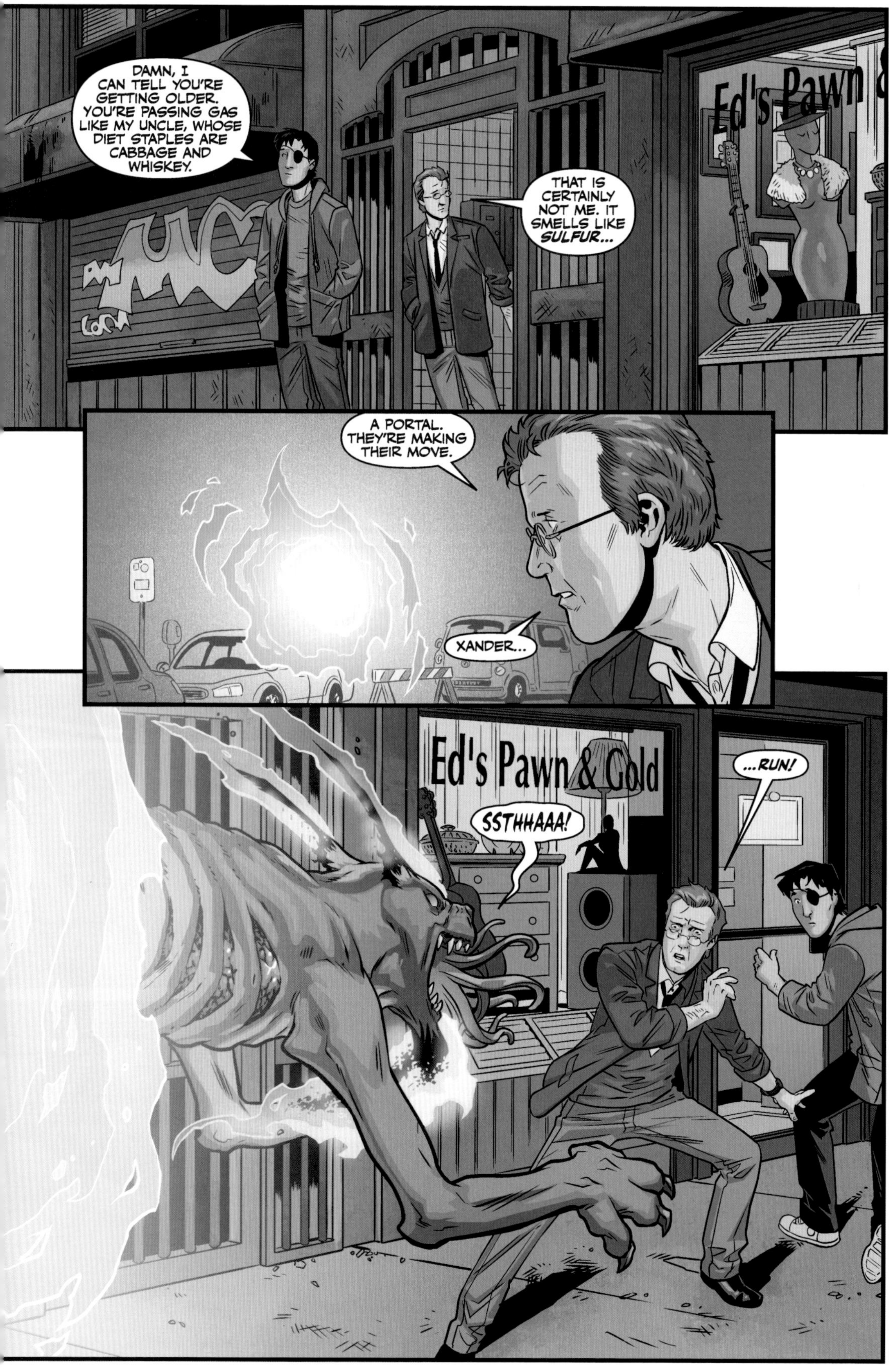
DAMN, I CAN TELL YOU'RE GETTING OLDER. YOU'RE PASSING GAS LIKE MY UNCLE, WHOSE DIET STAPLES ARE CABBAGE AND WHISKEY.
THAT IS CERTAINLY NOT ME. IT SMELLS LIKE SULFUR...
Ed's Pawn &
A PORTAL. THEY'RE MAKING THEIR MOVE.
XANDER...
Ed's Pawn & Gold
SSTHHAAA!
...RUN!

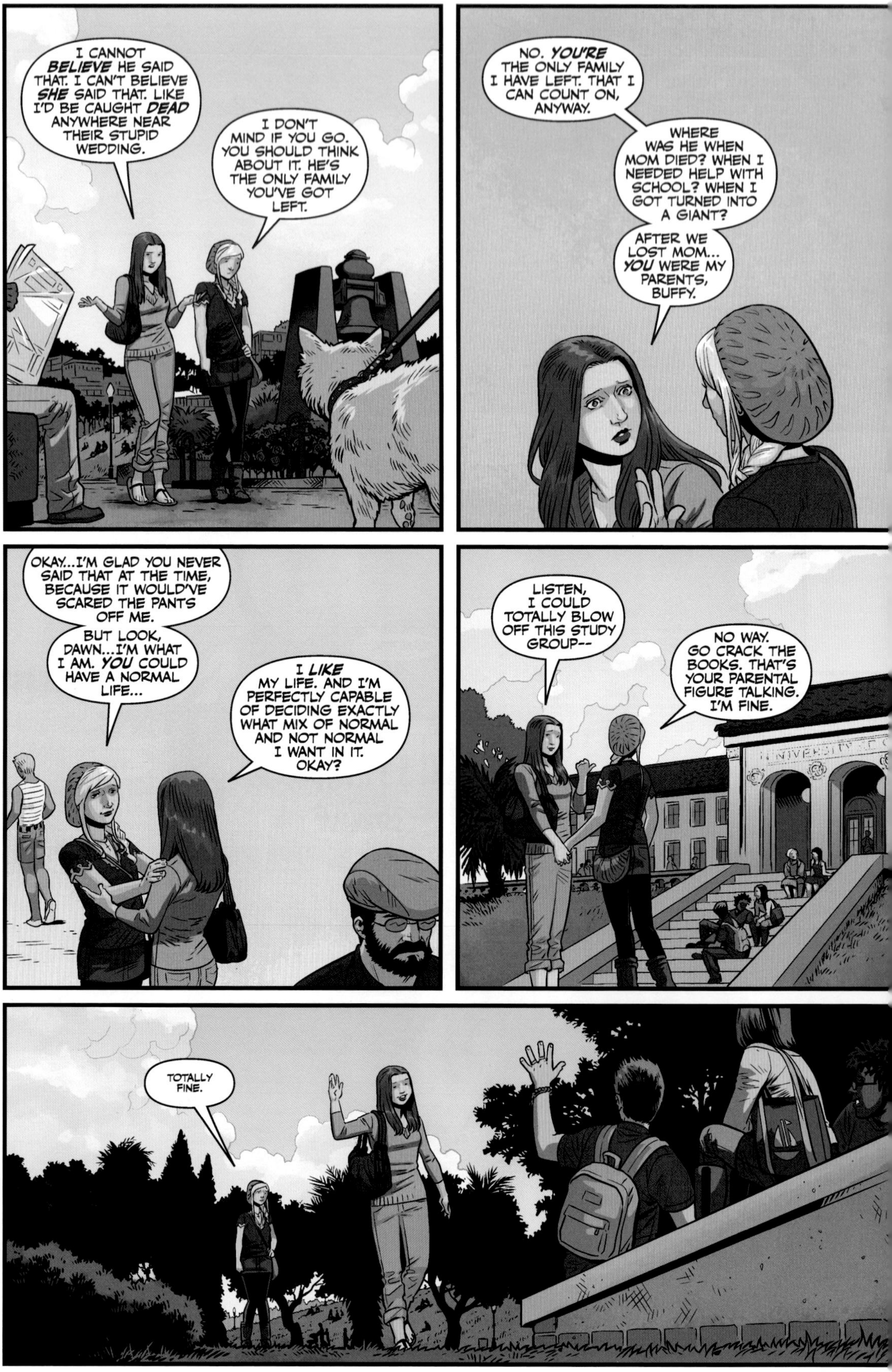
I CANNOT BELIEVE HE SAID THAT. I CAN'T BELIEVE SHE SAID THAT. LIKE I'D BE CAUGHT DEAD ANYWHERE NEAR THEIR STUPID WEDDING.
I DON'T MIND IF YOU GO. YOU SHOULD THINK ABOUT IT. HE'S THE ONLY FAMILY YOU'VE GOT LEFT.
NO. YOU'RE THE ONLY FAMILY I HAVE LEFT. THAT I CAN COUNT ON, ANYWAY.
WHERE WAS HE WHEN MOM DIED? WHEN I NEEDED HELP WITH SCHOOL? WHEN I GOT TURNED INTO A GIANT?
AFTER WE LOST MOM... YOU WERE MY PARENTS, BUFFY.
OKAY...I'M GLAD YOU NEVER SAID THAT AT THE TIME, BECAUSE IT WOULD'VE SCARED THE PANTS OFF ME.
BUT LOOK, DAWN...I'M WHAT I AM. YOU COULD HAVE A NORMAL LIFE...
I LIKE MY LIFE. AND I'M PERFECTLY CAPABLE OF DECIDING EXACTLY WHAT MIX OF NORMAL AND NOT NORMAL I WANT IN IT. OKAY?
LISTEN, I COULD TOTALLY BLOW OFF THIS STUDY GROUP--
NO WAY. GO CRACK THE BOOKS. THAT'S YOUR PARENTAL FIGURE TALKING. I'M FINE.
TOTALLY FINE.

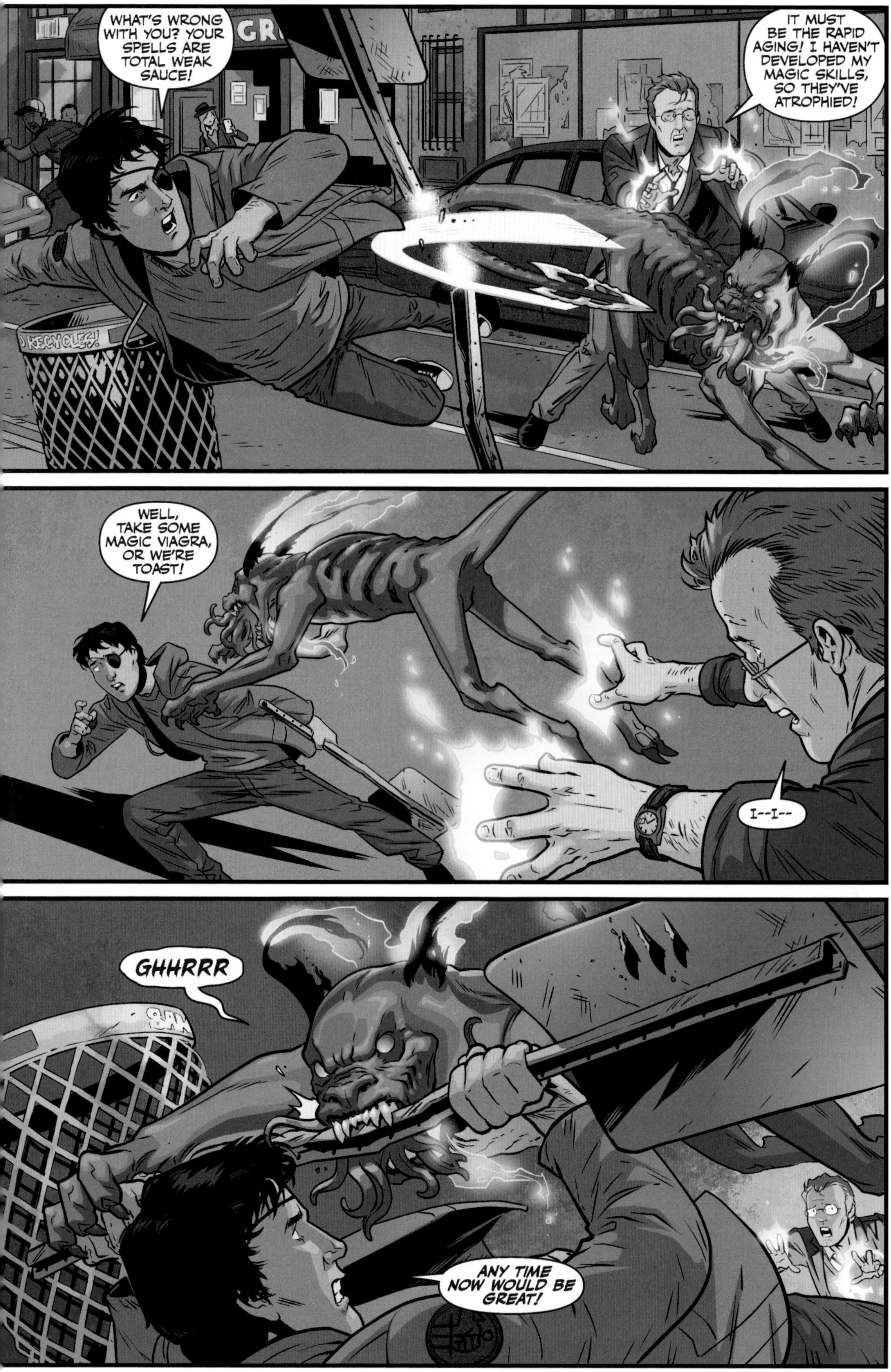
WHAT'S WRONG WITH YOU? YOUR SPELLS ARE TOTAL WEAK SAUCE!
IT MUST BE THE RAPID AGING! I HAVEN'T DEVELOPED MY MAGIC SKILLS, SO THEY'VE ATROPHIED!
RECYCLES!
WELL, TAKE SOME MAGIC VIAGRA, OR WE'RE TOAST!
I--I--
GHHRRR
ANY TIME NOW WOULD BE GREAT!

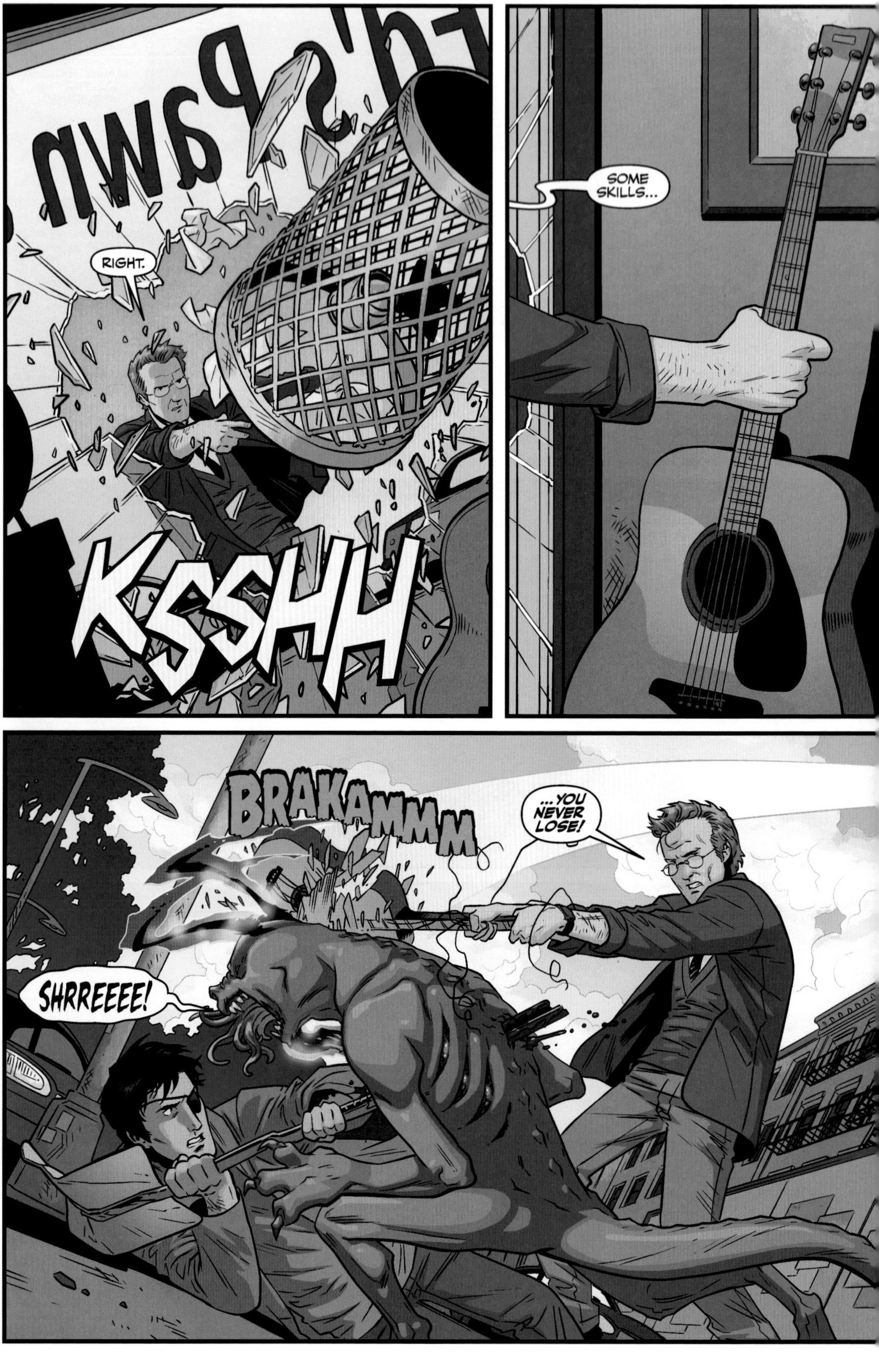
RIGHT.
KSSHH
SOME SKILLS...
BRAKAMMMM
...YOU NEVER LOSE!
SHRREEEE!

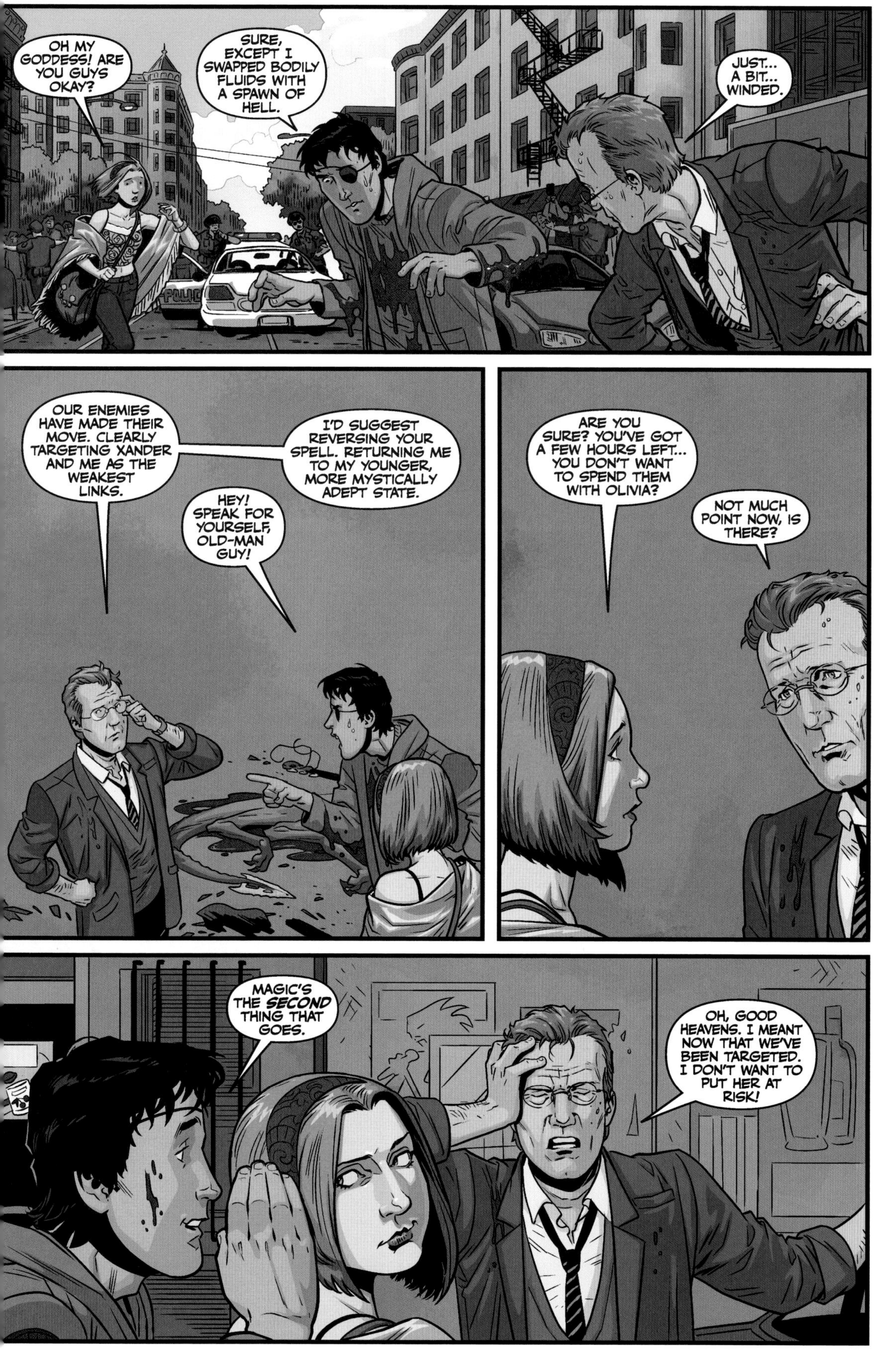
OH MY GODDESS! ARE YOU GUYS OKAY?
SURE, EXCEPT I SWAPPED BODILY FLUIDS WITH A SPAWN OF HELL.
JUST... A BIT... WINDED.
OUR ENEMIES HAVE MADE THEIR MOVE. CLEARLY TARGETING XANDER AND ME AS THE WEAKEST LINKS.
I'D SUGGEST REVERSING YOUR SPELL. RETURNING ME TO MY YOUNGER, MORE MYSTICALLY ADEPT STATE.
HEY! SPEAK FOR YOURSELF, OLD-MAN GUY!
ARE YOU SURE? YOU'VE GOT A FEW HOURS LEFT... YOU DON'T WANT TO SPEND THEM WITH OLIVIA?
NOT MUCH POINT NOW, IS THERE?
MAGIC'S THE SECOND THING THAT GOES.
OH, GOOD HEAVENS. I MEANT NOW THAT WE'VE BEEN TARGETED. I DON'T WANT TO PUT HER AT RISK!
POLICE

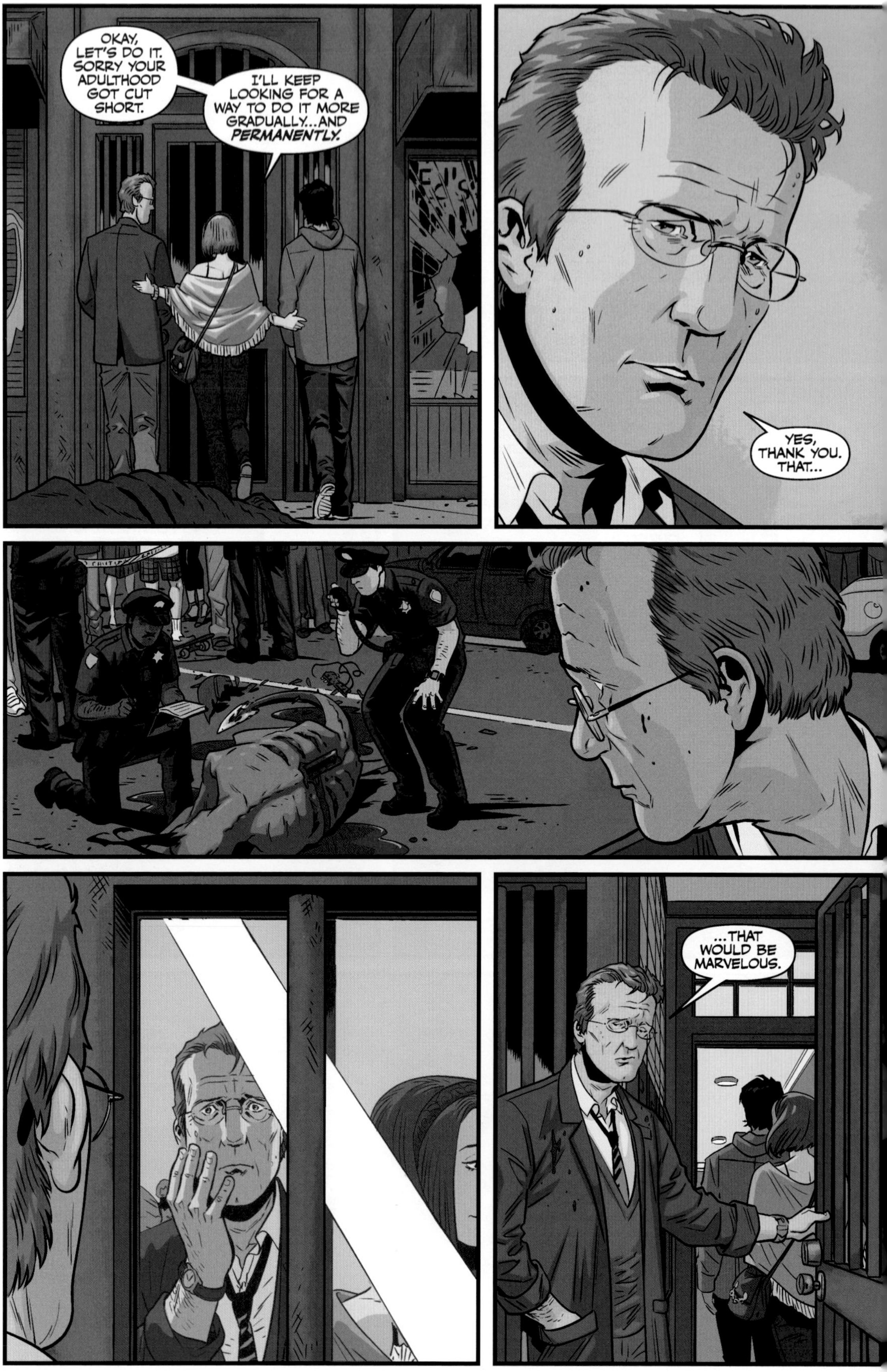
OKAY, LET'S DO IT. SORRY YOUR ADULTHOOD GOT CUT SHORT.
I'LL KEEP LOOKING FOR A WAY TO DO IT MORE GRADUALLY...AND PERMANENTLY.
YES, THANK YOU. THAT...
...THAT WOULD BE MARVELOUS.

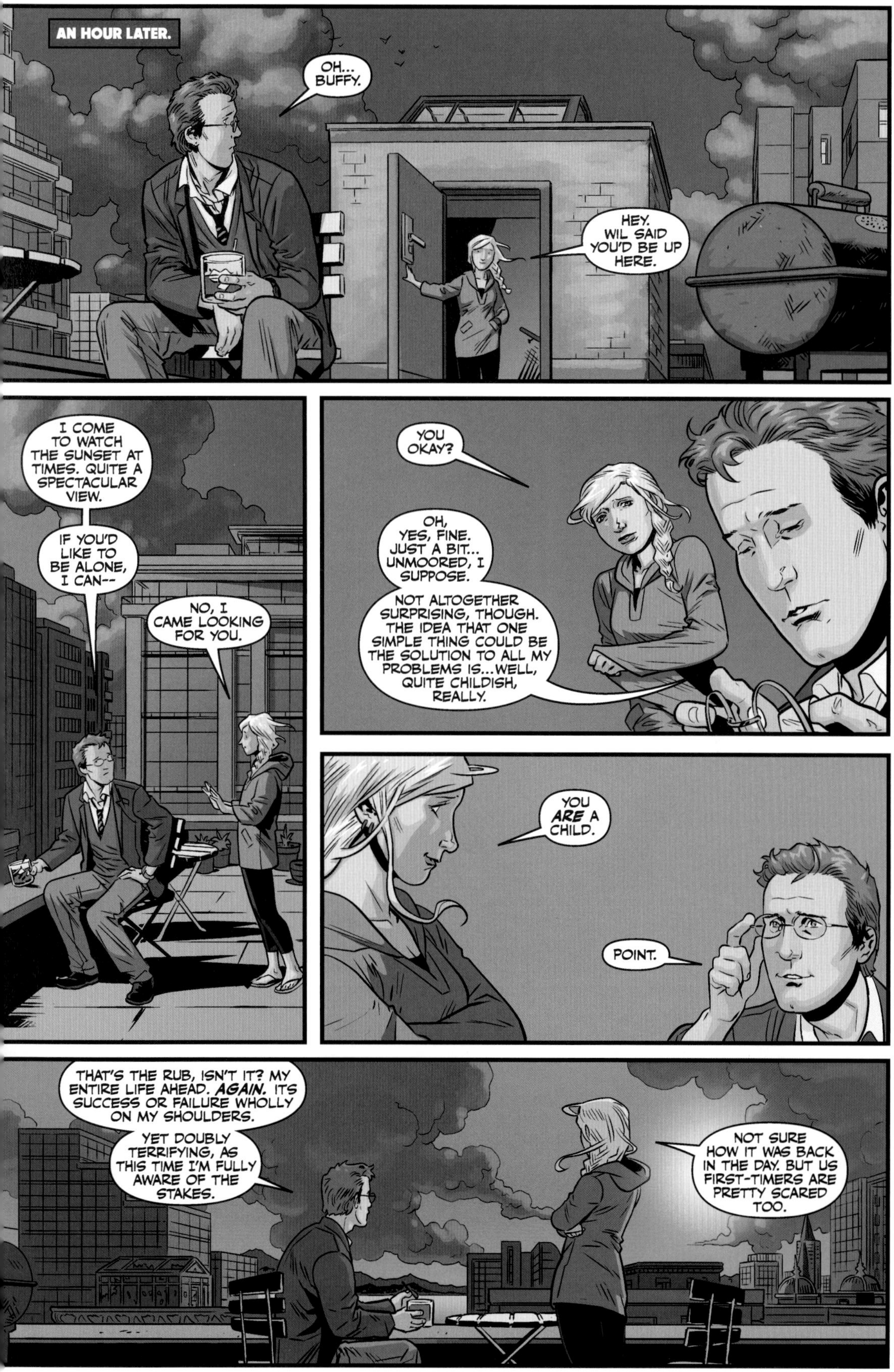
AN HOUR LATER.
OH... BUFFY.
HEY. WIL SAID YOU'D BE UP HERE.
I COME TO WATCH THE SUNSET AT TIMES. QUITE A SPECTACULAR VIEW.
IF YOU'D LIKE TO BE ALONE, I CAN--
NO, I CAME LOOKING FOR YOU.
YOU OKAY?
OH, YES, FINE. JUST A BIT... UNMOORED, I SUPPOSE.
NOT ALTOGETHER SURPRISING, THOUGH. THE IDEA THAT ONE SIMPLE THING COULD BE THE SOLUTION TO ALL MY PROBLEMS IS...WELL, QUITE CHILDISH, REALLY.
YOU ARE A CHILD.
POINT.
THAT'S THE RUB, ISN'T IT? MY ENTIRE LIFE AHEAD. AGAIN. ITS SUCCESS OR FAILURE WHOLLY ON MY SHOULDERS.
YET DOUBLY TERRIFYING, AS THIS TIME I'M FULLY AWARE OF THE STAKES.
NOT SURE HOW IT WAS BACK IN THE DAY. BUT US FIRST-TIMERS ARE PRETTY SCARED TOO.

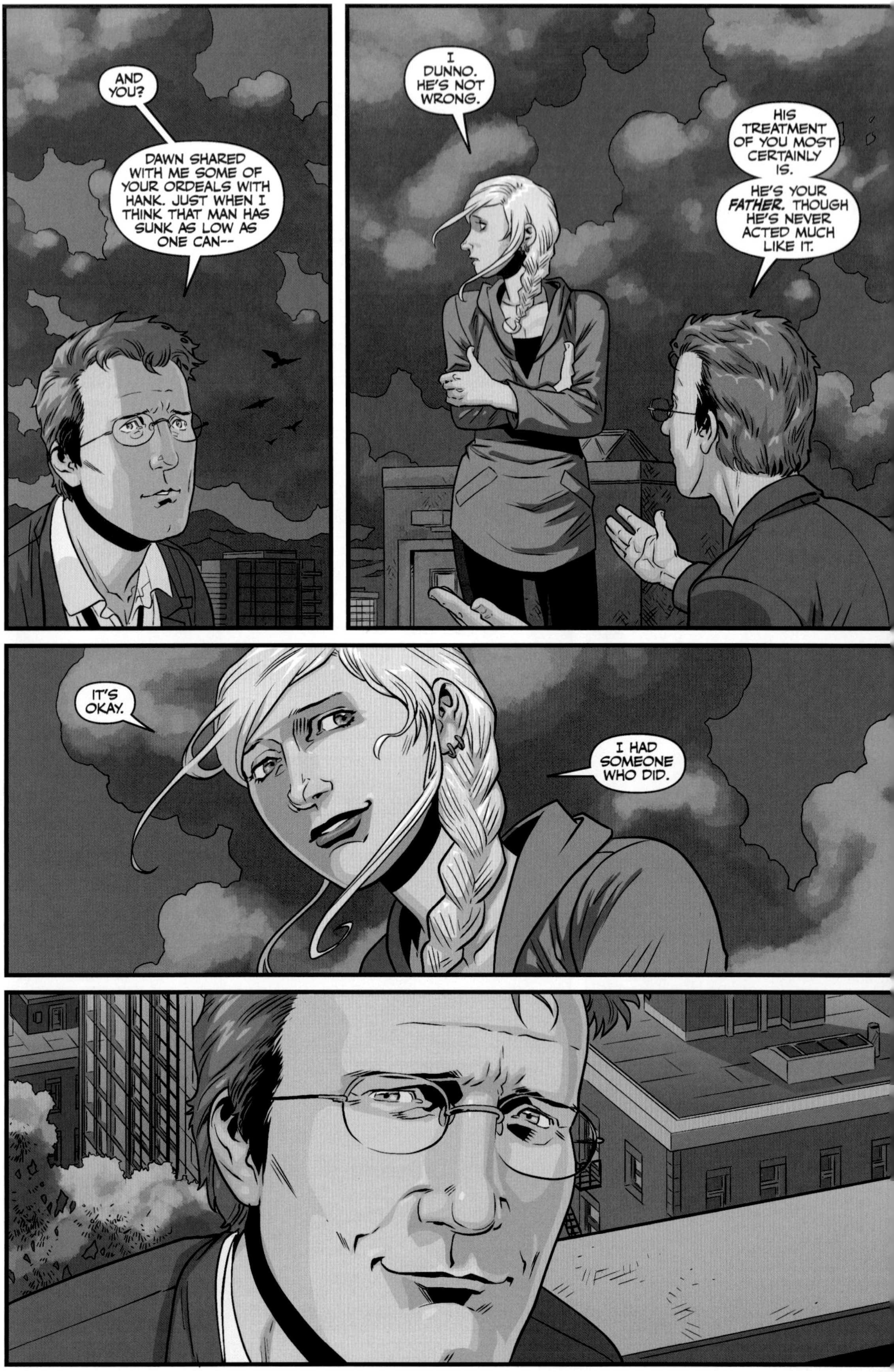
AND YOU?
DAWN SHARED WITH ME SOME OF YOUR ORDEALS WITH HANK. JUST WHEN I THINK THAT MAN HAS SUNK AS LOW AS ONE CAN--
I DUNNO. HE'S NOT WRONG.
HIS TREATMENT OF YOU MOST CERTAINLY IS.
HE'S YOUR FATHER. THOUGH HE'S NEVER ACTED MUCH LIKE IT.
IT'S OKAY.
I HAD SOMEONE WHO DID.

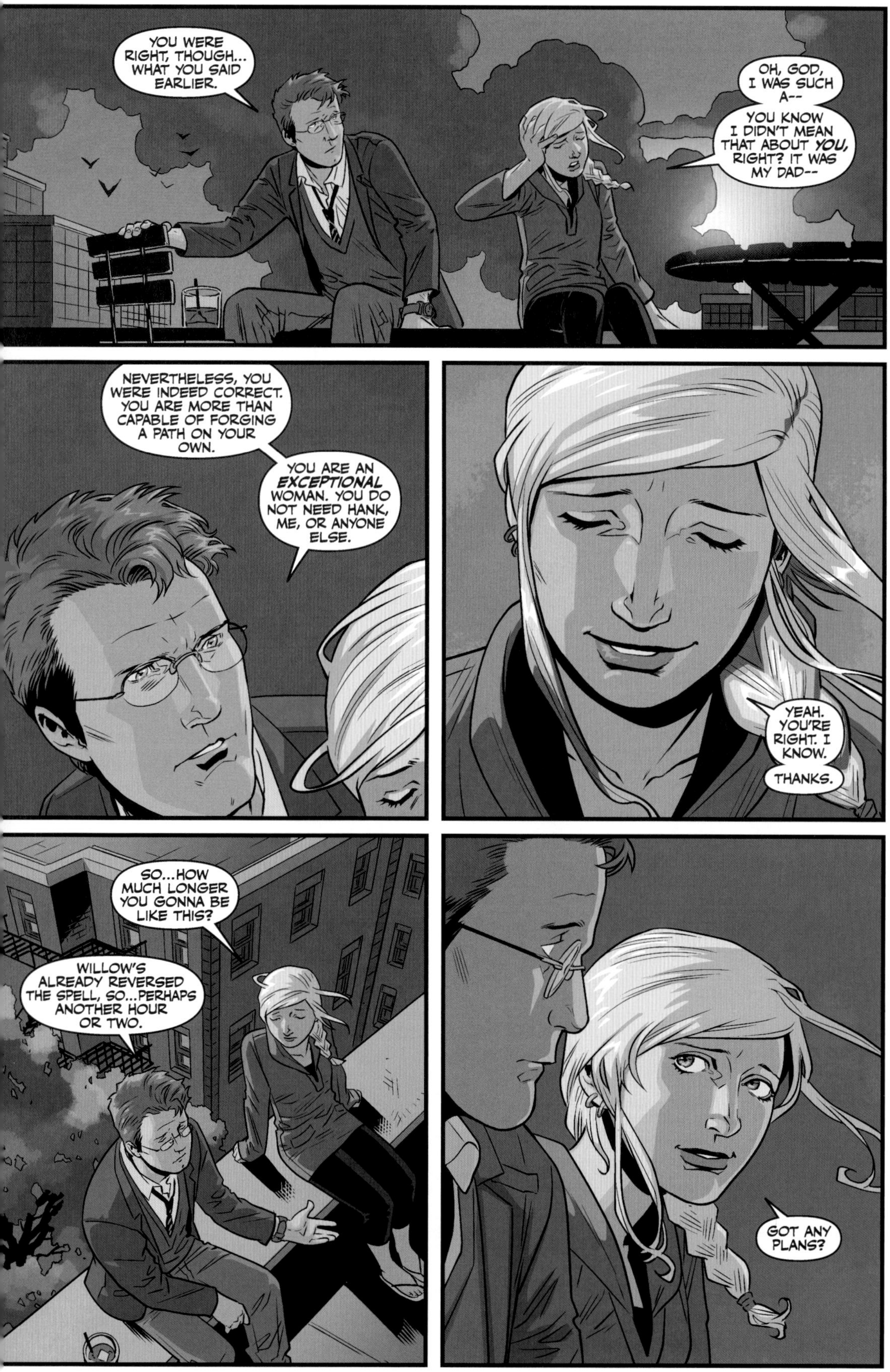
YOU WERE RIGHT, THOUGH... WHAT YOU SAID EARLIER.
OH, GOD, I WAS SUCH A--
YOU KNOW I DIDN'T MEAN THAT ABOUT *YOU*, RIGHT? IT WAS MY DAD--
NEVERTHELESS, YOU WERE INDEED CORRECT. YOU ARE MORE THAN CAPABLE OF FORGING A PATH ON YOUR OWN.
YOU ARE AN ***EXCEPTIONAL*** WOMAN. YOU DO NOT NEED HANK, ME, OR ANYONE ELSE.
YEAH. YOU'RE RIGHT. I KNOW.
THANKS.
SO...HOW MUCH LONGER YOU GONNA BE LIKE THIS?
WILLOW'S ALREADY REVERSED THE SPELL, SO...PERHAPS ANOTHER HOUR OR TWO.
GOT ANY PLANS?

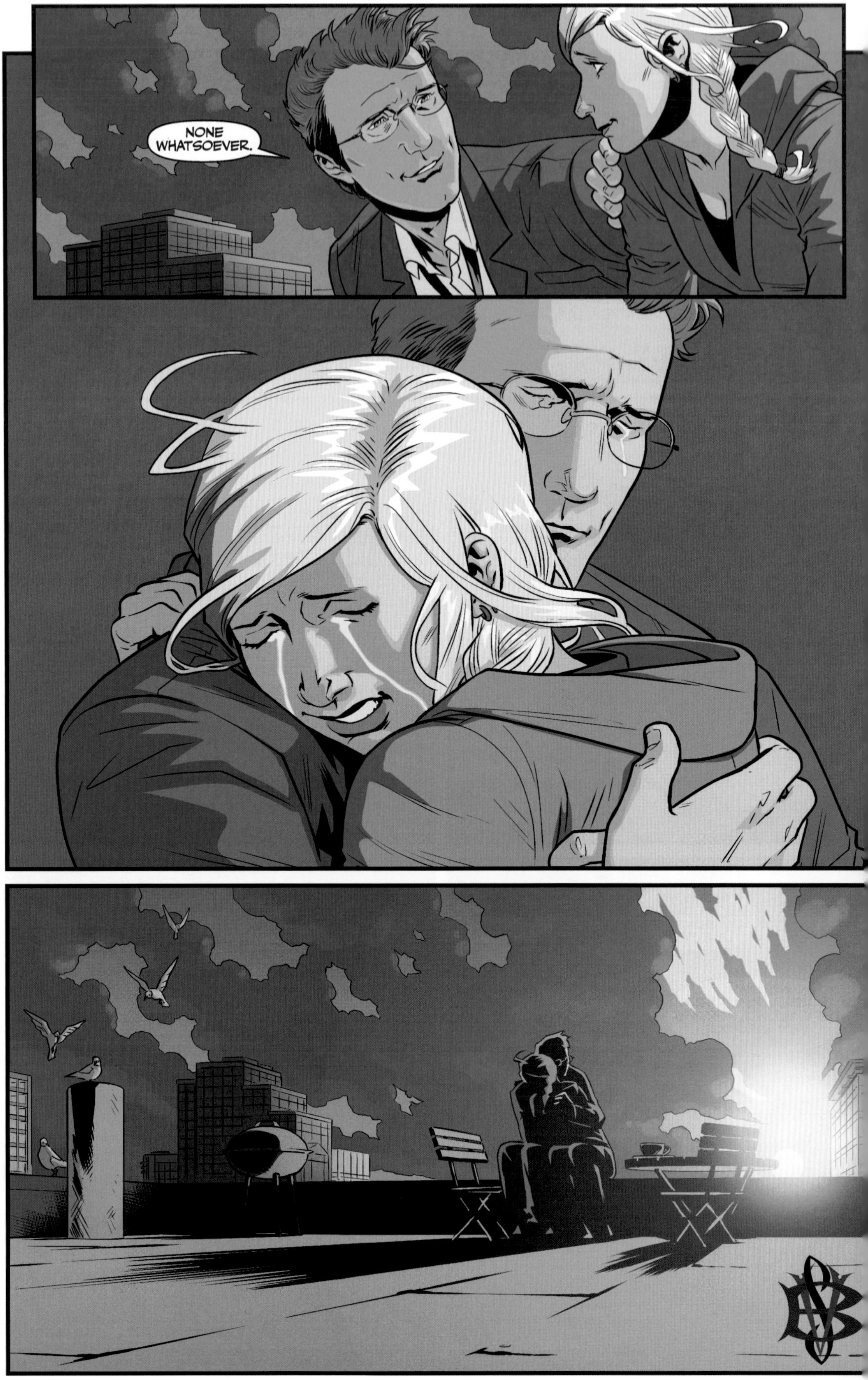
NONE WHATSOEVER.

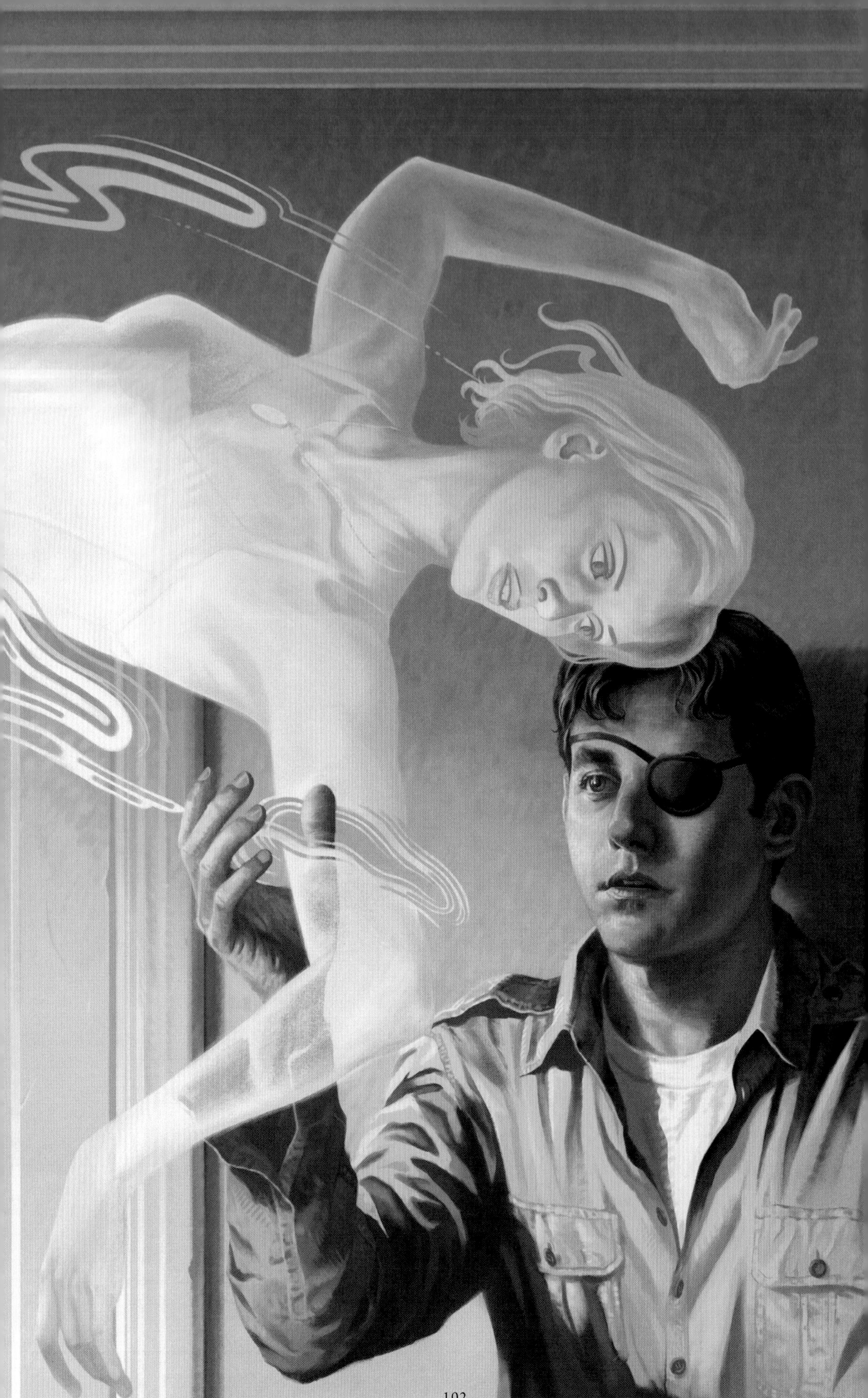

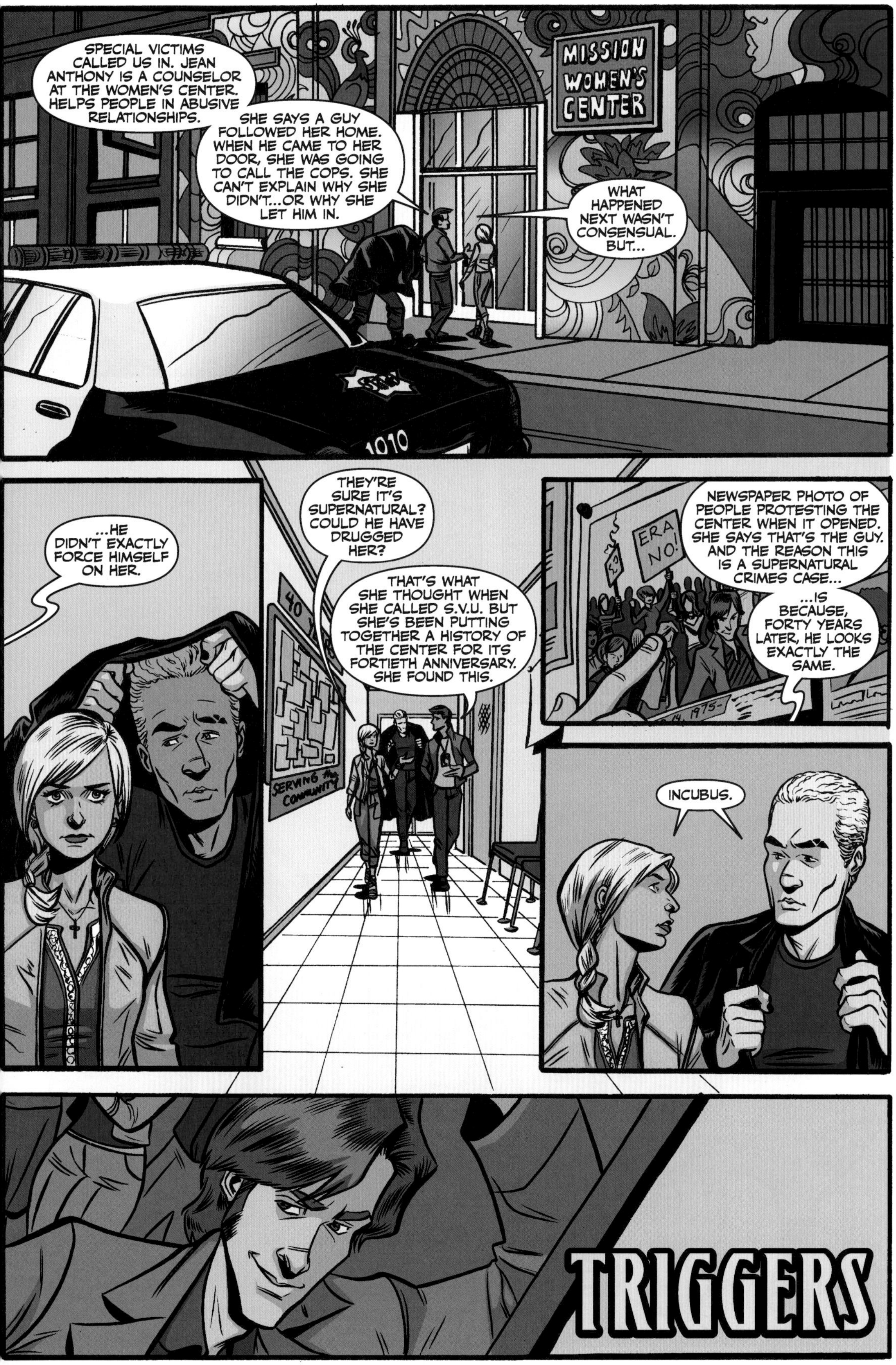
MISSION WOMEN'S CENTER
SPECIAL VICTIMS CALLED US IN. JEAN ANTHONY IS A COUNSELOR AT THE WOMEN'S CENTER. HELPS PEOPLE IN ABUSIVE RELATIONSHIPS.
SHE SAYS A GUY FOLLOWED HER HOME. WHEN HE CAME TO HER DOOR, SHE WAS GOING TO CALL THE COPS. SHE CAN'T EXPLAIN WHY SHE DIDN'T...OR WHY SHE LET HIM IN.
WHAT HAPPENED NEXT WASN'T CONSENSUAL. BUT...
1010
...HE DIDN'T EXACTLY FORCE HIMSELF ON HER.
THEY'RE SURE IT'S SUPERNATURAL? COULD HE HAVE DRUGGED HER?
THAT'S WHAT SHE THOUGHT WHEN SHE CALLED S.V.U. BUT SHE'S BEEN PUTTING TOGETHER A HISTORY OF THE CENTER FOR ITS FORTIETH ANNIVERSARY. SHE FOUND THIS.
SERVING the COMMUNITY
ERA NO!
NEWSPAPER PHOTO OF PEOPLE PROTESTING THE CENTER WHEN IT OPENED. SHE SAYS THAT'S THE GUY. AND THE REASON THIS IS A SUPERNATURAL CRIMES CASE...
...IS BECAUSE, FORTY YEARS LATER, HE LOOKS EXACTLY THE SAME.
INCUBUS.
TRIGGERS

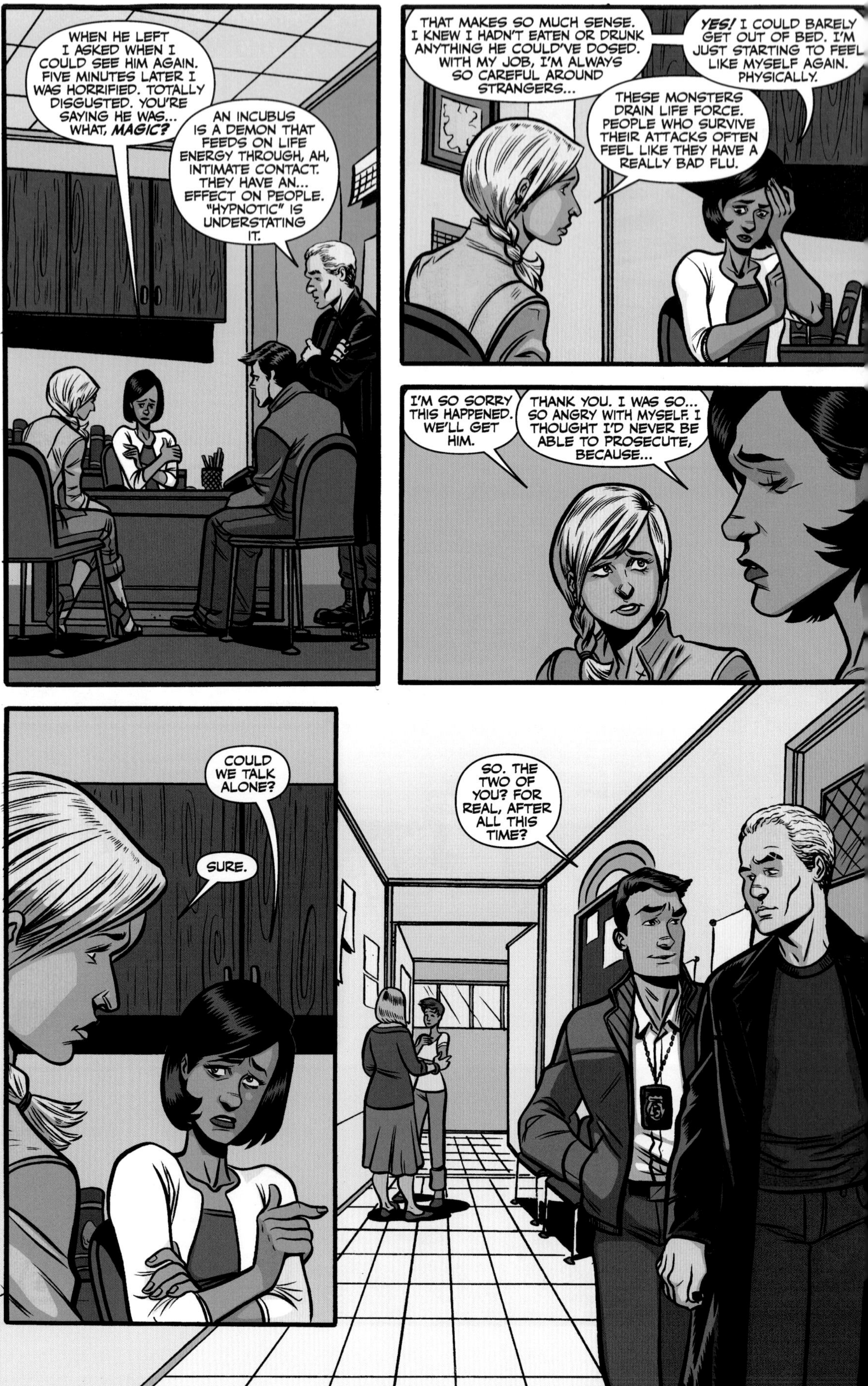
WHEN HE LEFT I ASKED WHEN I COULD SEE HIM AGAIN. FIVE MINUTES LATER I WAS HORRIFIED. TOTALLY DISGUSTED. YOU'RE SAYING HE WAS... WHAT, MAGIC?
AN INCUBUS IS A DEMON THAT FEEDS ON LIFE ENERGY THROUGH, AH, INTIMATE CONTACT. THEY HAVE AN... EFFECT ON PEOPLE. "HYPNOTIC" IS UNDERSTATING IT.
THAT MAKES SO MUCH SENSE. I KNEW I HADN'T EATEN OR DRUNK ANYTHING HE COULD'VE DOSED. WITH MY JOB, I'M ALWAYS SO CAREFUL AROUND STRANGERS...
YES! I COULD BARELY GET OUT OF BED. I'M JUST STARTING TO FEEL LIKE MYSELF AGAIN. PHYSICALLY.
THESE MONSTERS DRAIN LIFE FORCE. PEOPLE WHO SURVIVE THEIR ATTACKS OFTEN FEEL LIKE THEY HAVE A REALLY BAD FLU.
I'M SO SORRY THIS HAPPENED. WE'LL GET HIM.
THANK YOU. I WAS SO... SO ANGRY WITH MYSELF. I THOUGHT I'D NEVER BE ABLE TO PROSECUTE, BECAUSE...
COULD WE TALK ALONE?
SURE.
SO. THE TWO OF YOU? FOR REAL, AFTER ALL THIS TIME?

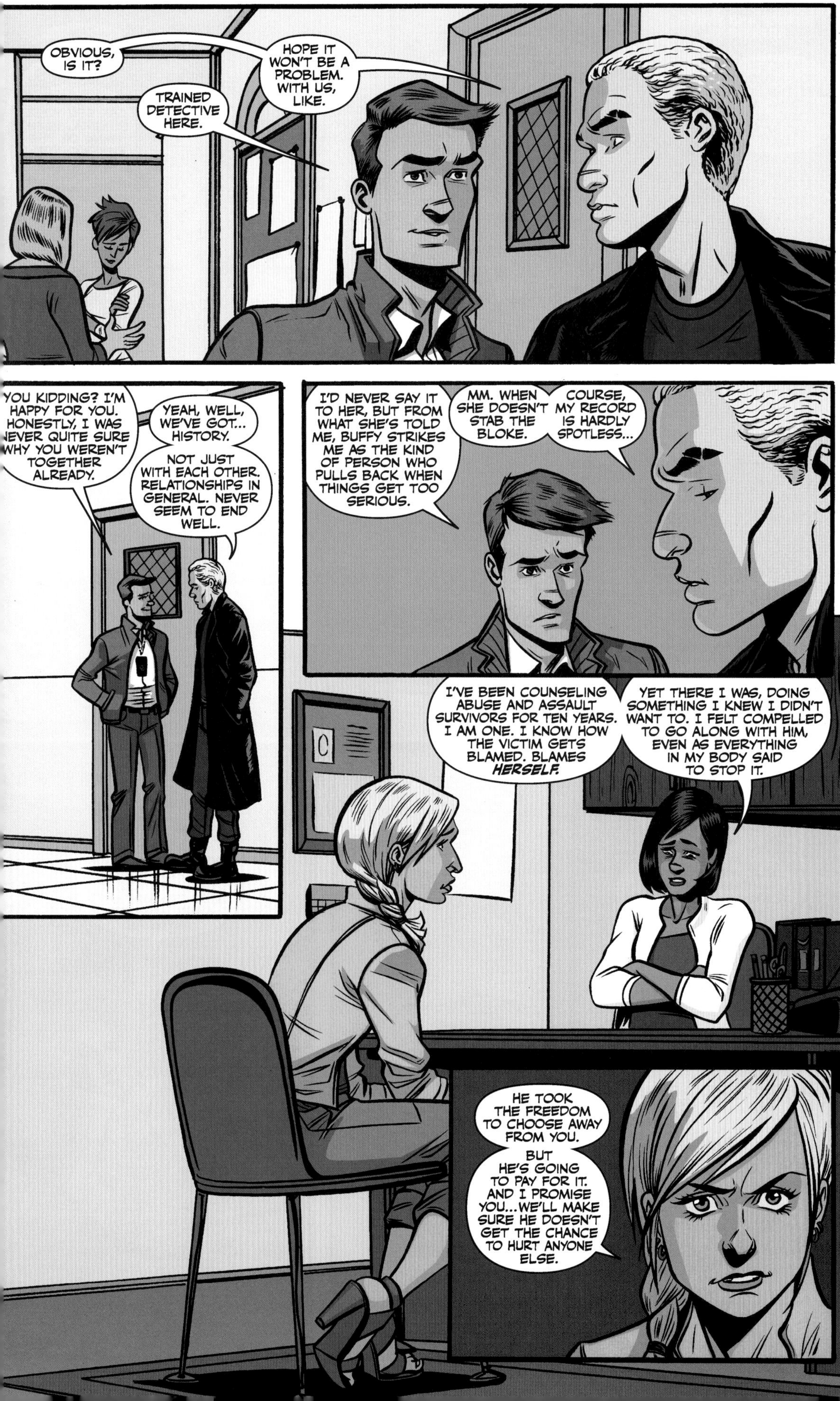
OBVIOUS, IS IT?
TRAINED DETECTIVE HERE.
HOPE IT WON'T BE A PROBLEM. WITH US, LIKE.
YOU KIDDING? I'M HAPPY FOR YOU. HONESTLY, I WAS NEVER QUITE SURE WHY YOU WEREN'T TOGETHER ALREADY.
YEAH, WELL, WE'VE GOT... HISTORY.
NOT JUST WITH EACH OTHER. RELATIONSHIPS IN GENERAL. NEVER SEEM TO END WELL.
I'D NEVER SAY IT TO HER, BUT FROM WHAT SHE'S TOLD ME, BUFFY STRIKES ME AS THE KIND OF PERSON WHO PULLS BACK WHEN THINGS GET TOO SERIOUS.
MM. WHEN SHE DOESN'T STAB THE BLOKE.
COURSE, MY RECORD IS HARDLY SPOTLESS...
I'VE BEEN COUNSELING ABUSE AND ASSAULT SURVIVORS FOR TEN YEARS. I AM ONE. I KNOW HOW THE VICTIM GETS BLAMED. BLAMES *HERSELF*.
YET THERE I WAS, DOING SOMETHING I KNEW I DIDN'T WANT TO. I FELT COMPELLED TO GO ALONG WITH HIM, EVEN AS EVERYTHING IN MY BODY SAID TO STOP IT.
HE TOOK THE FREEDOM TO CHOOSE AWAY FROM YOU.
BUT HE'S GOING TO PAY FOR IT. AND I PROMISE YOU...WE'LL MAKE SURE HE DOESN'T GET THE CHANCE TO HURT ANYONE ELSE.

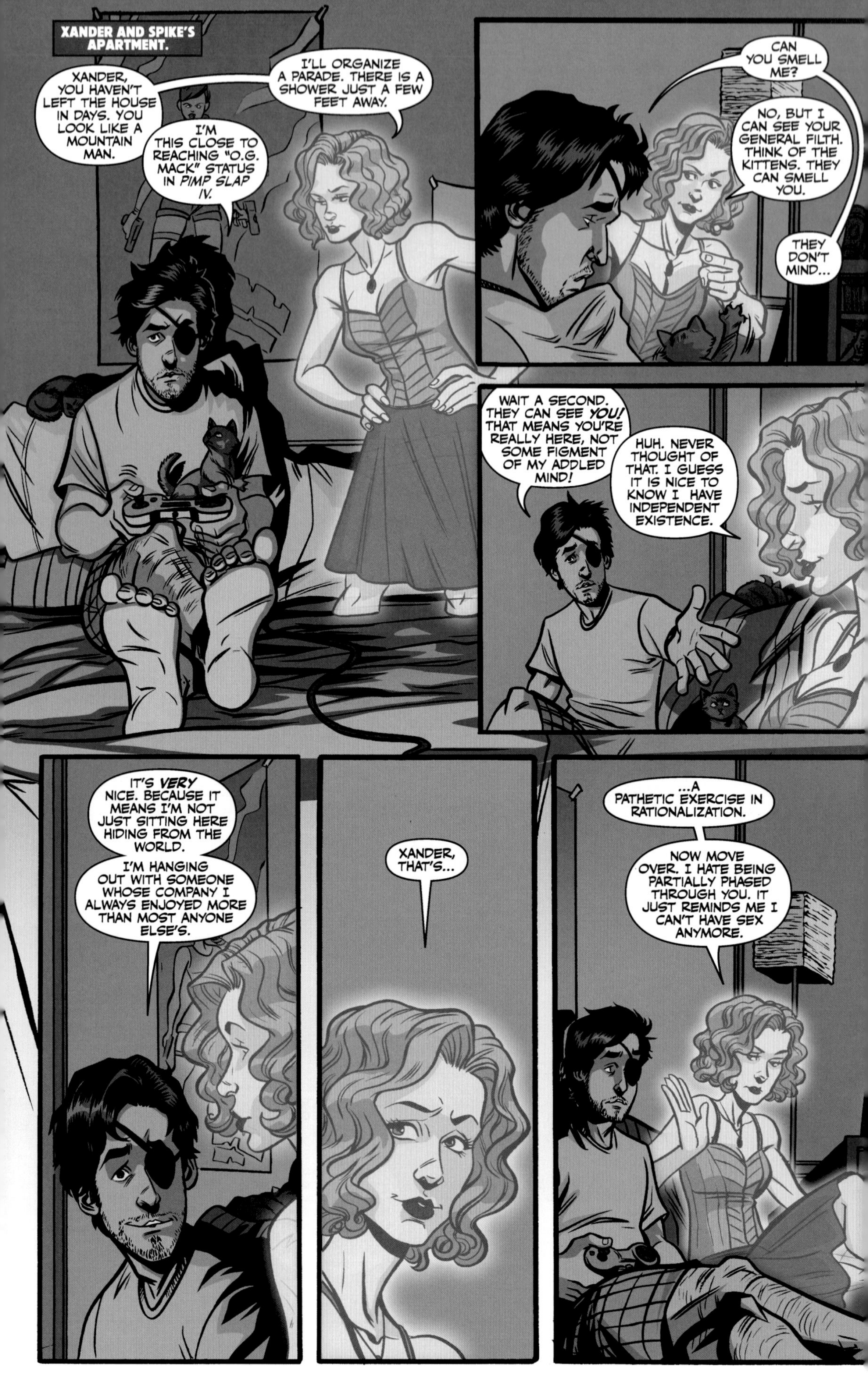
XANDER AND SPIKE'S APARTMENT.
XANDER, YOU HAVEN'T LEFT THE HOUSE IN DAYS. YOU LOOK LIKE A MOUNTAIN MAN.
I'M THIS CLOSE TO REACHING "O.G. MACK" STATUS IN *PIMP SLAP IV.*
I'LL ORGANIZE A PARADE. THERE IS A SHOWER JUST A FEW FEET AWAY.
CAN YOU SMELL ME?
NO, BUT I CAN SEE YOUR GENERAL FILTH. THINK OF THE KITTENS. THEY CAN SMELL YOU.
THEY DON'T MIND...
WAIT A SECOND. THEY CAN SEE *YOU!* THAT MEANS YOU'RE REALLY HERE, NOT SOME FIGMENT OF MY ADDLED MIND!
HUH. NEVER THOUGHT OF THAT. I GUESS IT IS NICE TO KNOW I HAVE INDEPENDENT EXISTENCE.
IT'S ***VERY*** NICE. BECAUSE IT MEANS I'M NOT JUST SITTING HERE HIDING FROM THE WORLD.
I'M HANGING OUT WITH SOMEONE WHOSE COMPANY I ALWAYS ENJOYED MORE THAN MOST ANYONE ELSE'S.
XANDER, THAT'S...
...A PATHETIC EXERCISE IN RATIONALIZATION.
NOW MOVE OVER. I HATE BEING PARTIALLY PHASED THROUGH YOU. IT JUST REMINDS ME I CAN'T HAVE SEX ANYMORE.

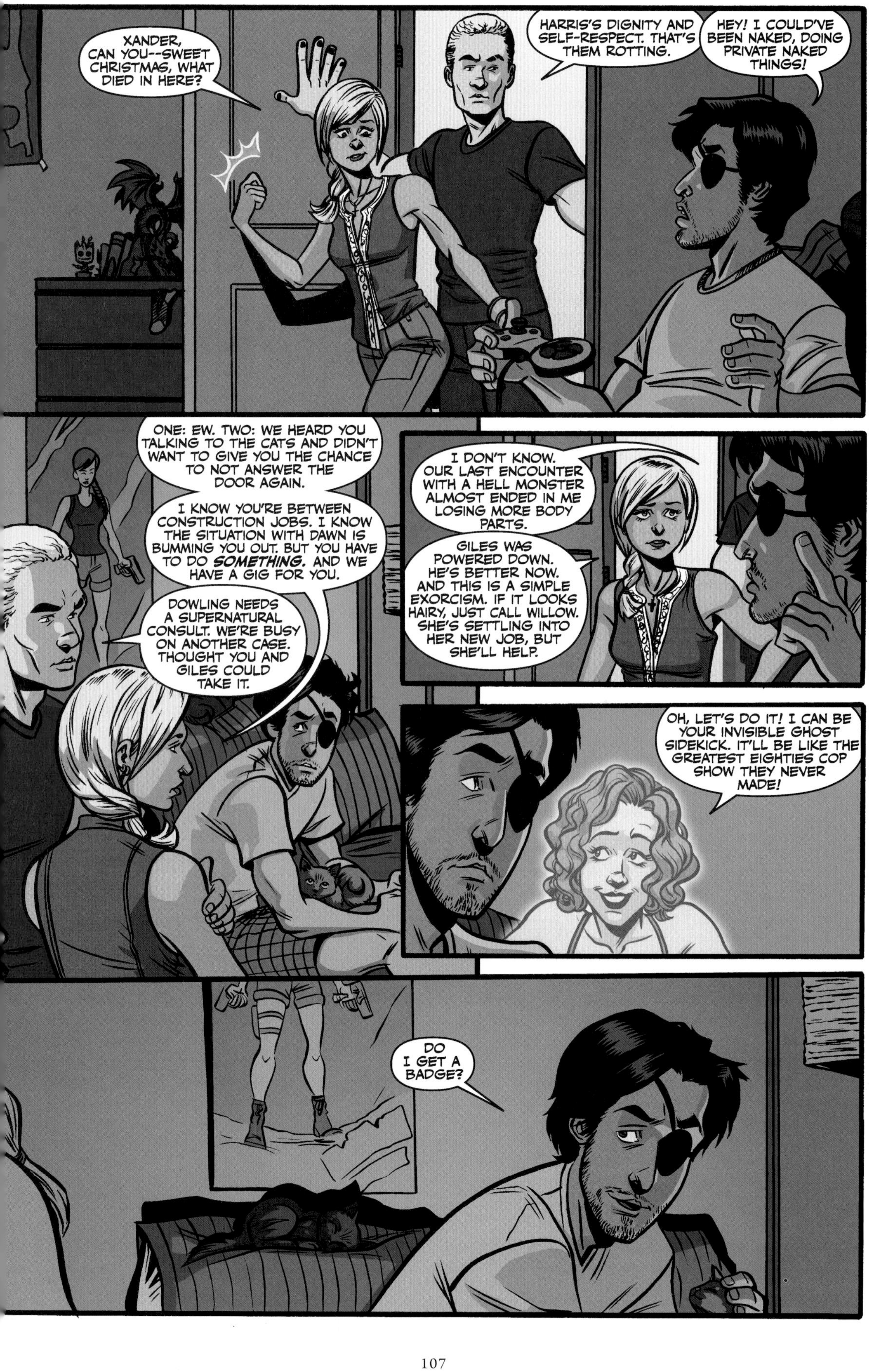

XANDER, CAN YOU--SWEET CHRISTMAS, WHAT DIED IN HERE?
HARRIS'S DIGNITY AND SELF-RESPECT. THAT'S THEM ROTTING.
HEY! I COULD'VE BEEN NAKED, DOING PRIVATE NAKED THINGS!
ONE: EW. TWO: WE HEARD YOU TALKING TO THE CATS AND DIDN'T WANT TO GIVE YOU THE CHANCE TO NOT ANSWER THE DOOR AGAIN.
I KNOW YOU'RE BETWEEN CONSTRUCTION JOBS. I KNOW THE SITUATION WITH DAWN IS BUMMING YOU OUT. BUT YOU HAVE TO DO SOMETHING. AND WE HAVE A GIG FOR YOU.
DOWLING NEEDS A SUPERNATURAL CONSULT. WE'RE BUSY ON ANOTHER CASE. THOUGHT YOU AND GILES COULD TAKE IT.
I DON'T KNOW. OUR LAST ENCOUNTER WITH A HELL MONSTER ALMOST ENDED IN ME LOSING MORE BODY PARTS.
GILES WAS POWERED DOWN. HE'S BETTER NOW. AND THIS IS A SIMPLE EXORCISM. IF IT LOOKS HAIRY, JUST CALL WILLOW. SHE'S SETTLING INTO HER NEW JOB, BUT SHE'LL HELP.
OH, LET'S DO IT! I CAN BE YOUR INVISIBLE GHOST SIDEKICK. IT'LL BE LIKE THE GREATEST EIGHTIES COP SHOW THEY NEVER MADE!
DO I GET A BADGE?

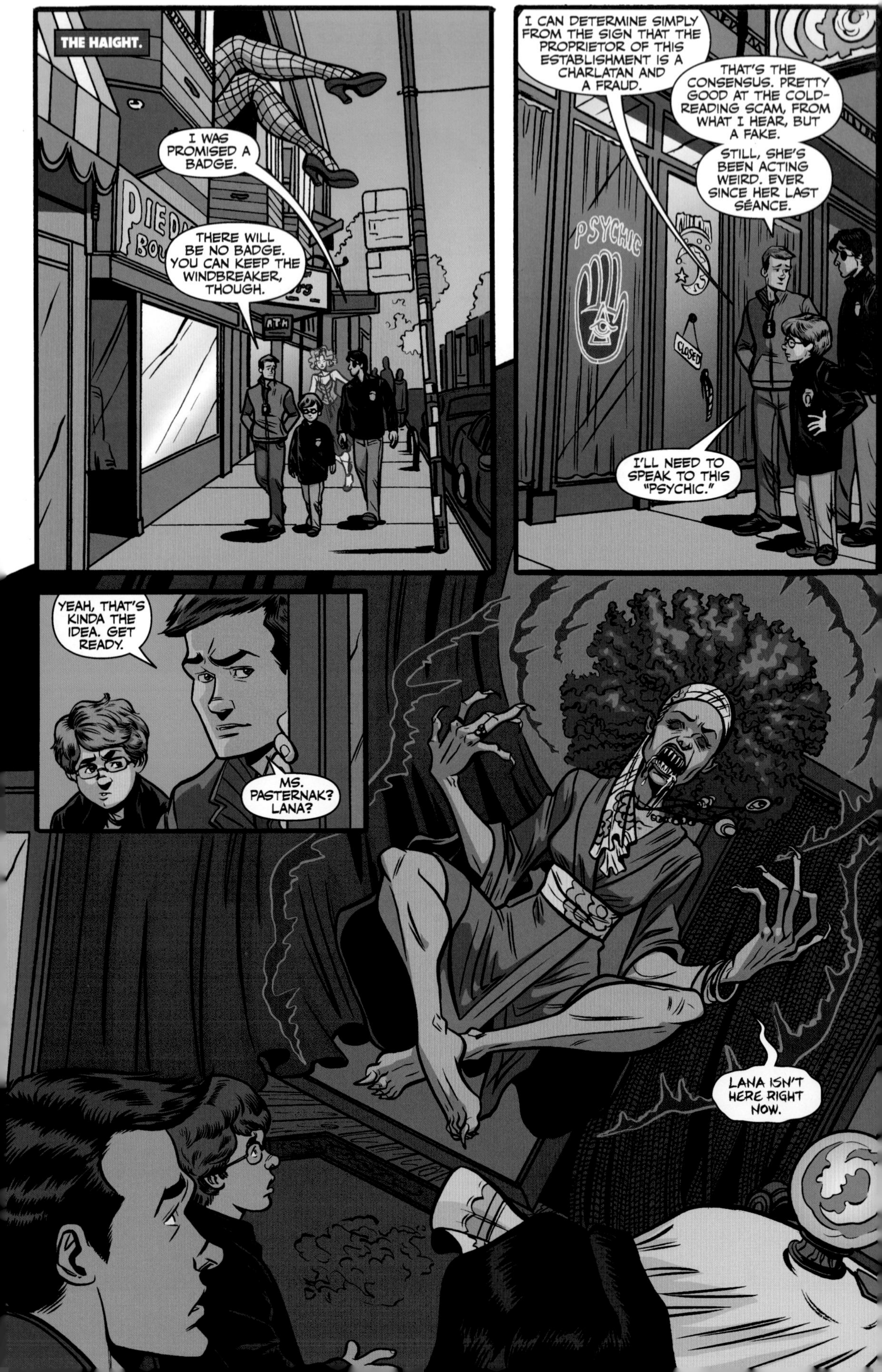
THE HAIGHT.
I WAS PROMISED A BADGE.
THERE WILL BE NO BADGE. YOU CAN KEEP THE WINDBREAKER, THOUGH.
ATM
I CAN DETERMINE SIMPLY FROM THE SIGN THAT THE PROPRIETOR OF THIS ESTABLISHMENT IS A CHARLATAN AND A FRAUD.
THAT'S THE CONSENSUS. PRETTY GOOD AT THE COLD-READING SCAM, FROM WHAT I HEAR, BUT A FAKE.
STILL, SHE'S BEEN ACTING WEIRD. EVER SINCE HER LAST SÉANCE.
PSYCHIC
CLOSED
I'LL NEED TO SPEAK TO THIS "PSYCHIC."
YEAH, THAT'S KINDA THE IDEA. GET READY.
MS. PASTERNAK? LANA?
LANA ISN'T HERE RIGHT NOW.

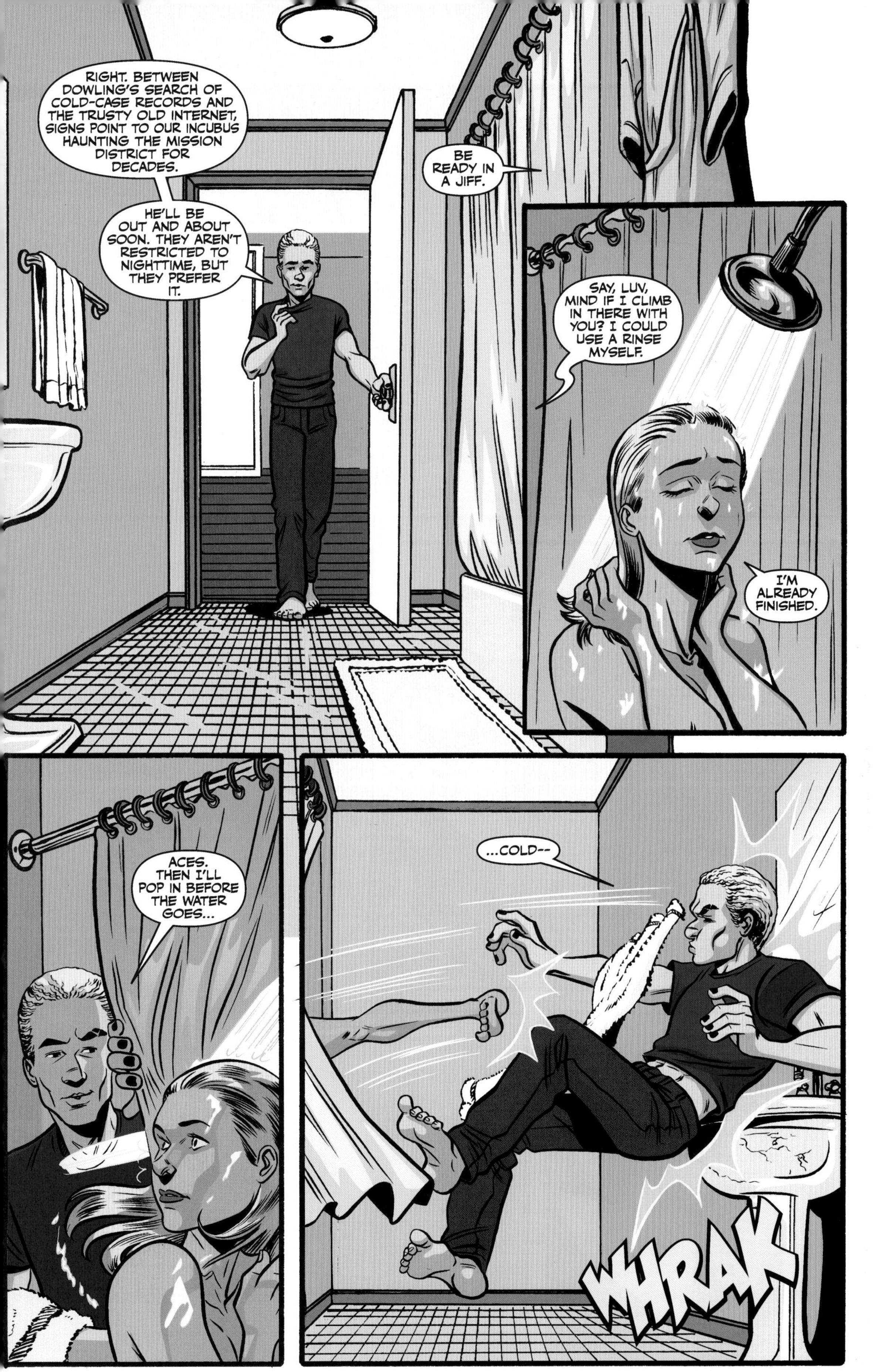
RIGHT. BETWEEN DOWLING'S SEARCH OF COLD-CASE RECORDS AND THE TRUSTY OLD INTERNET, SIGNS POINT TO OUR INCUBUS HAUNTING THE MISSION DISTRICT FOR DECADES.
HE'LL BE OUT AND ABOUT SOON. THEY AREN'T RESTRICTED TO NIGHTTIME, BUT THEY PREFER IT.
BE READY IN A JIFF.
SAY, LUV, MIND IF I CLIMB IN THERE WITH YOU? I COULD USE A RINSE MYSELF.
I'M ALREADY FINISHED.
ACES. THEN I'LL POP IN BEFORE THE WATER GOES...
...COLD--
WHRAK

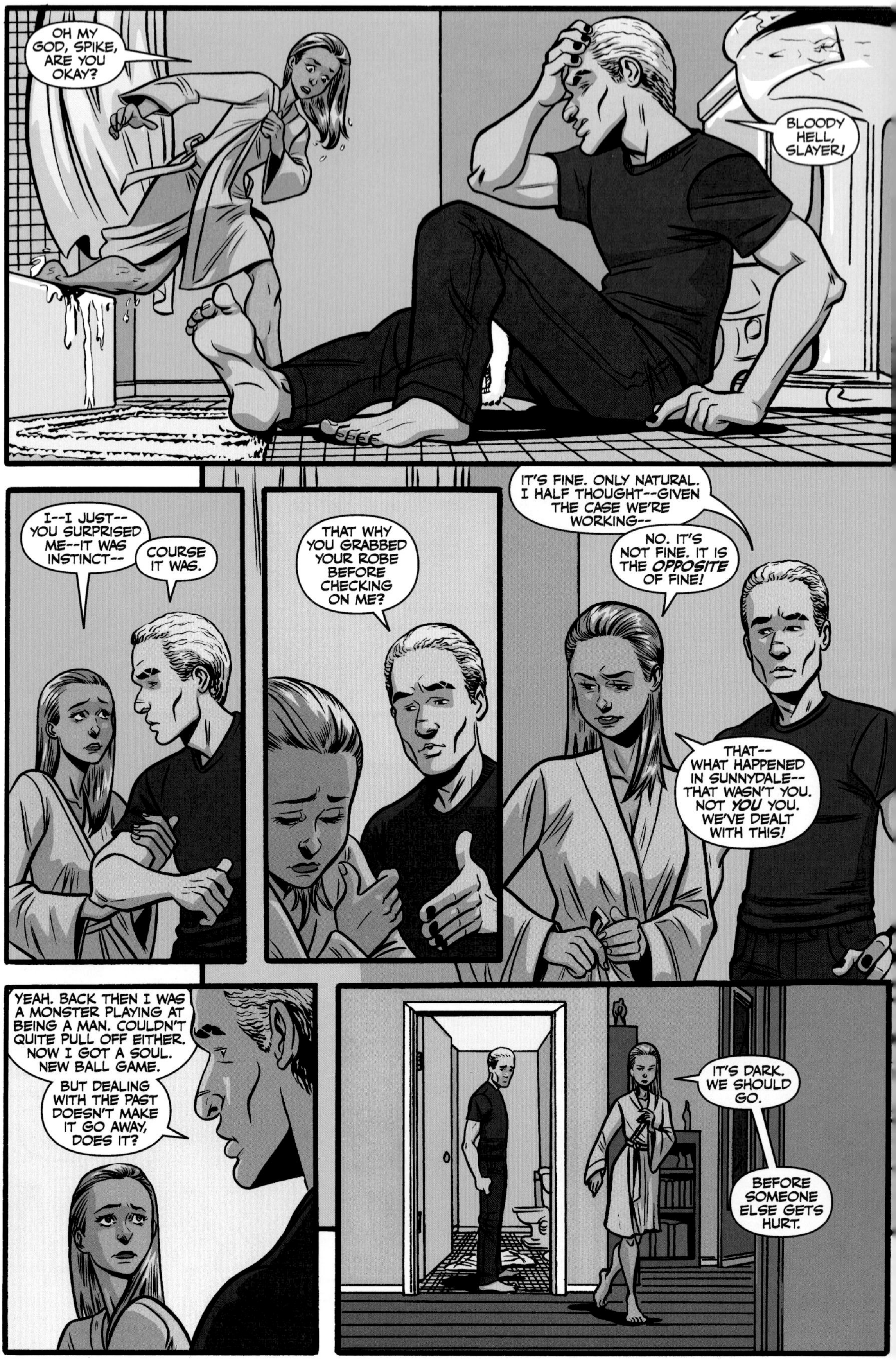
OH MY GOD, SPIKE, ARE YOU OKAY?
BLOODY HELL, SLAYER!
I--I JUST-- YOU SURPRISED ME--IT WAS INSTINCT--
COURSE IT WAS.
THAT WHY YOU GRABBED YOUR ROBE BEFORE CHECKING ON ME?
IT'S FINE. ONLY NATURAL. I HALF THOUGHT--GIVEN THE CASE WE'RE WORKING--
NO. IT'S NOT FINE. IT IS THE *OPPOSITE* OF FINE!
THAT-- WHAT HAPPENED IN SUNNYDALE-- THAT WASN'T YOU. NOT *YOU* YOU. WE'VE DEALT WITH THIS!
YEAH. BACK THEN I WAS A MONSTER PLAYING AT BEING A MAN. COULDN'T QUITE PULL OFF EITHER. NOW I GOT A SOUL. NEW BALL GAME.
BUT DEALING WITH THE PAST DOESN'T MAKE IT GO AWAY, DOES IT?
IT'S DARK. WE SHOULD GO.
BEFORE SOMEONE ELSE GETS HURT.

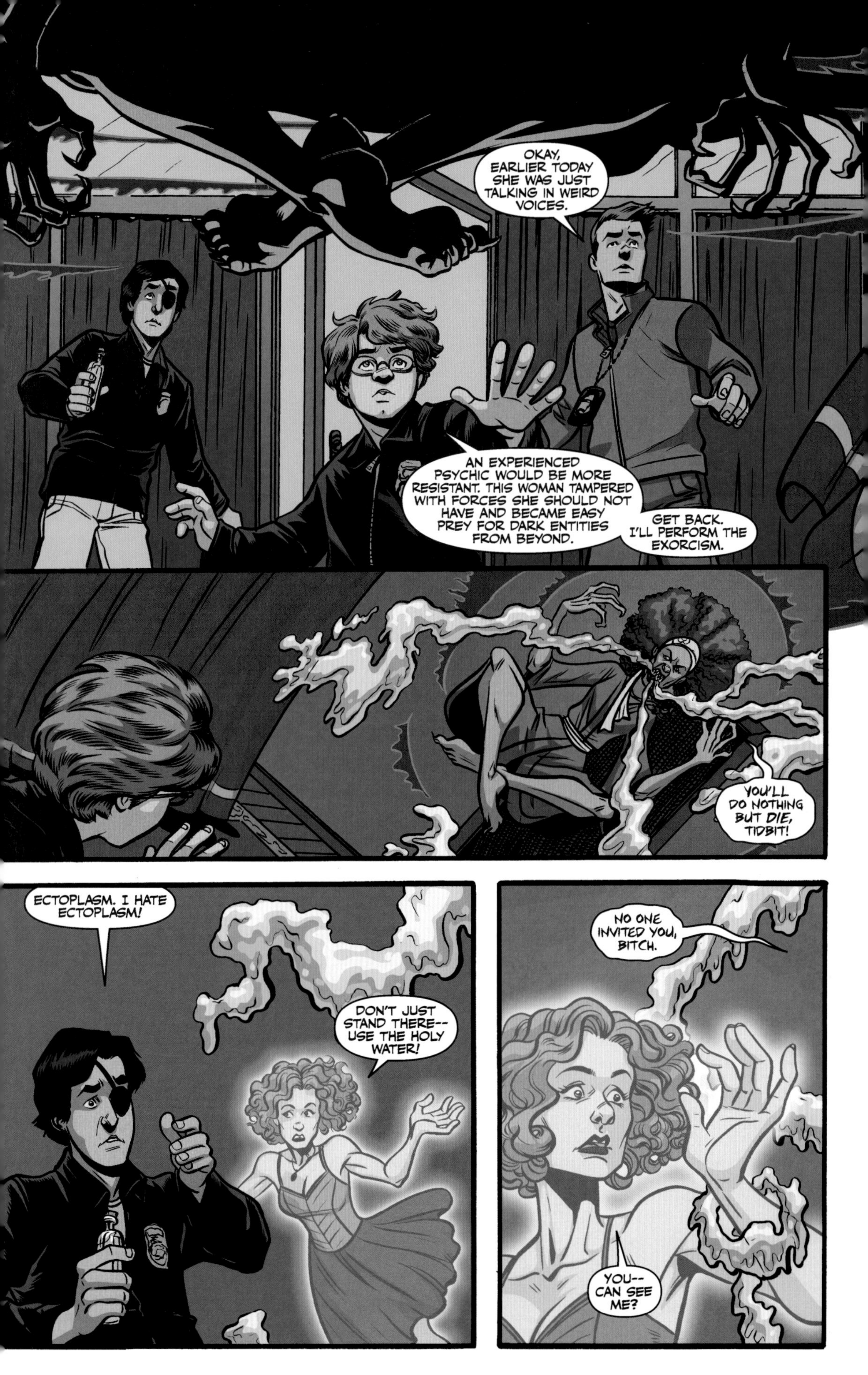
OKAY, EARLIER TODAY SHE WAS JUST TALKING IN WEIRD VOICES.
AN EXPERIENCED PSYCHIC WOULD BE MORE RESISTANT. THIS WOMAN TAMPERED WITH FORCES SHE SHOULD NOT HAVE AND BECAME EASY PREY FOR DARK ENTITIES FROM BEYOND.
GET BACK. I'LL PERFORM THE EXORCISM.
YOU'LL DO NOTHING BUT DIE, TIDBIT!
ECTOPLASM. I HATE ECTOPLASM!
DON'T JUST STAND THERE-- USE THE HOLY WATER!
NO ONE INVITED YOU, BITCH.
YOU-- CAN SEE ME?

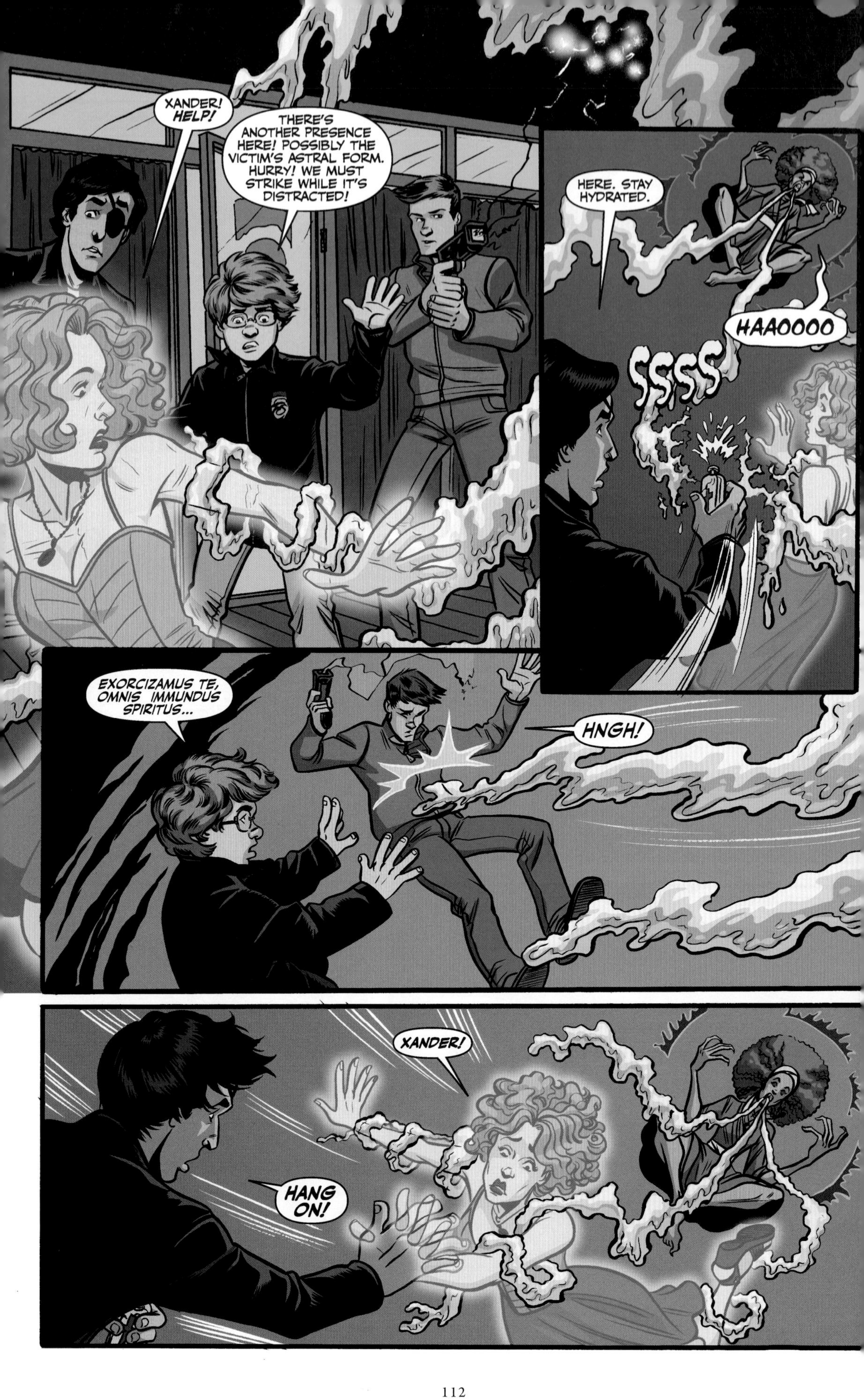
XANDER! HELP!
THERE'S ANOTHER PRESENCE HERE! POSSIBLY THE VICTIM'S ASTRAL FORM. HURRY! WE MUST STRIKE WHILE IT'S DISTRACTED!
HERE. STAY HYDRATED.
HAAOOOO
SSSS
EXORCIZAMUS TE, OMNIS IMMUNDUS SPIRITUS...
HNGH!
XANDER!
HANG ON!

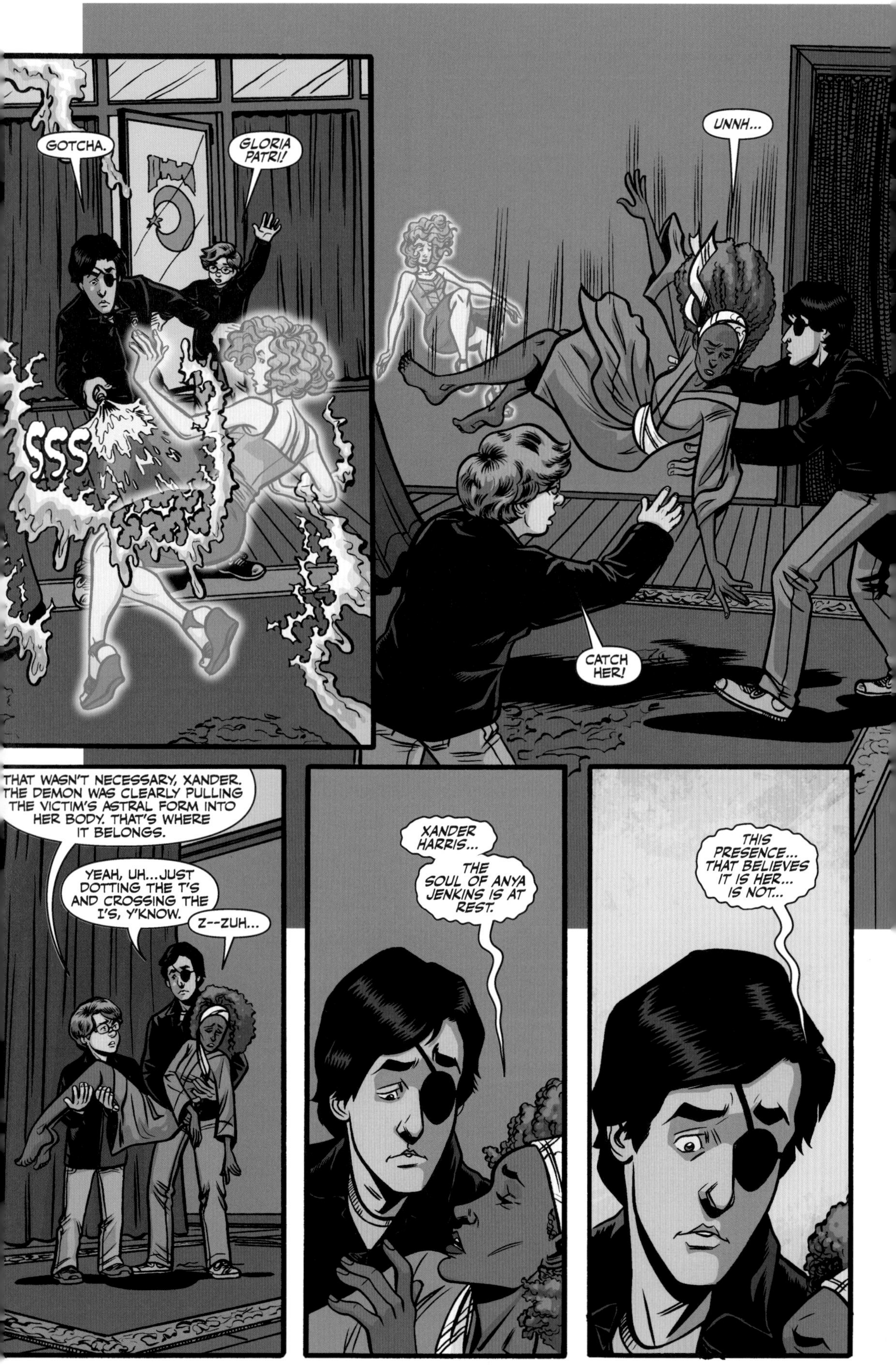
GOTCHA.
GLORIA PATRI!
SSS
UNNH...
CATCH HER!
THAT WASN'T NECESSARY, XANDER. THE DEMON WAS CLEARLY PULLING THE VICTIM'S ASTRAL FORM INTO HER BODY. THAT'S WHERE IT BELONGS.
YEAH, UH...JUST DOTTING THE T'S AND CROSSING THE I'S, Y'KNOW.
Z--ZUH...
XANDER HARRIS...
THE SOUL OF ANYA JENKINS IS AT REST.
THIS PRESENCE... THAT BELIEVES IT IS HER... IS NOT...

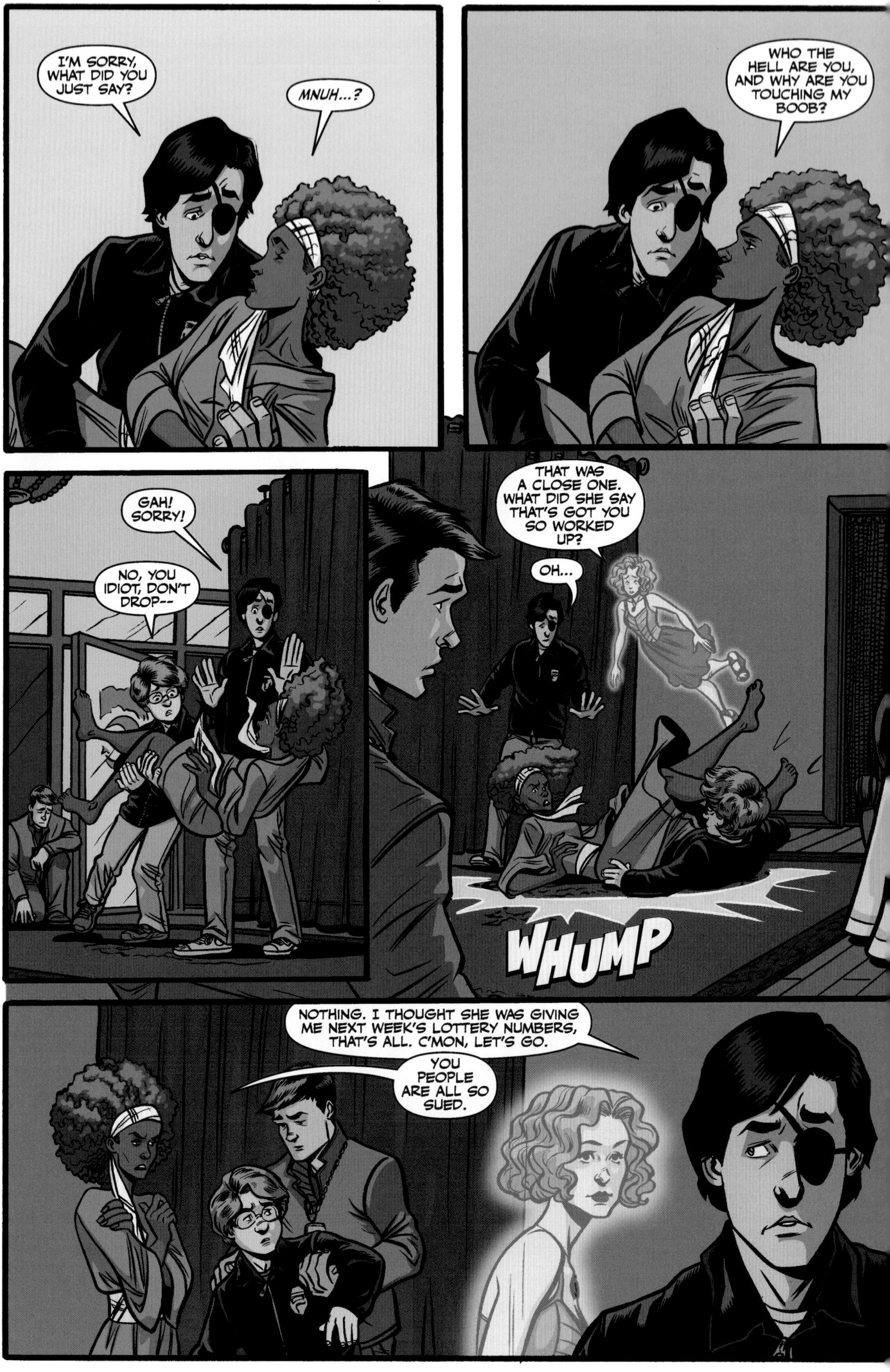
I'M SORRY, WHAT DID YOU JUST SAY?
MNUH...?
WHO THE HELL ARE YOU, AND WHY ARE YOU TOUCHING MY BOOB?
GAH! SORRY!
NO, YOU IDIOT, DON'T DROP--
THAT WAS A CLOSE ONE. WHAT DID SHE SAY THAT'S GOT YOU SO WORKED UP?
OH...
WHUMP
NOTHING. I THOUGHT SHE WAS GIVING ME NEXT WEEK'S LOTTERY NUMBERS, THAT'S ALL. C'MON, LET'S GO.
YOU PEOPLE ARE ALL SO SUED.

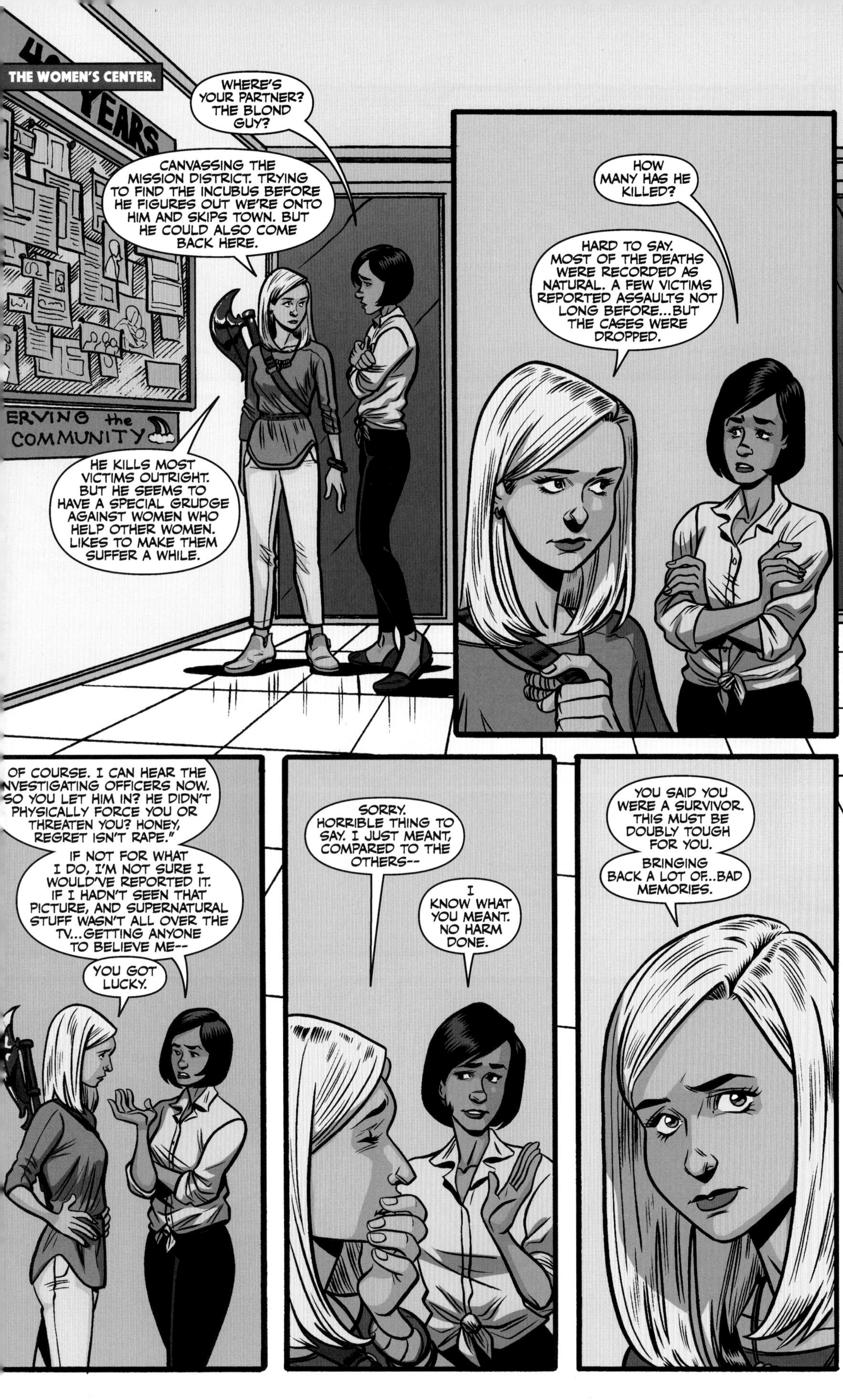
THE WOMEN'S CENTER.
YEARS
WHERE'S YOUR PARTNER? THE BLOND GUY?
CANVASSING THE MISSION DISTRICT. TRYING TO FIND THE INCUBUS BEFORE HE FIGURES OUT WE'RE ONTO HIM AND SKIPS TOWN. BUT HE COULD ALSO COME BACK HERE.
ERVING the COMMUNITY
HE KILLS MOST VICTIMS OUTRIGHT. BUT HE SEEMS TO HAVE A SPECIAL GRUDGE AGAINST WOMEN WHO HELP OTHER WOMEN. LIKES TO MAKE THEM SUFFER A WHILE.
HOW MANY HAS HE KILLED?
HARD TO SAY. MOST OF THE DEATHS WERE RECORDED AS NATURAL. A FEW VICTIMS REPORTED ASSAULTS NOT LONG BEFORE...BUT THE CASES WERE DROPPED.
OF COURSE. I CAN HEAR THE NVESTIGATING OFFICERS NOW. SO YOU LET HIM IN? HE DIDN'T PHYSICALLY FORCE YOU OR THREATEN YOU? HONEY, REGRET ISN'T RAPE."
IF NOT FOR WHAT I DO, I'M NOT SURE I WOULD'VE REPORTED IT. IF I HADN'T SEEN THAT PICTURE, AND SUPERNATURAL STUFF WASN'T ALL OVER THE TV...GETTING ANYONE TO BELIEVE ME--
YOU GOT LUCKY.
SORRY. HORRIBLE THING TO SAY. I JUST MEANT, COMPARED TO THE OTHERS--
I KNOW WHAT YOU MEANT. NO HARM DONE.
YOU SAID YOU WERE A SURVIVOR. THIS MUST BE DOUBLY TOUGH FOR YOU.
BRINGING BACK A LOT OF...BAD MEMORIES.

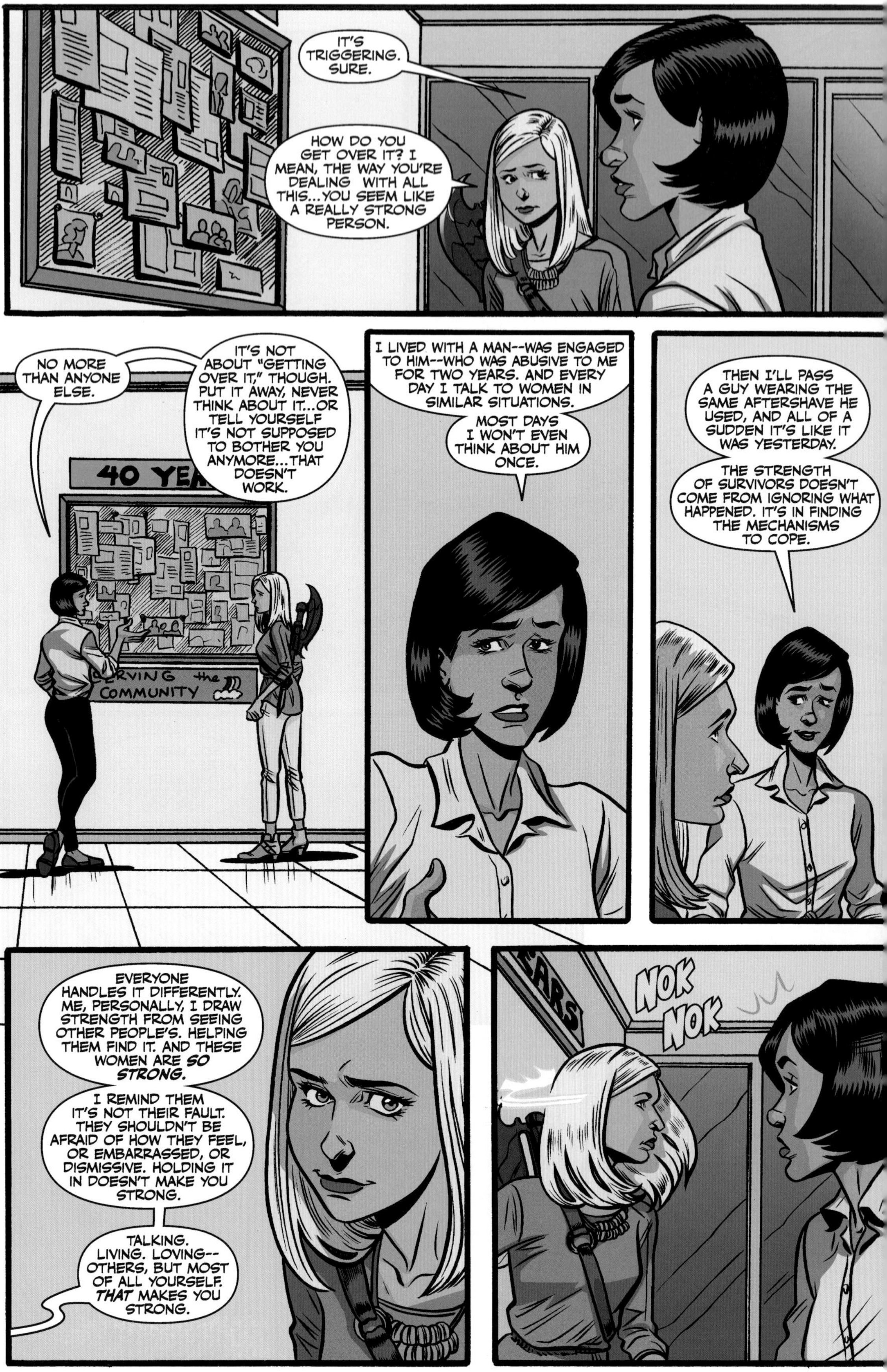
IT'S TRIGGERING. SURE.
HOW DO YOU GET OVER IT? I MEAN, THE WAY YOU'RE DEALING WITH ALL THIS...YOU SEEM LIKE A REALLY STRONG PERSON.
NO MORE THAN ANYONE ELSE.
IT'S NOT ABOUT "GETTING OVER IT," THOUGH. PUT IT AWAY, NEVER THINK ABOUT IT...OR TELL YOURSELF IT'S NOT SUPPOSED TO BOTHER YOU ANYMORE...THAT DOESN'T WORK.
COMMUNITY
I LIVED WITH A MAN--WAS ENGAGED TO HIM--WHO WAS ABUSIVE TO ME FOR TWO YEARS. AND EVERY DAY I TALK TO WOMEN IN SIMILAR SITUATIONS.
MOST DAYS I WON'T EVEN THINK ABOUT HIM ONCE.
THEN I'LL PASS A GUY WEARING THE SAME AFTERSHAVE HE USED, AND ALL OF A SUDDEN IT'S LIKE IT WAS YESTERDAY.
THE STRENGTH OF SURVIVORS DOESN'T COME FROM IGNORING WHAT HAPPENED. IT'S IN FINDING THE MECHANISMS TO COPE.
EVERYONE HANDLES IT DIFFERENTLY. ME, PERSONALLY, I DRAW STRENGTH FROM SEEING OTHER PEOPLE'S. HELPING THEM FIND IT. AND THESE WOMEN ARE *SO STRONG.*
I REMIND THEM IT'S NOT THEIR FAULT. THEY SHOULDN'T BE AFRAID OF HOW THEY FEEL, OR EMBARRASSED, OR DISMISSIVE. HOLDING IT IN DOESN'T MAKE YOU STRONG.
TALKING. LIVING. LOVING-- OTHERS, BUT MOST OF ALL YOURSELF. *THAT* MAKES YOU STRONG.
NOK NOK

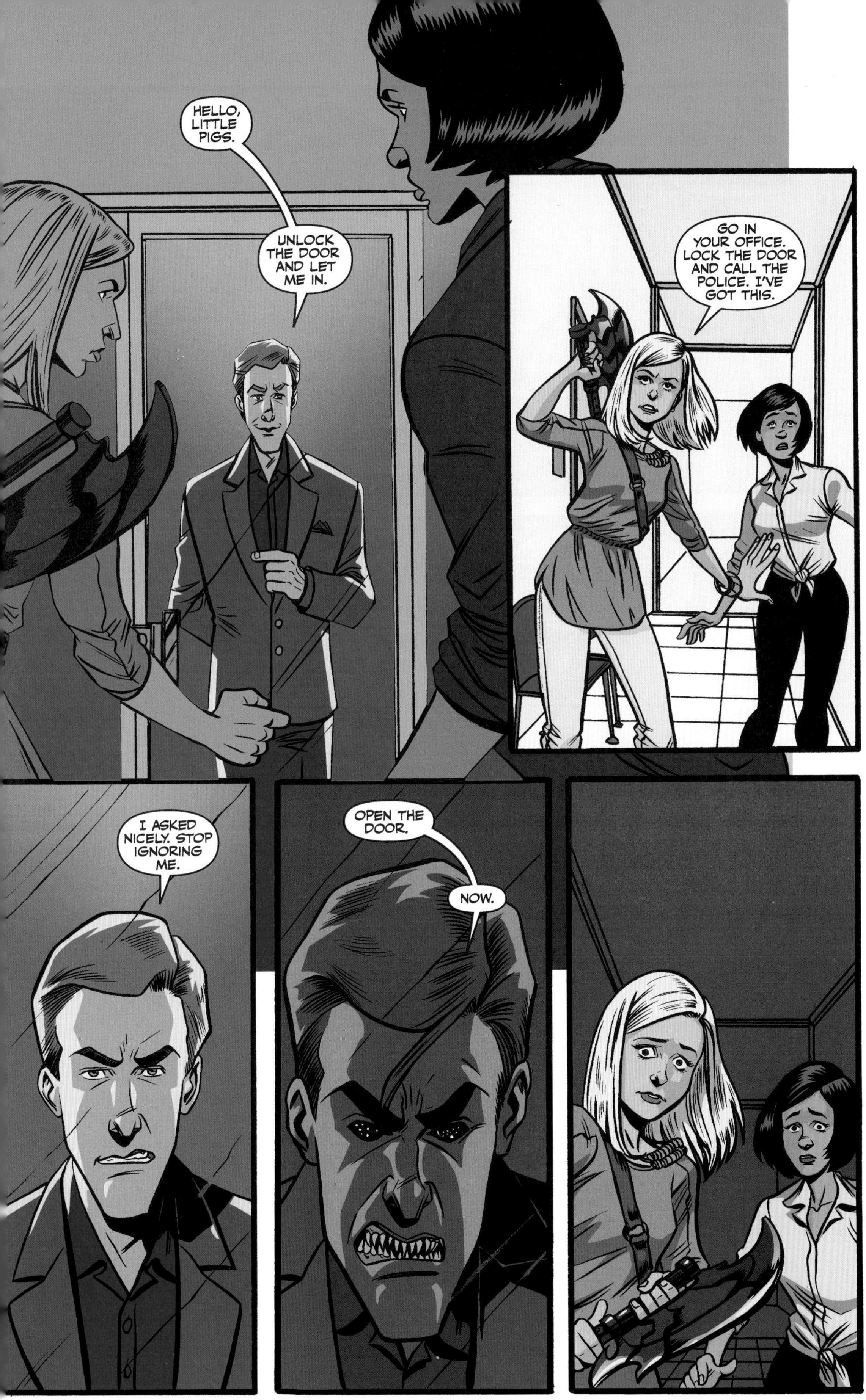
HELLO, LITTLE PIGS.
UNLOCK THE DOOR AND LET ME IN.
GO IN YOUR OFFICE. LOCK THE DOOR AND CALL THE POLICE. I'VE GOT THIS.
I ASKED NICELY. STOP IGNORING ME.
OPEN THE DOOR.
NOW.

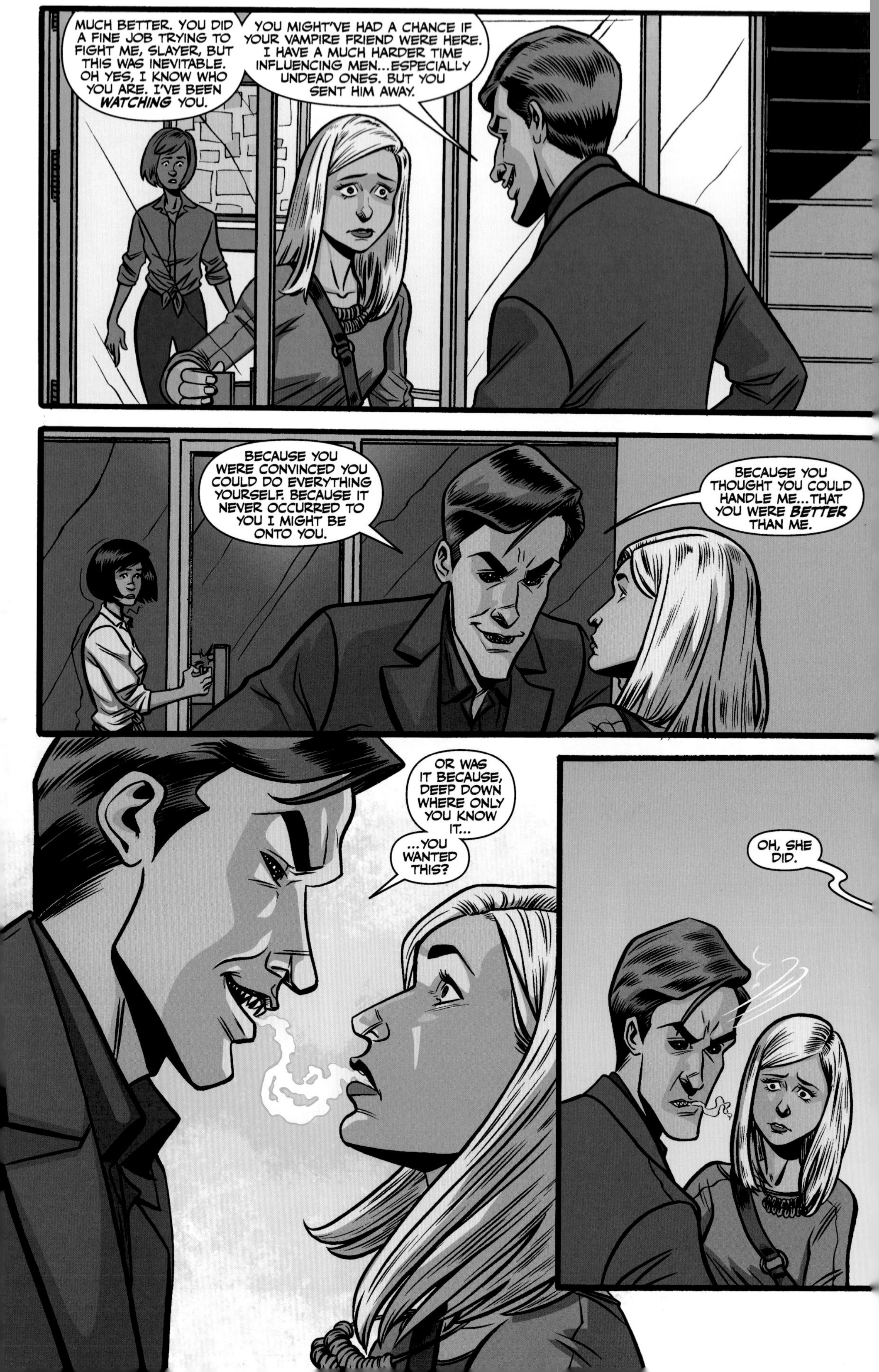
MUCH BETTER. YOU DID A FINE JOB TRYING TO FIGHT ME, SLAYER, BUT THIS WAS INEVITABLE. OH YES, I KNOW WHO YOU ARE. I'VE BEEN *WATCHING* YOU.
YOU MIGHT'VE HAD A CHANCE IF YOUR VAMPIRE FRIEND WERE HERE. I HAVE A MUCH HARDER TIME INFLUENCING MEN...ESPECIALLY UNDEAD ONES. BUT YOU SENT HIM AWAY.
BECAUSE YOU WERE CONVINCED YOU COULD DO EVERYTHING YOURSELF. BECAUSE IT NEVER OCCURRED TO YOU I MIGHT BE ONTO YOU.
BECAUSE YOU THOUGHT YOU COULD HANDLE ME...THAT YOU WERE *BETTER* THAN ME.
OR WAS IT BECAUSE, DEEP DOWN WHERE ONLY YOU KNOW IT...
...YOU WANTED THIS?
OH, SHE DID.

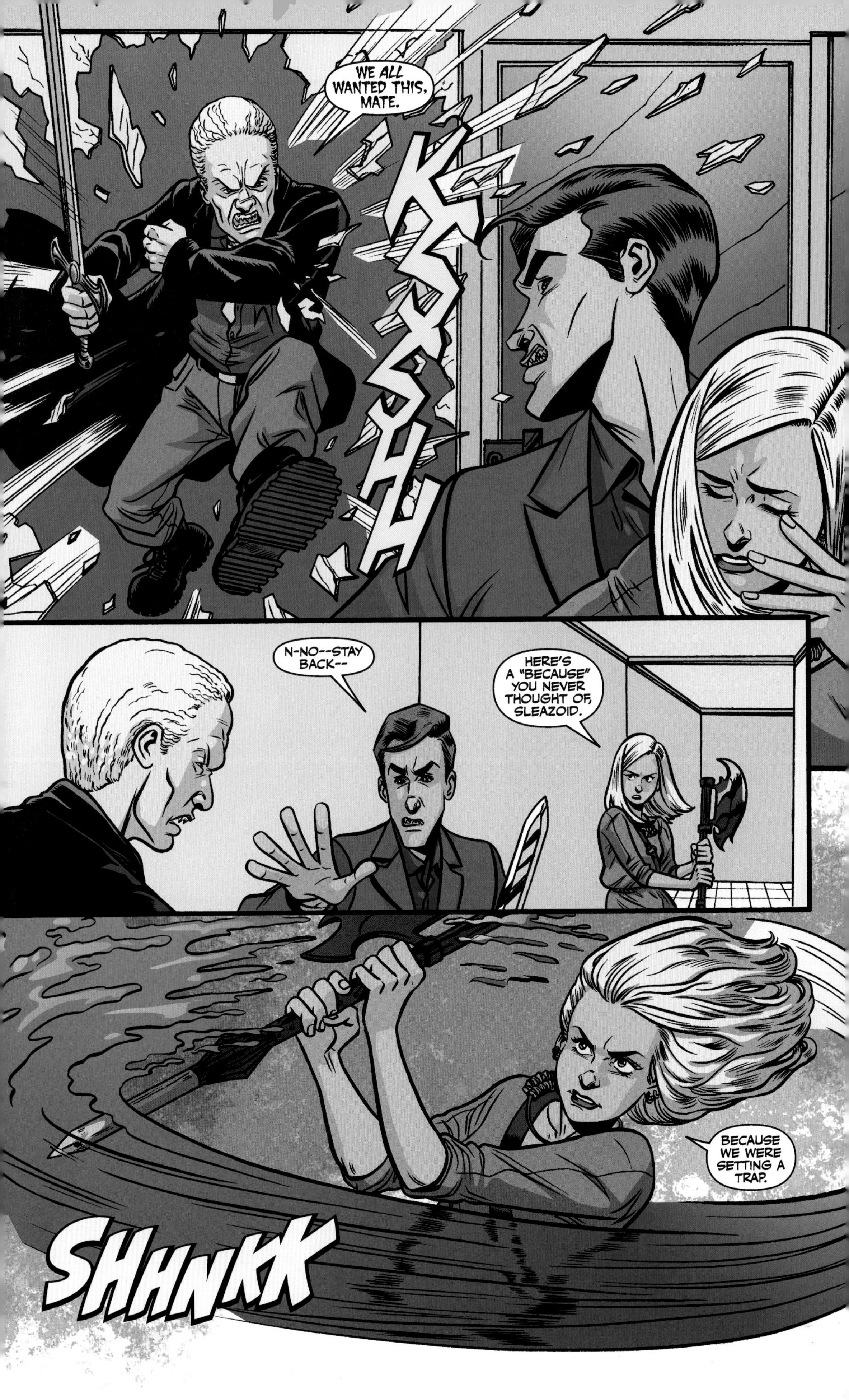
WE ALL WANTED THIS, MATE.
KSSHHH
N-NO--STAY BACK--
HERE'S A "BECAUSE" YOU NEVER THOUGHT OF, SLEAZOID.
BECAUSE WE WERE SETTING A TRAP.
SHNKK

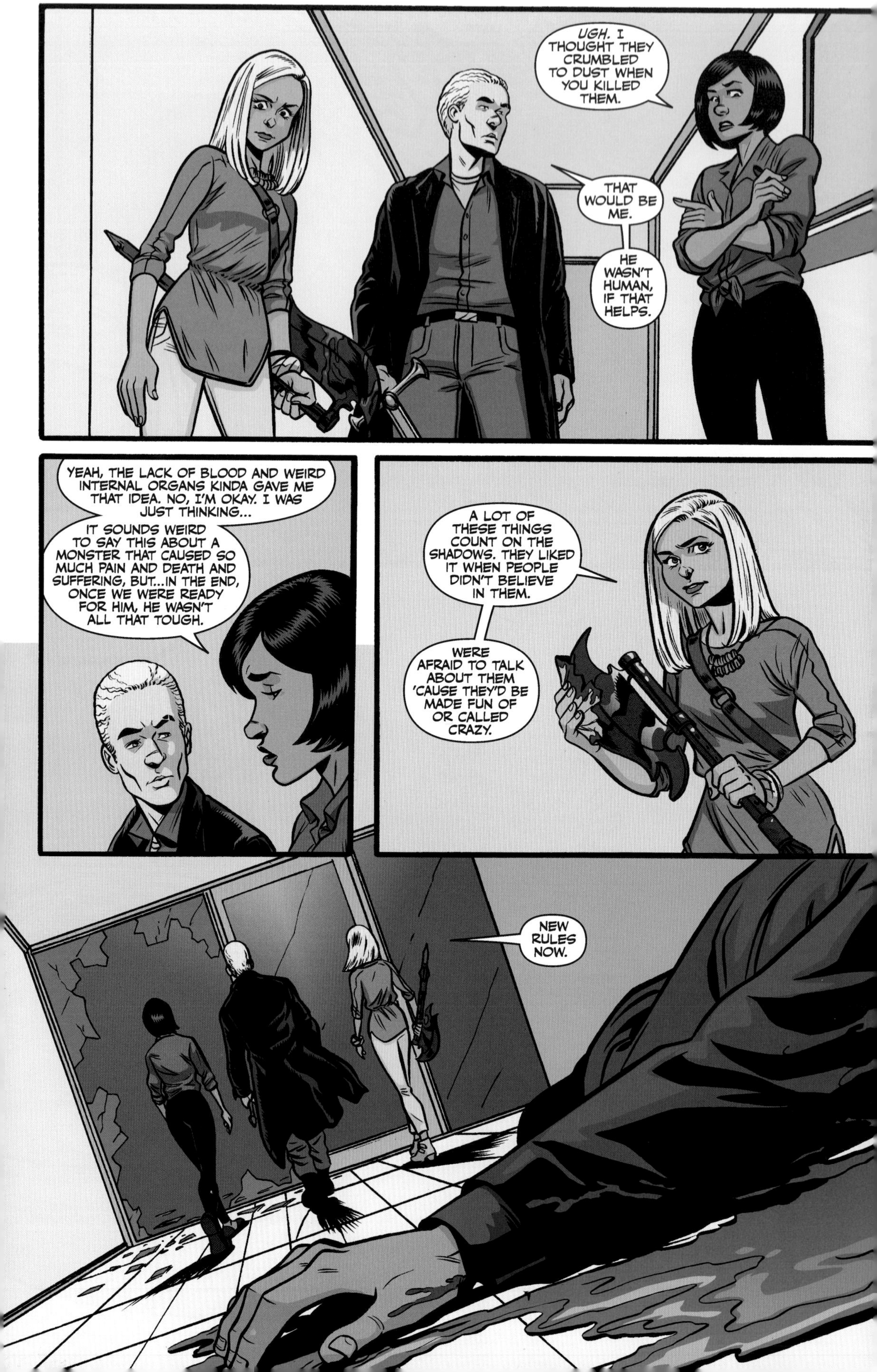
UGH. I THOUGHT THEY CRUMBLED TO DUST WHEN YOU KILLED THEM.
THAT WOULD BE ME.
HE WASN'T HUMAN, IF THAT HELPS.
YEAH, THE LACK OF BLOOD AND WEIRD INTERNAL ORGANS KINDA GAVE ME THAT IDEA. NO, I'M OKAY. I WAS JUST THINKING...
IT SOUNDS WEIRD TO SAY THIS ABOUT A MONSTER THAT CAUSED SO MUCH PAIN AND DEATH AND SUFFERING, BUT...IN THE END, ONCE WE WERE READY FOR HIM, HE WASN'T ALL THAT TOUGH.
A LOT OF THESE THINGS COUNT ON THE SHADOWS. THEY LIKED IT WHEN PEOPLE DIDN'T BELIEVE IN THEM.
WERE AFRAID TO TALK ABOUT THEM 'CAUSE THEY'D BE MADE FUN OF OR CALLED CRAZY.
NEW RULES NOW.

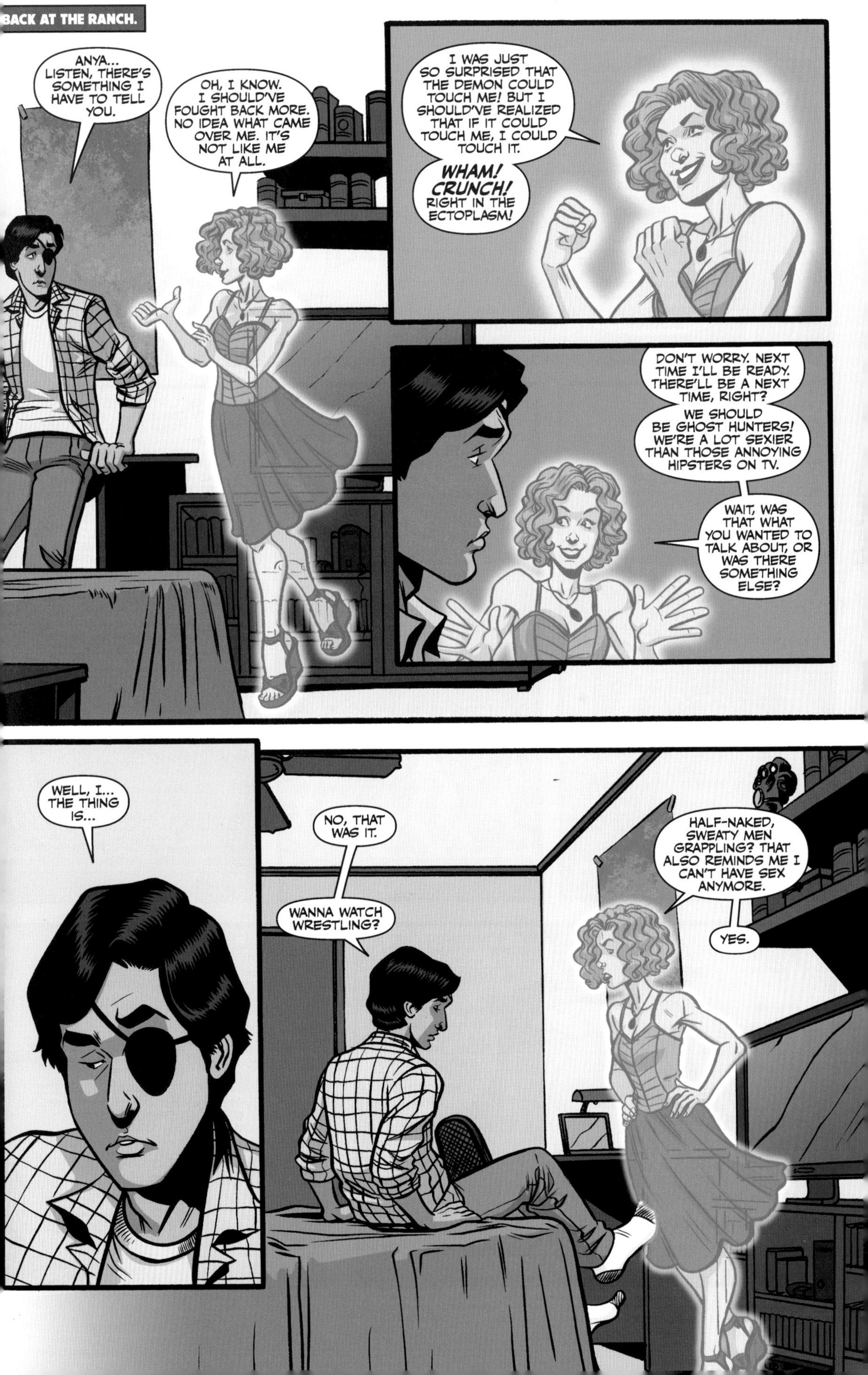
BACK AT THE RANCH.
ANYA... LISTEN, THERE'S SOMETHING I HAVE TO TELL YOU.
OH, I KNOW. I SHOULD'VE FOUGHT BACK MORE. NO IDEA WHAT CAME OVER ME. IT'S NOT LIKE ME AT ALL.
I WAS JUST SO SURPRISED THAT THE DEMON COULD TOUCH ME! BUT I SHOULD'VE REALIZED THAT IF IT COULD TOUCH ME, I COULD TOUCH IT.
WHAM! CRUNCH! RIGHT IN THE ECTOPLASM!
DON'T WORRY. NEXT TIME I'LL BE READY. THERE'LL BE A NEXT TIME, RIGHT?
WE SHOULD BE GHOST HUNTERS! WE'RE A LOT SEXIER THAN THOSE ANNOYING HIPSTERS ON TV.
WAIT, WAS THAT WHAT YOU WANTED TO TALK ABOUT, OR WAS THERE SOMETHING ELSE?
WELL, I... THE THING IS...
NO, THAT WAS IT.
WANNA WATCH WRESTLING?
HALF-NAKED, SWEATY MEN GRAPPLING? THAT ALSO REMINDS ME I CAN'T HAVE SEX ANYMORE.
YES.

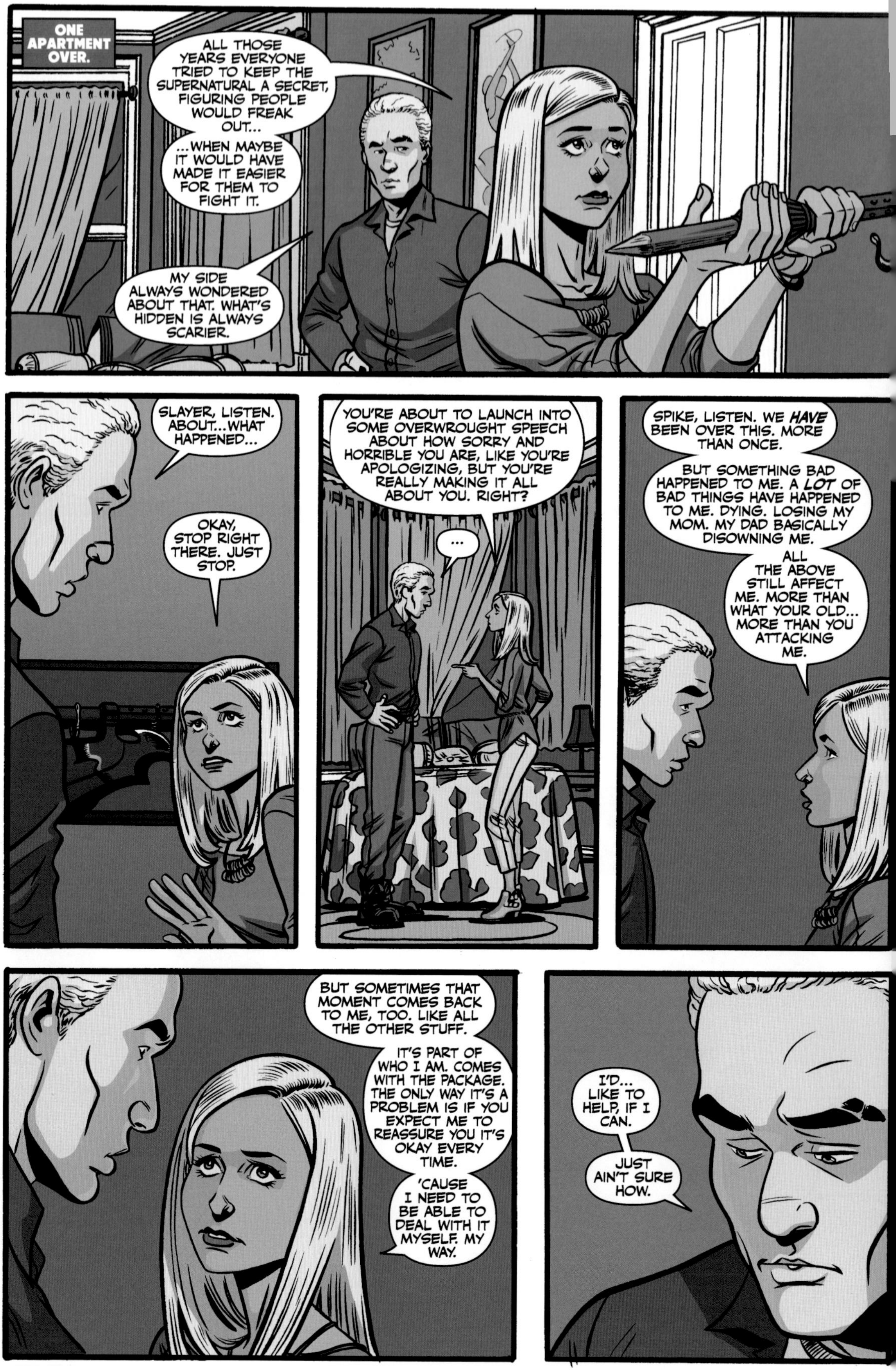
ONE APARTMENT OVER.
ALL THOSE YEARS EVERYONE TRIED TO KEEP THE SUPERNATURAL A SECRET, FIGURING PEOPLE WOULD FREAK OUT...
...WHEN MAYBE IT WOULD HAVE MADE IT EASIER FOR THEM TO FIGHT IT.
MY SIDE ALWAYS WONDERED ABOUT THAT. WHAT'S HIDDEN IS ALWAYS SCARIER.
SLAYER, LISTEN. ABOUT...WHAT HAPPENED...
OKAY, STOP RIGHT THERE. JUST STOP.
YOU'RE ABOUT TO LAUNCH INTO SOME OVERWROUGHT SPEECH ABOUT HOW SORRY AND HORRIBLE YOU ARE, LIKE YOU'RE APOLOGIZING, BUT YOU'RE REALLY MAKING IT ALL ABOUT YOU. RIGHT?
...
SPIKE, LISTEN. WE *HAVE* BEEN OVER THIS. MORE THAN ONCE.
BUT SOMETHING BAD HAPPENED TO ME. A *LOT* OF BAD THINGS HAVE HAPPENED TO ME. DYING. LOSING MY MOM. MY DAD BASICALLY DISOWNING ME.
ALL THE ABOVE STILL AFFECT ME. MORE THAN WHAT YOUR OLD... MORE THAN YOU ATTACKING ME.
BUT SOMETIMES THAT MOMENT COMES BACK TO ME, TOO. LIKE ALL THE OTHER STUFF.
IT'S PART OF WHO I AM. COMES WITH THE PACKAGE. THE ONLY WAY IT'S A PROBLEM IS IF YOU EXPECT ME TO REASSURE YOU IT'S OKAY EVERY TIME.
'CAUSE I NEED TO BE ABLE TO DEAL WITH IT MYSELF. MY WAY.
I'D... LIKE TO HELP, IF I CAN.
JUST AIN'T SURE HOW.

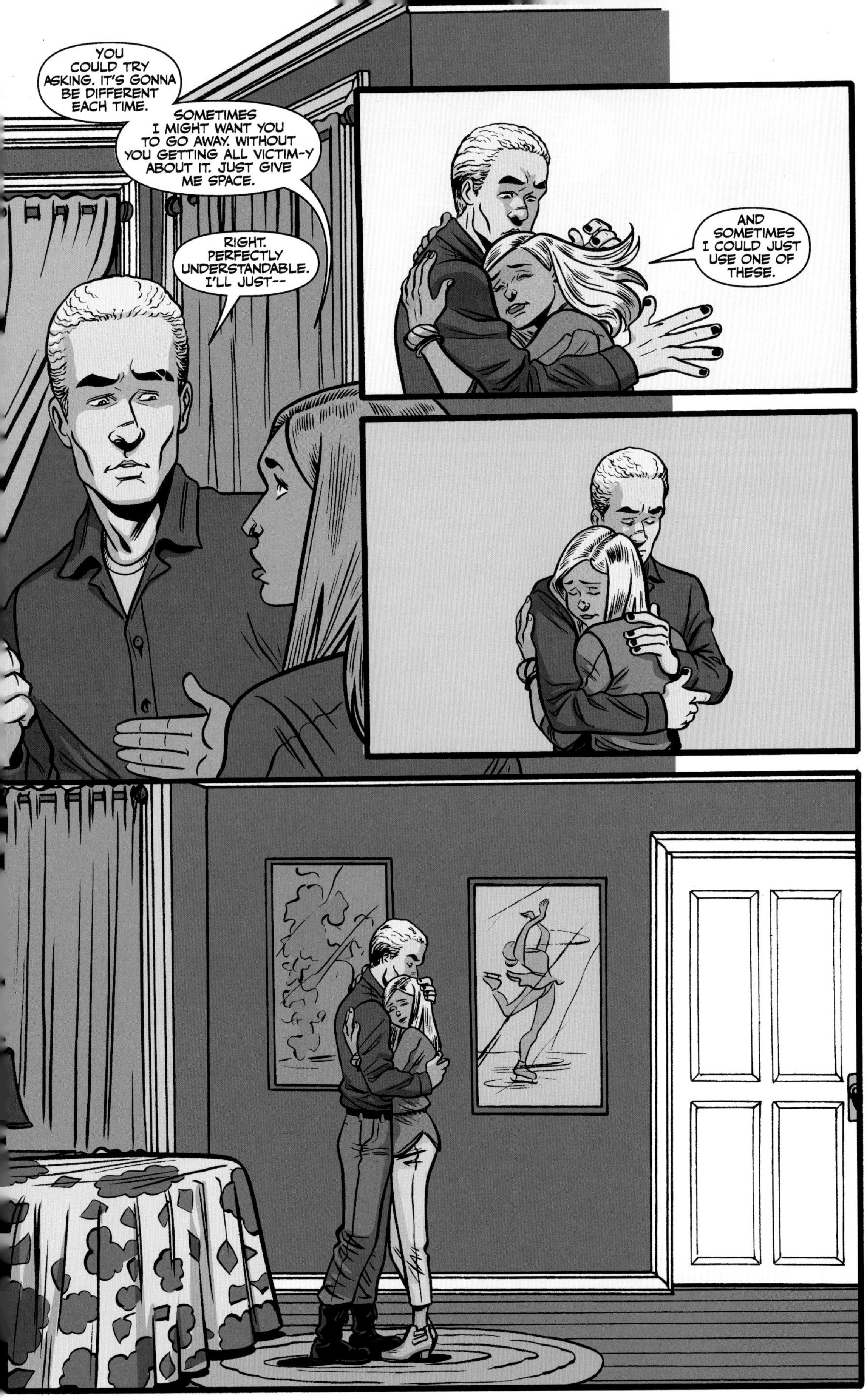
YOU COULD TRY ASKING. IT'S GONNA BE DIFFERENT EACH TIME.
SOMETIMES I MIGHT WANT YOU TO GO AWAY. WITHOUT YOU GETTING ALL VICTIM-Y ABOUT IT. JUST GIVE ME SPACE.
RIGHT. PERFECTLY UNDERSTANDABLE. I'LL JUST--
AND SOMETIMES I COULD JUST USE ONE OF THESE.

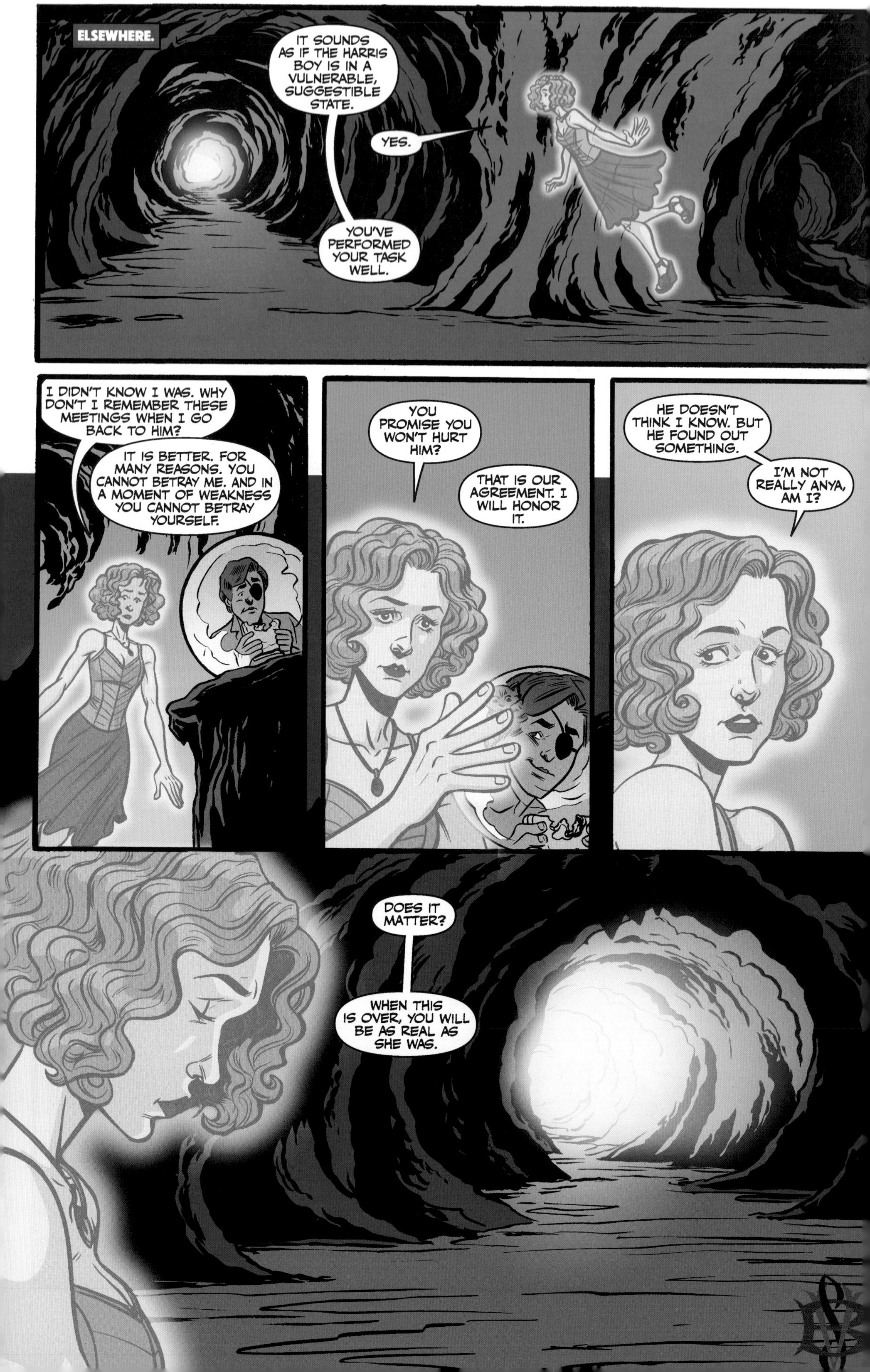
ELSEWHERE.
IT SOUNDS AS IF THE HARRIS BOY IS IN A VULNERABLE, SUGGESTIBLE STATE.
YES.
YOU'VE PERFORMED YOUR TASK WELL.
I DIDN'T KNOW I WAS. WHY DON'T I REMEMBER THESE MEETINGS WHEN I GO BACK TO HIM?
IT IS BETTER. FOR MANY REASONS. YOU CANNOT BETRAY ME. AND IN A MOMENT OF WEAKNESS YOU CANNOT BETRAY YOURSELF.
YOU PROMISE YOU WON'T HURT HIM?
THAT IS OUR AGREEMENT. I WILL HONOR IT.
HE DOESN'T THINK I KNOW. BUT HE FOUND OUT SOMETHING.
I'M NOT REALLY ANYA, AM I?
DOES IT MATTER?
WHEN THIS IS OVER, YOU WILL BE AS REAL AS SHE WAS.

BUFFY *the* VAMPIRE SLAYER

COVER GALLERY and SKETCHBOOK

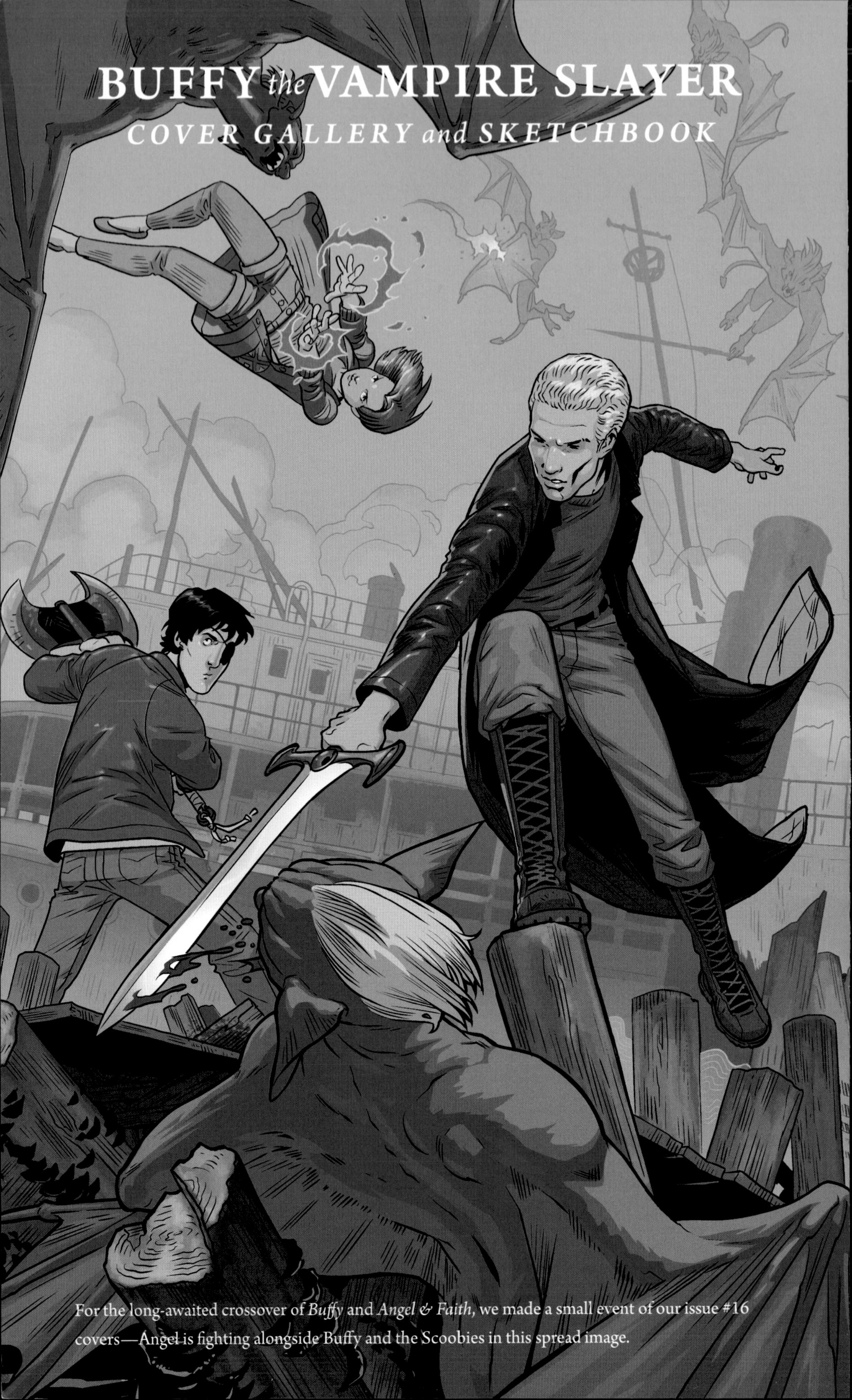

For the long-awaited crossover of *Buffy* and *Angel & Faith,* we made a small event of our issue #16 covers—Angel is fighting alongside Buffy and the Scoobies in this spread image.

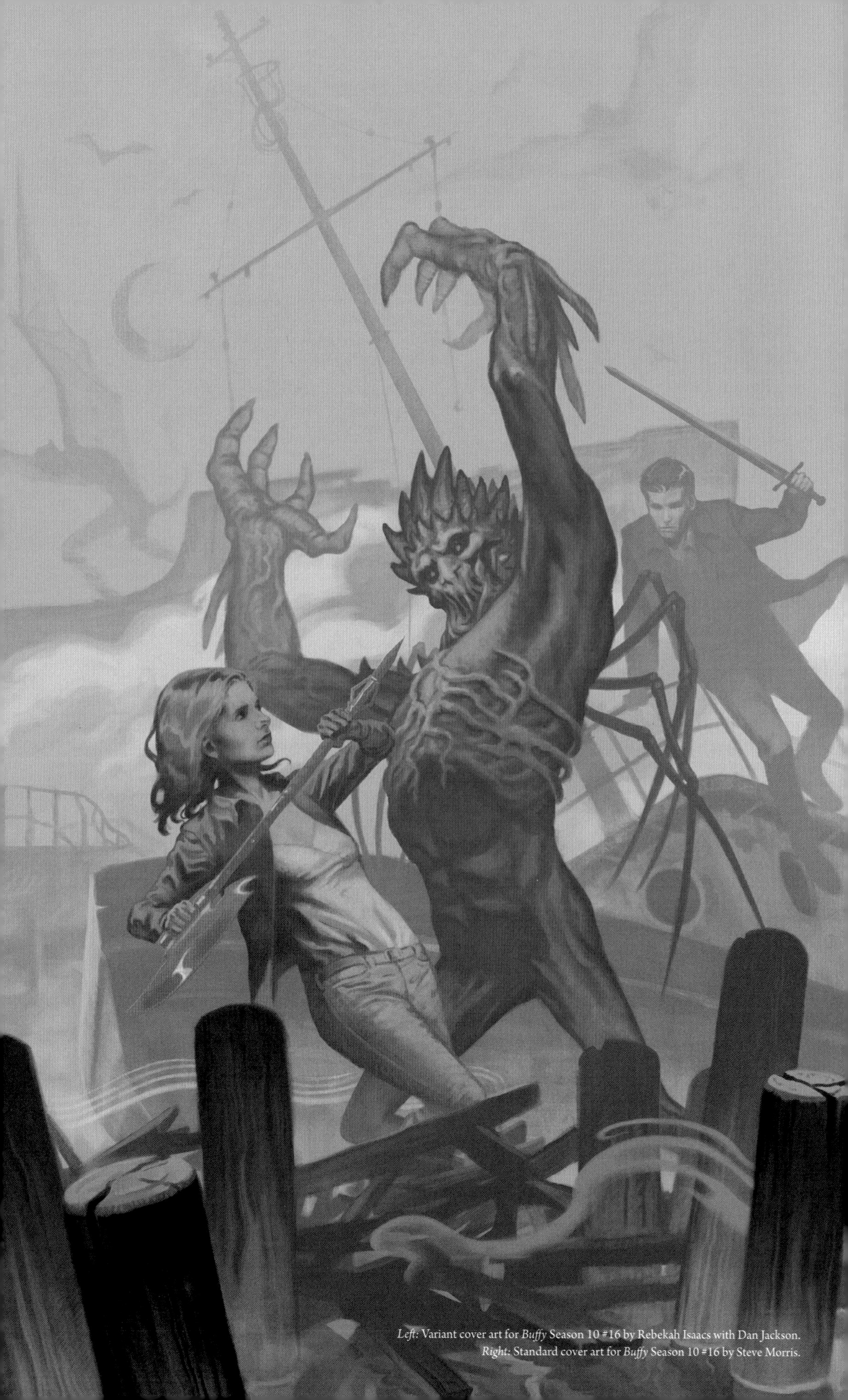

Left: Variant cover art for *Buffy* Season 10 #16 by Rebekah Isaacs with Dan Jackson.
Right: Standard cover art for *Buffy* Season 10 #16 by Steve Morris.

Thumbnail concepts and variant cover pencils for *Buffy* Season 10 #17 by Rebekah Isaacs. Buffy and Willow fighty together!

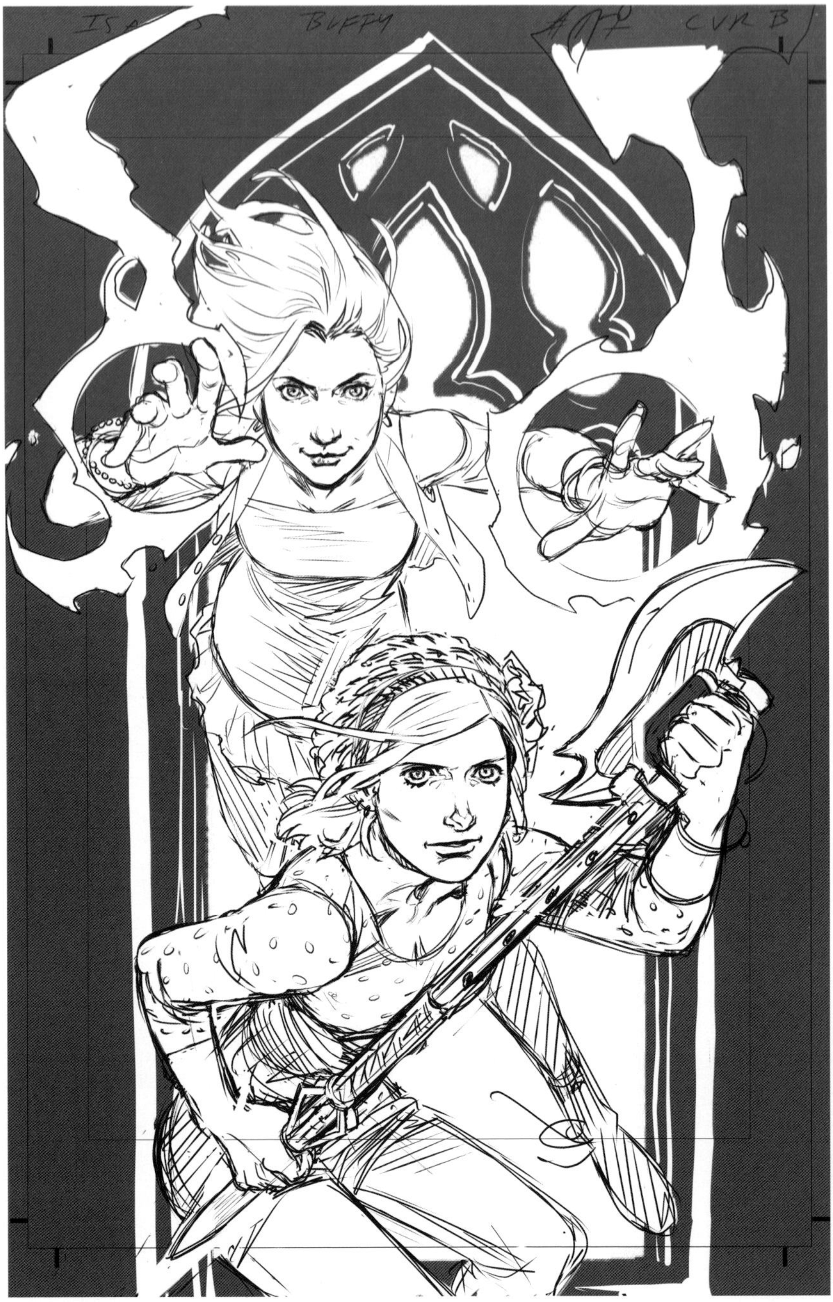

BUFFY
CVR B

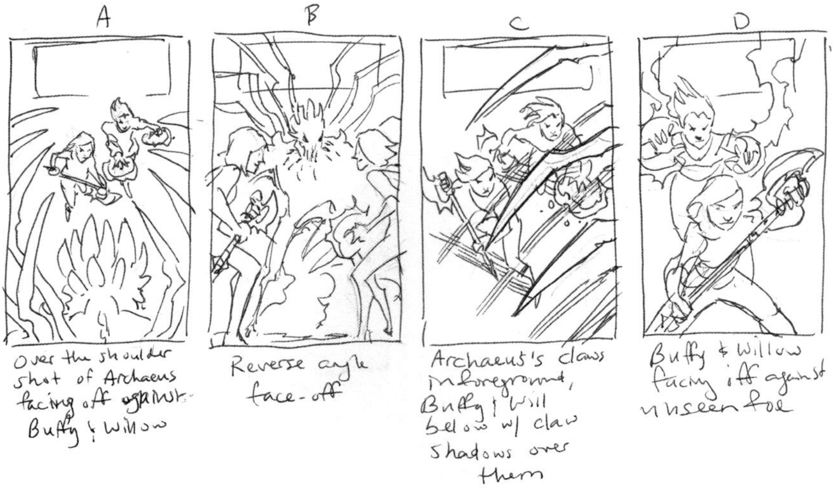

A
B
C
D
Over the shoulder shot of Archaeus facing off against Buffy & Willow
Reverse angle face-off
Archaeus's claws in foreground, Buffy & Will below w/ claw shadows over them
Buffy & Willow facing off against unseen foe

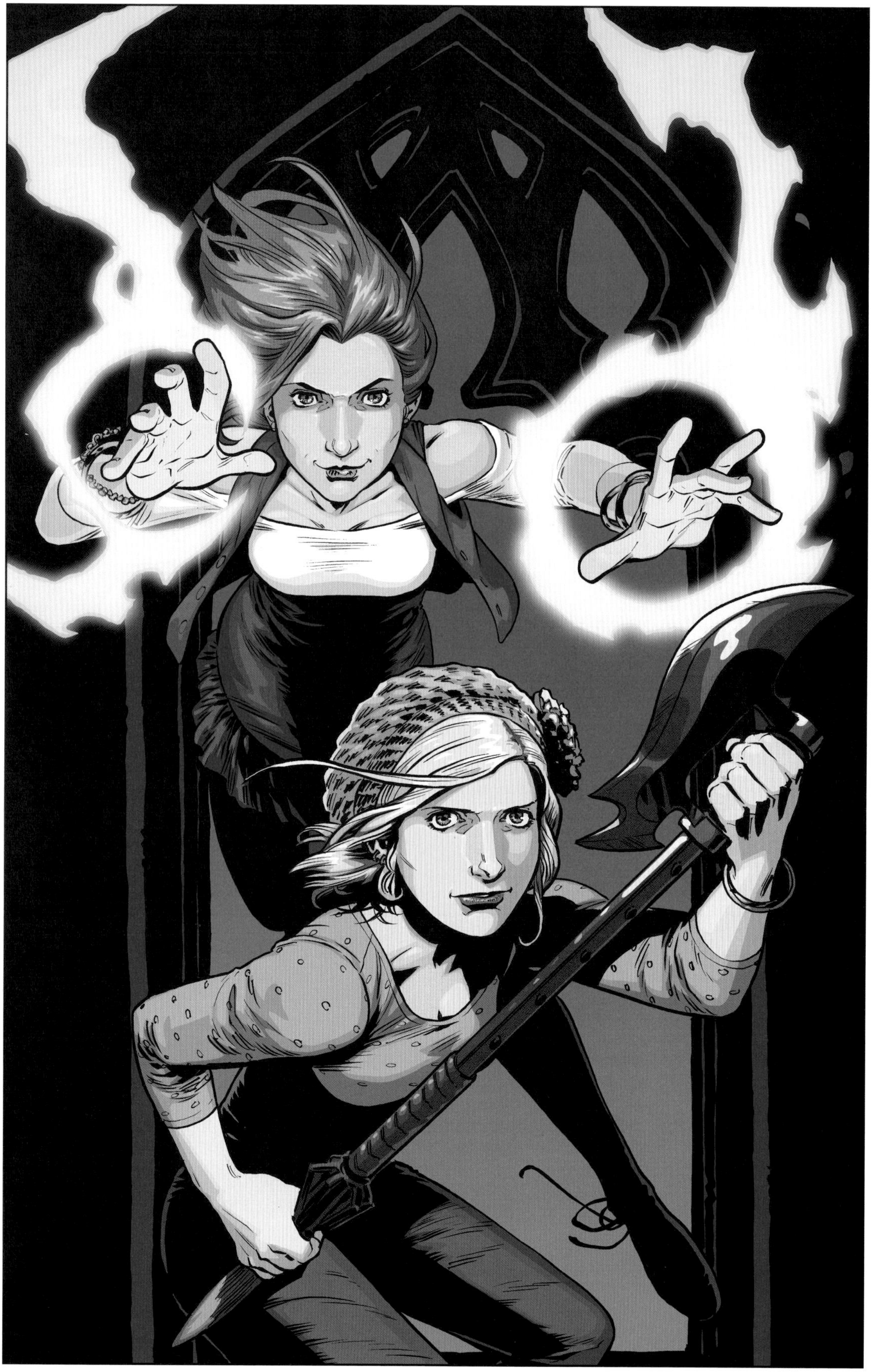

Variant cover art for *Buffy* Season 10 #17, by Rebekah Isaacs with Dan Jackson.

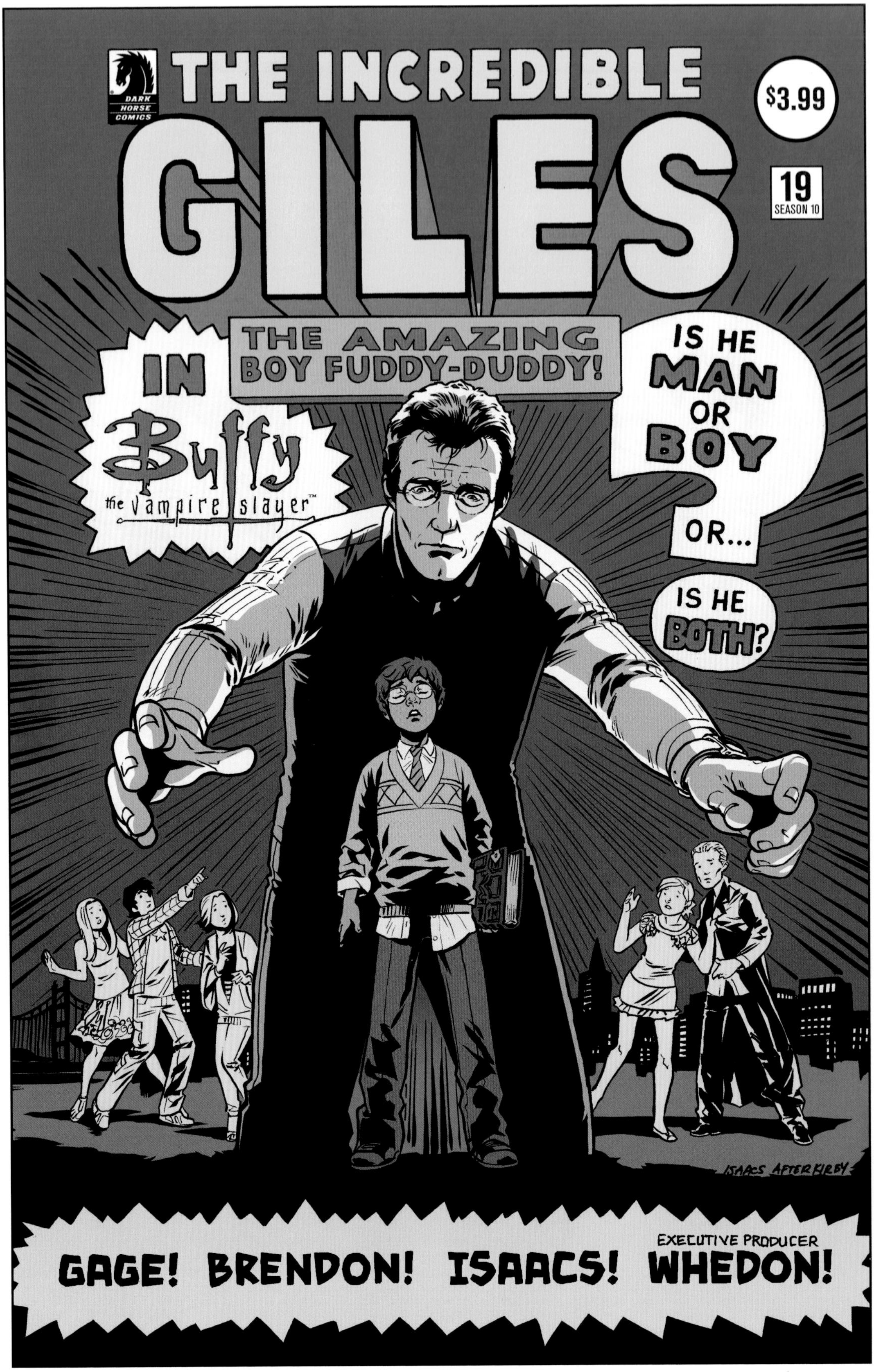
DARK HORSE COMICS
THE INCREDIBLE
GILES
$3.99
19
SEASON 10
IN
THE AMAZING BOY FUDDY-DUDDY!
Buffy the vampire slayer™
IS HE MAN OR BOY
OR...
IS HE BOTH?
ISAACS AFTER KIRBY
GAGE! BRENDON! ISAACS! EXECUTIVE PRODUCER WHEDON!

Fully designed variant cover art for *Buffy* Season 10 #19, by Rebekah Isaacs with Dan Jackson. After the 1962 cover to *The Incredible Hulk* #1 by Jack Kirby.

Opposite: Pencils for this variant by Rebekah.

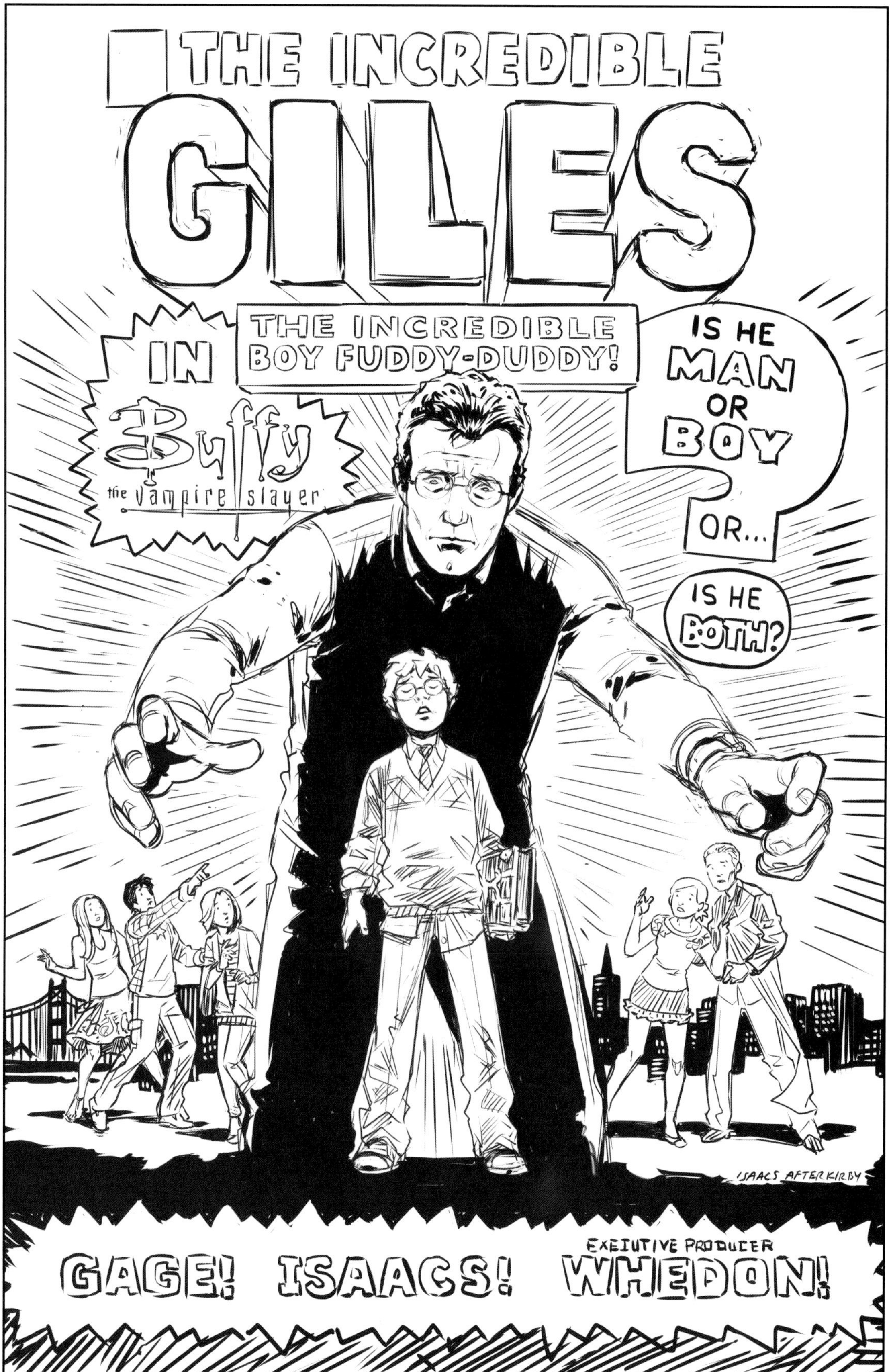
THE INCREDIBLE
GILES
IN
Buffy the vampire slayer
THE INCREDIBLE BOY FUDDY-DUDDY!
IS HE MAN OR BOY
OR...
IS HE BOTH?
ISAACS AFTER KIRBY
GAGE! ISAACS! EXECUTIVE PRODUCER WHEDON!

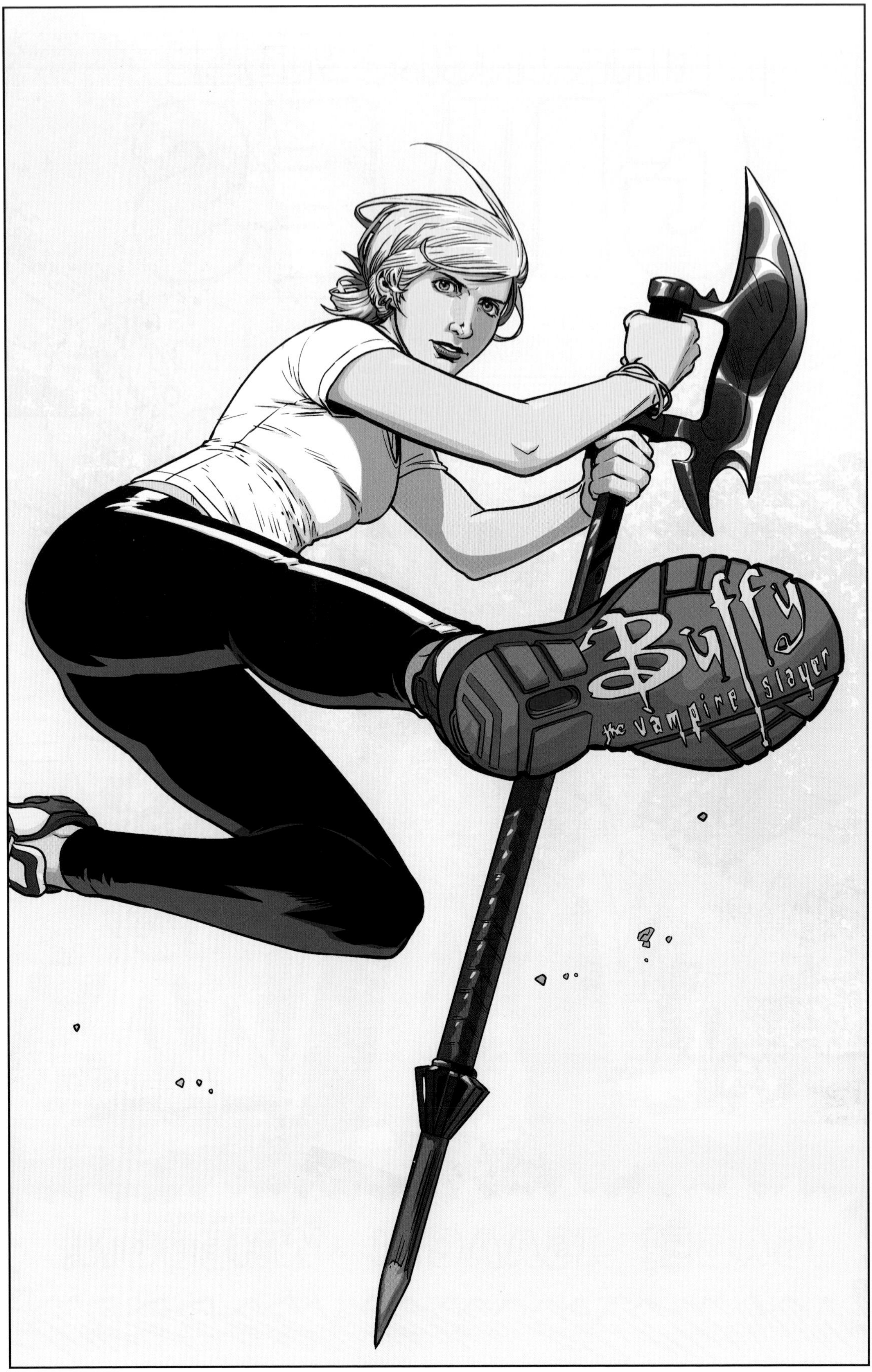
Buffy
the vampire slayer
Variant cover art for *Buffy* Season 10 #20, by Rebekah Isaacs with Dan Jackson.

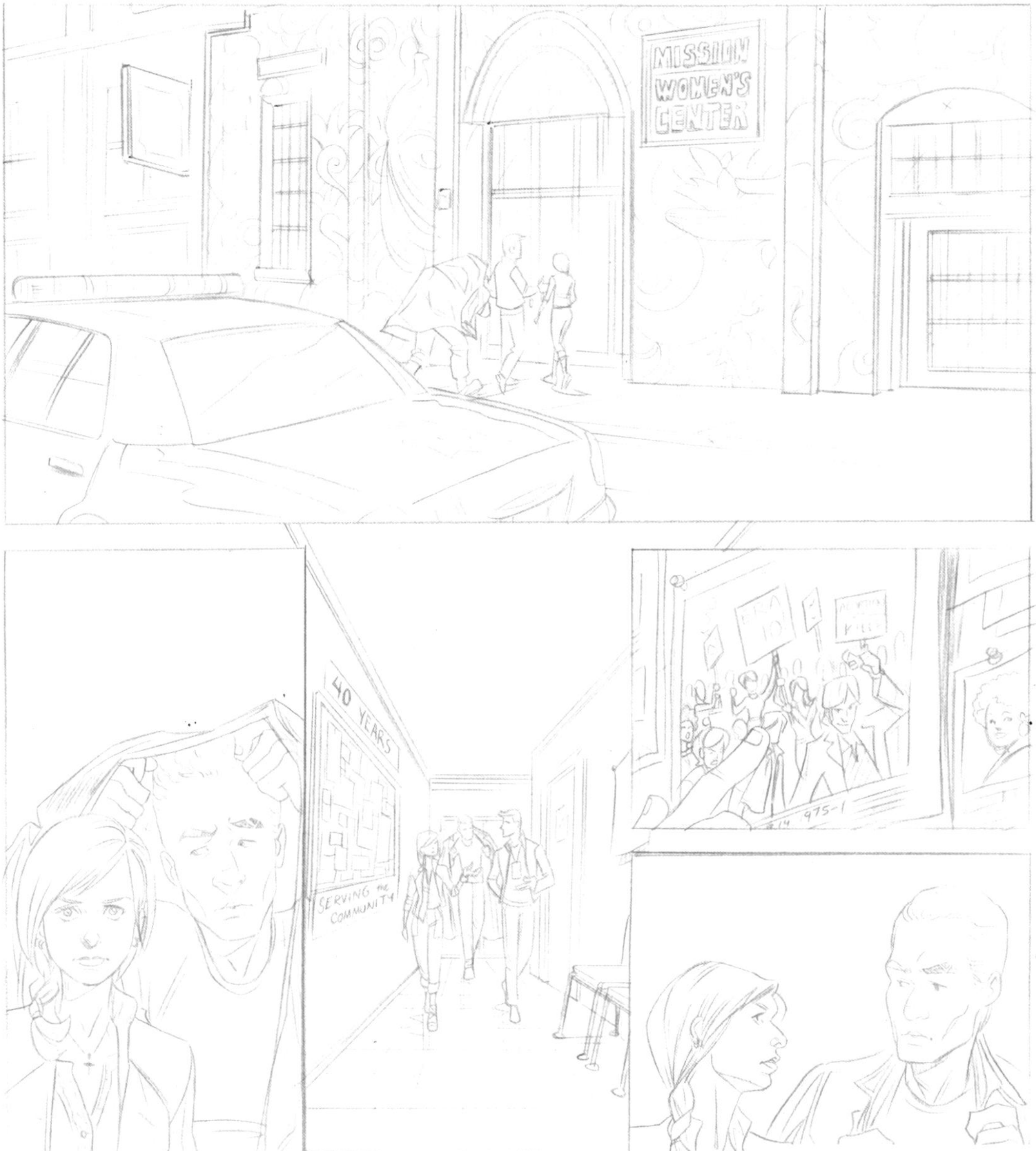
MISSION WOMEN'S CENTER
40 YEARS
SERVING the COMMUNITY

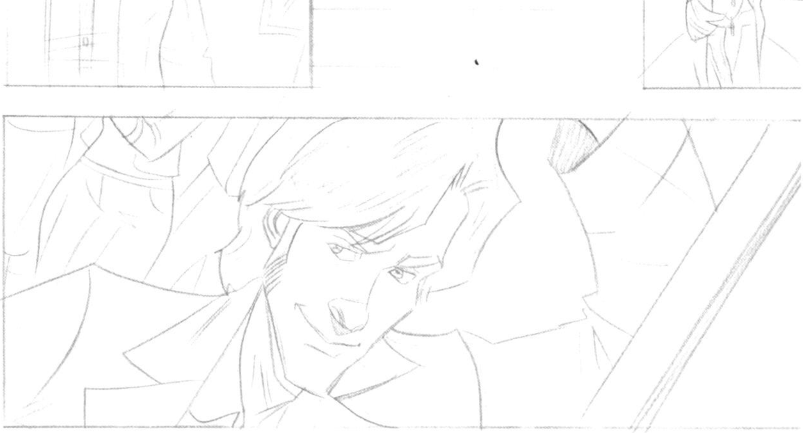

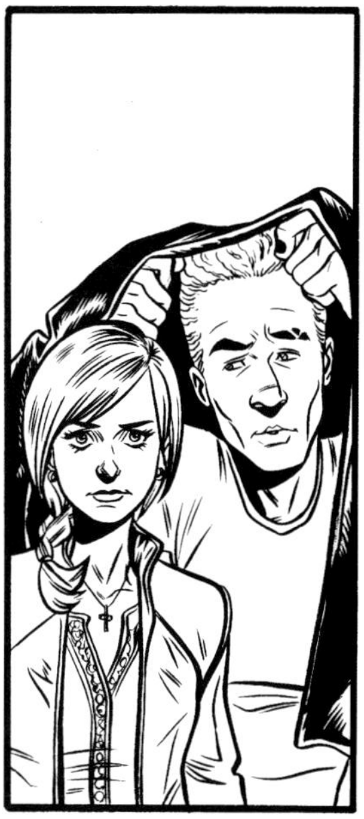

Guest artist Megan Levens took on the duty of penciling and inking issue #20, where Buffy and Spike tackled a Special Victims crime that concerned an incubus demon—bringing back some difficult memories for the pair. Here are pencils for page 1 of the issue, where the scene was set for *Triggers*.

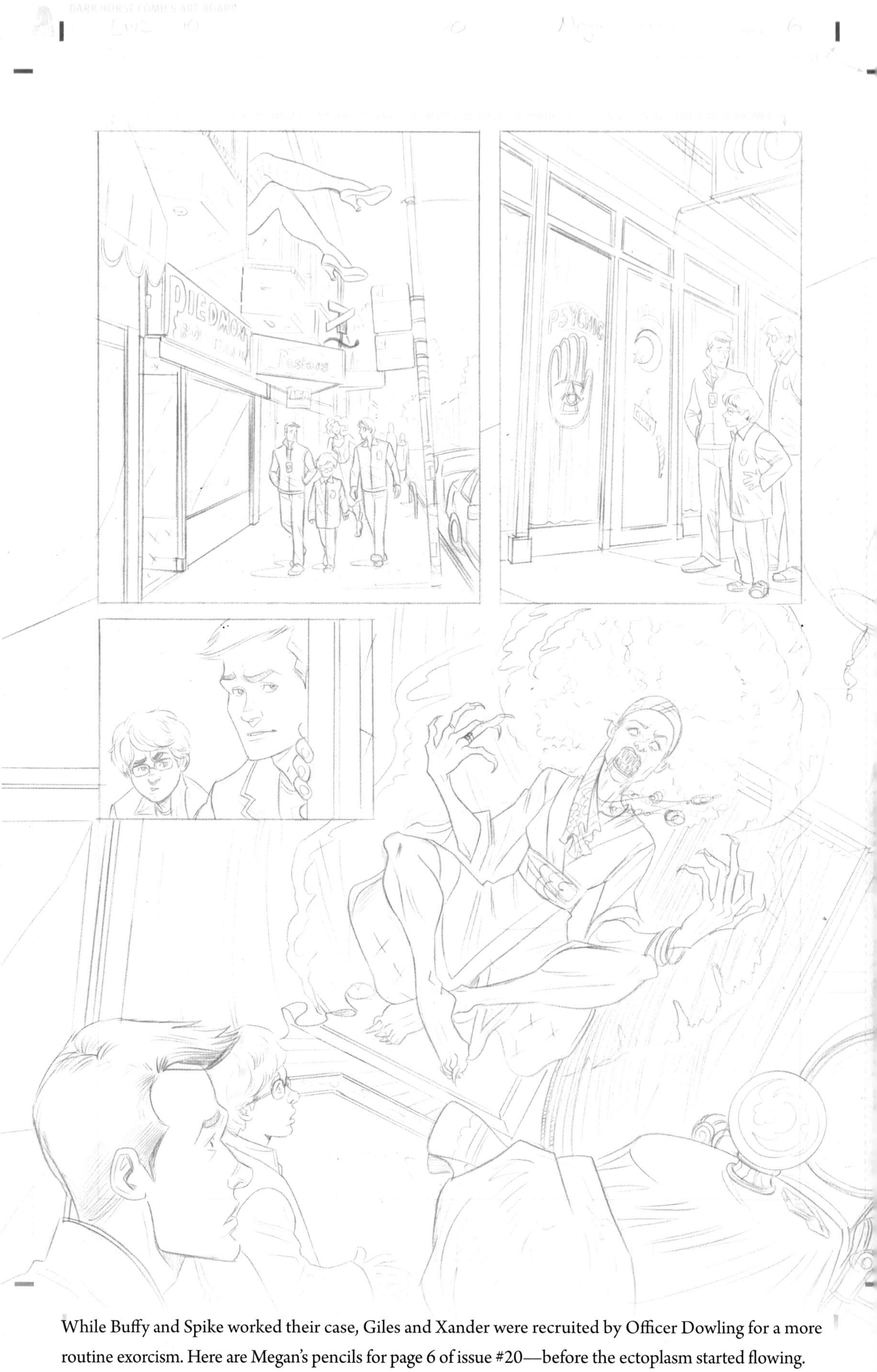
Posters
PSYCHIC

While Buffy and Spike worked their case, Giles and Xander were recruited by Officer Dowling for a more routine exorcism. Here are Megan's pencils for page 6 of issue #20—before the ectoplasm started flowing.

BUFFY THE VAMPIRE SLAYER SEASON 8

VOLUME 1: THE LONG WAY HOME
Joss Whedon and Georges Jeanty
ISBN 978-1-59307-822-5 | $15.99

VOLUME 2: NO FUTURE FOR YOU
Brian K. Vaughan, Georges Jeanty, and Joss Whedon
ISBN 978-1-59307-963-5 | $15.99

VOLUME 3: WOLVES AT THE GATE
Drew Goddard, Georges Jeanty, and Joss Whedon
ISBN 978-1-59582-165-2 | $15.99

VOLUME 4: TIME OF YOUR LIFE
Joss Whedon, Jeph Loeb, Georges Jeanty, and others
ISBN 978-1-59582-310-6 | $15.99

VOLUME 5: PREDATORS AND PREY
Joss Whedon, Jane Espenson, Georges Jeanty, Cliff Richards, and others
ISBN 978-1-59582-342-7 | $15.99

VOLUME 6: RETREAT
Joss Whedon, Jane Espenson, Georges Jeanty, Karl Moline, and others
ISBN 978-1-59582-415-8 | $15.99

VOLUME 7: TWILIGHT
Joss Whedon, Brad Meltzer, and Georges Jeanty
ISBN 978-1-59582-558-2 | $16.99

VOLUME 8: LAST GLEAMING
Joss Whedon, Scott Allie, and Georges Jeanty
ISBN 978-1-59582-610-7 | $16.99

BUFFY THE VAMPIRE SLAYER SEASON 8 LIBRARY EDITION

VOLUME 1 ISBN 978-1-59582-888-0 | $29.99
VOLUME 2 ISBN 978-1-59582-935-1 | $29.99
VOLUME 3 ISBN 978-1-59582-978-8 | $29.99
VOLUME 4 ISBN 978-1-61655-127-8 | $29.99

BUFFY THE VAMPIRE SLAYER SEASON 9

VOLUME 1: FREEFALL
Joss Whedon, Andrew Chambliss, Georges Jeanty, and others
ISBN 978-1-59582-922-1 | $17.99

VOLUME 2: ON YOUR OWN
Andrew Chambliss, Scott Allie, Georges Jeanty, and others
ISBN 978-1-59582-990-0 | $17.99

VOLUME 3: GUARDED
Joss Whedon, Jane Espenson, Drew Z. Greenberg, Georges Jeanty, and others
ISBN 978-1-61655-099-8 | $17.99

VOLUME 4: WELCOME TO THE TEAM
Andrew Chambliss, Georges Jeanty, Karl Moline, and others
ISBN 978-1-61655-166-7 | $17.99

VOLUME 5: THE CORE
Andrew Chambliss, Georges Jeanty, and others
ISBN 978-1-61655-254-1 | $17.99

BUFFY THE VAMPIRE SLAYER SEASON 9 LIBRARY EDITION

VOLUME 1 ISBN 978-1-61655-715-7 | $29.99
VOLUME 2 ISBN 978-1-61655-716-4 | $29.99
VOLUME 3 ISBN 978-1-61655-717-1 | $29.99

BUFFY THE VAMPIRE SLAYER SEASON 10

VOLUME 1: NEW RULES
Christos Gage, Rebekah Isaacs, Nicholas Brendon, and others
ISBN 978-1-61655-490-3 | $18.99

VOLUME 2: I WISH
Christos Gage, Rebekah Isaacs, Nicholas Brendon, and others
ISBN 978-1-61655-600-6 | $18.99

VOLUME 3: LOVE DARES YOU
Christos Gage, Rebekah Isaacs, Nicholas Brendon, and Megan Levens
ISBN 978-1-61655-758-4 | $18.99

VOLUME 4: OLD DEMONS
Christos Gage and Rebekah Isaacs
ISBN 978-1-61655-802-4 | $18.99

ANGEL & FAITH SEASON 9

VOLUME 1: LIVE THROUGH THIS
Christos Gage, Rebekah Isaacs, and Phil Noto
ISBN 978-1-59582-887-3 | $17.99

VOLUME 2: DADDY ISSUES
Christos Gage, Rebekah Isaacs, and Chris Samnee
ISBN 978-1-59582-960-3 | $17.99

VOLUME 3: FAMILY REUNION
Christos Gage, Rebekah Isaacs, Lee Garbett, and David Lapham
ISBN 978-1-61655-079-0 | $17.99

VOLUME 4: DEATH AND CONSEQUENCES
Christos Gage and Rebekah Isaacs
ISBN 978-1-61655-165-0 | $17.99

VOLUME 5: WHAT YOU WANT, NOT WHAT YOU NEED
Christos Gage and Rebekah Isaacs
ISBN 978-1-61655-253-4 | $17.99

ANGEL & FAITH SEASON 9 LIBRARY EDITION

VOLUME 1 ISBN 978-1-61655-712-6 | $29.99
VOLUME 2 ISBN 978-1-61655-713-3 | $29.99
VOLUME 3 ISBN 978-1-61655-714-0 | $29.99

ANGEL & FAITH SEASON 10

VOLUME 1: WHERE THE RIVER MEETS THE SEA
Victor Gischler, Will Conrad, Derlis Santacruz, and others
ISBN 978-1-61655-503-0 | $18.99

VOLUME 2: LOST AND FOUND
Victor Gischler and Will Conrad
ISBN 978-1-61655-601-3 | $18.99

VOLUME 3: UNITED
Victor Gischler and Will Conrad
ISBN 978-1-61655-766-9 | $18.99

SPIKE

VOLUME 1: A DARK PLACE
Victor Gischler and Paul Lee
ISBN 978-1-61655-109-4 | $17.99

SPIKE: INTO THE LIGHT
James Marsters and Derlis Santacruz
ISBN 978-1-61655-421-7 | $14.99

WILLOW

VOLUME 1: WONDERLAND
Jeff Parker, Christos Gage, and Brian Ching
ISBN 978-1-61655-145-2 | $17.99

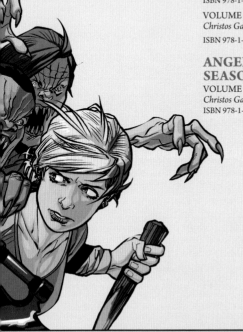

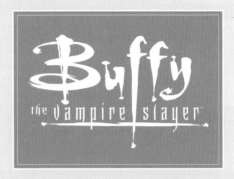

JOSS WHEDON

Serenity
FIREFLY CLASS 03-K64
THOSE LEFT BEHIND

DR. HORRIBLE
AND OTHER HORRIBLE STORIES BY ZACK WHEDON

JOSS WHEDON'S
dollhouse
EPITAPHS

Buffy
the vampire slayer
OMNIBUS
VOLUME 1

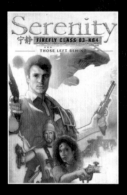

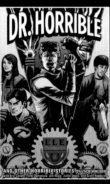

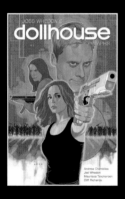

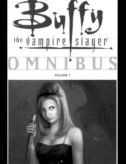

SERENITY VOLUME 1: THOSE LEFT BEHIND SECOND EDITON HC
Joss Whedon, Brett Matthews, and Will Conrad
978-1-59582-914-6 | $17.99

SERENITY VOLUME 2: BETTER DAYS AND OTHER STORIES HC
Joss Whedon, Patton Oswalt, Zack Whedon, Patric Reynolds, and others
978-1-59582-739-5 | $19.99

SERENITY VOLUME 3: THE SHEPHERD'S TALE HC
Joss Whedon, Zack Whedon, and Chris Samnee
978-1-59582-561-2 | $14.99

SERENITY VOLUME 4: LEAVES ON THE WIND
Zack Whedon, Georges Jeanty, and Karl Story
978-1-61655-489-7 | $19.99

DR. HORRIBLE AND OTHER HORRIBLE STORIES
Joss Whedon, Zack Whedon, Joëlle Jones, and others
978-1-59582-577-3 | $9.99

DOLLHOUSE: EPITAPHS
Andrew Chambliss, Jed Whedon, Maurissa Tancharoen, and Cliff Richards
978-1-59582-863-7 | $18.99

BUFFY THE VAMPIRE SLAYER: TALES
978-1-59582-644-2 | $29.99

ANGEL OMNIBUS
Christopher Golden, Eric Powell, and others
978-1-59582-706-7 | $24.99

BUFFY THE VAMPIRE SLAYER OMNIBUS
Volume 1 978-1-59307-784-6 | $24.99
Volume 2 978-1-59307-826-3 | $24.99
Volume 3 978-1-59307-885-0 | $24.99
Volume 4 978-1-59307-968-0 | $24.99
Volume 5 978-1-59582-225-3 | $24.99
Volume 6 978-1-59582-242-0 | $24.99
Volume 7 978-1-59582-331-1 | $24.99

BUFFY THE VAMPIRE SLAYER: PANEL TO PANEL
978-1-59307-836-2 | $19.99

BUFFY THE VAMPIRE SLAYER: PANEL TO PANEL—SEASONS 8 & 9
978-1-61655-743-0 | $24.99

SPIKE VOLUME 1: A DARK PLACE
Victor Gischler, Paul Lee, Andy Owens, and Dexter Vines
978-1-61655-109-4 | $17.99

SPIKE: INTO THE LIGHT
James Marsters, Derlis Santacruz, Andy Owens, and Steve Morris
978-1-61655-421-7 | $14.99

WILLOW VOLUME 1: WONDERLAND
Jeff Parker, Christos Gage, Brian Ching, and Jason Gorder
978-1-61655-145-2 | $17.99